Researching School Experience
Ethnographic Studies of Teaching and Learning

Edited by Martyn Hammersley

Contributors: Jennifer Nias, Geoff Troman, Bob Jeffrey, Bethan Marshall and Stephen J. Ball, Andy Hargreaves, Pat Sikes, Ivor F. Goodson, Alex Moore, Andrew Pollard and Ann Filer, Lynda Measor, and Martyn Denscombe

London and New York

First published 1999
by Falmer Press
11 New Fetter Lane, London EC4P 4EE

Simultaneously published in the USA and Canada
by Garland Inc.
19 Union Square West, New York, NY 10003

Falmer Press is an imprint of the Taylor & Francis Group

Typeset in Times by
J&L Composition Ltd, Filey, North Yorkshire
Printed and bound in Great Britain by
Biddles Ltd, Guildford and King's Lynn

British Library Cataloguing in Publication Data
A catalogue record for this book is available from the British Library

Library of Congress Cataloging in Publication Data
Researching school experience: ethnographic studies of teaching and
    learning / edited by Martyn Hammersley.
    Includes bibliographical references and index.
    1. Teaching—Social aspects. 2. Teachers—Social conditions.
3. Learning.   4. Educational sociology.   5. Ethnology.
I. Hammersley, Martyn.
LB1027.R453   1999
306.43'2–dc21   99–28141

ISBN 0–7507–0915–4 (hbk)
ISBN 0–7507–0914–6 (pbk)

Contents

Acknowledgments

The editor would like to thank Dr Ved Varma for encouragement in preparing this book. He also gratefully acknowledges permission from Elsevier Science Ltd to reprint Ivor Goodson's article 'Representing teachers', which previously appeared in *Teaching and Teacher Education*, **13**, 1, 1991, pp. 111–17; and from Demos for permission to reprint Table 3.1 on page 68 from M. Power, *The Audit Explosion*, London: Demos, 1994, p. 8.

Introduction

Martyn Hammersley

Teaching and learning are at the heart of education; that is a matter of wide agreement. But, sometimes, they are seen in overly instrumental and cognitive terms: there is neglect of the way they are embedded in the lives of both children and teachers. Closely associated with this is an exaggerated emphasis on the *outputs* of education, at the expense of the process itself. Over the past three decades, pedagogy and learning in both primary and secondary schools have acquired a high political profile. Where once they were treated as the exclusive domain of the teaching profession, a mysterious matter of art and judgment, they have become subject to public debate about the merits of different approaches, along with demands for quantitative research designed to test the effectiveness of different techniques. As a counterpoint to this, however, since the 1970s qualitative research has provided us with an increasingly subtle and complex picture of what is involved in the teaching–learning process.

An early theme emerging from this research was that teachers and pupils are not solely, and in some cases not even primarily, concerned with the business of education – narrowly defined. In the words of Peter Woods, they both employ survival strategies and engage in adaptations shaped by circumstances and the requirements of self. While initially this theme was rather negative in character, treating coping and survival as alternatives to the furtherance of education, in recent years there has been growing recognition of the extent to which education necessarily has a social context, and involves the articulation of selves, not just the playing out of roles.

The authors of the chapters in this book have all been strongly influenced by an approach to the study of education that emphasizes its processual, personal and social character – what is often referred to as 'interactionist ethnography'. This involves a commitment to documenting what actually goes on in learning situations, through first-hand observation and/or in-depth interviews with those directly involved. There is resistance among interactionists to viewing those situations through the spectacles of what is *assumed* to be going on, what *ought* to go on, or what *must* be going on according to some prior theoretical perspective. In short, there is an assumption of complexity, and a reluctance to reduce that complexity to simplistic schemes. What this produces is a recognition of diversity, change and potential or actual conflict.

Alongside this, there is a concern with exploring the perspectives of the people involved rather than rushing to judgments about them and what they are doing. This concern is premissed in part on the assumption that people's behaviour is structured by how they interpret the world and the particular situations they face. But it is also based on a belief in the essential rationality of all people: that if we make the effort we can understand why they do what they do, even if their behaviour is initially incomprehensible, and even if we personally disapprove of it. What is required for proper understanding, then, is tolerance of uncertainty and of transgression, and a capacity for taking pleasure in the detail of things, finding there neither devils nor gods but rather the very nature of human society, a society in which we are all involved.

The emphasis of interactionist ethnography in education is on researching the experience, perspectives and actions of those involved: teachers, children, students and others. This is to be done not in abstract terms, but by treating perspectives and actions as socially grounded, both in the immediate contexts in which people live and work, and within the wider framework of global society. The interactionist idea that people construct their perspectives about the world and build lines of action on the basis of these, rather than simply responding to events in a passive way, has recently been reinforced by the influence of feminism and postmodernism, with their heightened concern for the role of the self and their stress on the social construction of cognition, motivation and action. These changes in focus and orientation have occurred over a period when, from many points of view, the conditions of work for teachers in Britain have worsened. The result is that recognition of the constraints imposed by recent education policies has been complemented by an emphasis on the ways in which these policies have been read, and often reinterpreted and adapted, by teachers. In particular, the stress has been on the ways in which teachers have not only managed to sustain their emotional survival, but have also kept open some space to make available crucial opportunities for learning by children and young people.

A key figure in the early application of the interactionist approach to understanding teaching and learning, and in subsequent developments of it, has been Peter Woods. The origin of this book lies in the desire of the contributors to honour his work on the occasion of his formal retirement. It was decided that the best way to do this was to produce a book that makes a direct contribution to the literature. That there is no tension involved in this dual commitment reflects the scale and character of Woods' academic contributions to the field.

In this brief introduction I will outline something of the history of interactionist research, and of Peter Woods' role within it, before providing brief summaries of the individual chapters.

The Development of Interactionist Ethnography

The immediate source of the considerable body of ethnographic work on teaching and learning that is now available was the change that occurred in British sociology of education in the late 1960s and early 1970s, often labelled as the emergence of the 'new sociology of education' (for an overview, see Atkinson, Delamont and Hammersley, 1993). Prior to this, sociological research on education had given little attention to teaching and learning. The focus had been primarily on social class inequalities in achievement and their causes – investigated in aggregate terms – and subsequently on schools as organizations. However, under the growing influence of interpretive theoretical ideas – notably, symbolic interactionism, phenomenology and ethnomethodology – sociologists began to look in detail at classroom processes and at the perspectives of teachers and pupils. Of course, they were not the first researchers to pay attention to what went on in the classroom. There was already a substantial psychological literature (see Morrison and McIntyre, 1969 and 1971). But the new sociologists adopted a very different approach. Where before there had been a concern with measuring learning and documenting those features of teachers and teaching that maximized it, among the sociologists the primary concern was to *explore* the world of the classroom, to document it, and to do so in a way that did not take for granted conventional educational assumptions about what counted as learning or teaching. This approach was encouraged by the tenor of the times, in which progressive educational ideas competed with even more radical ones, like deschooling. These ideas presented teaching and schooling as potentially, if not actually, *anti*-educational. The effect of this was to encourage sociologists to suspend belief in many of the assumptions on which the education system was founded, and to investigate the form that teaching and learning actually took in classrooms, and why.

Out of this mix of new theoretical ideas in sociology with radical political questioning of educational shibboleths, interactionist ethnography emerged in the early 1970s. Peter Woods was an influential contributor to this. He produced a series of articles on teachers' perspectives and strategies, and on pupils' experience of school; and at the end of that decade his first book *The Divided School* appeared. From the beginning, his voice was a distinctive one. While his work exemplifies the application of an interactionist approach to the study of schooling, he was less oppositional to earlier forms of research than were some other 'new sociologists'. Indeed, the spirit that lies behind Woods' approach, then and now, is an eclectic one. Ideas and methods are selected for use solely according to whether they seem to illuminate the data; their origin is not held against them. Thus, over the course of his career, we find Woods drawing on diverse sources, not just interactionist ideas but also those of functionalist sociologists, like Merton and Bell, and of anthropologists.

As the field of work developed, Woods steamed ahead, charting a strategic route through the narrow passage between the excesses of voluntarism and determinism, between an overemphasis on the micro or on the macro, between a concern with immediate practical relevance and the tendency to academicism, between subjectivism and objectivism. As a result, his work can be used as a kind of tracer with which to chart change in the field of ethnographic research on teaching and learning, from the early 1970s through to the late 1990s.

One aspect of this change is the way in which the focus of interactionist ethnography has expanded over time. At the beginning, the concern was almost exclusively with secondary education. And, in examining pupils' perspectives, there was a preoccupation with the overtly oppositional attitudes and behaviour of many working-class boys. This was no accident: they were the most vociferous group whom the education system seemed to be failing. Here, interactionist researchers built on the earlier work of Hargreaves and Lacey, which had shown how streaming and other sorts of differentiation structured pupils' experience of, and responses to, school (Hargreaves, 1967; Lacey, 1970). The result of this narrow focus, however, was a perspective that neglected the experiences of others, most notably girls but also working- and middle-class pupils who were more 'conformist' in their orientation to school.[1]

Early work also gave attention to teachers' perspectives and classroom strategies, these often being seen to play a central role in shaping the environment in which pupils' behaviour and learning took the forms they did. Over time, however, there also came to be an emphasis on the way in which teachers' orientations, like those of pupils, are shaped by the contexts they face – and the material and ideological constraints built into these.

The focus of research thus expanded considerably. Early on, Woods investigated what was a key aspect of the organization of secondary schools at the time – the option choice system. He also opened up investigation of the staffroom, looking at what could be learned from interaction there about the way in which teachers' attitudes are formed and sustained. Later, with Lynda Measor, he extended the study of pupils' perspectives by investigating their experience of entering secondary schools, their anticipations of this change, and how they coped with the realities of it. Similarly, working again with Measor and also with Pat Sikes, Woods was one of the pioneers of life history work on teachers – looking at how their perspectives are structured by experience in different types of school, and shaped across the life cycle by critical incidents. In the past 10 years, with another small team of researchers – including Mari Boyle, Bob Jeffrey, and Geoff Troman

– Woods has played a key role in extending an interactionist approach to the study of teaching and learning in primary schools, and to investigating the impact of various aspects of the 'new regime' in the education system of England and Wales inaugurated by the 1988 Act and subsequent legislation.

However, what has changed over the past 30 years is not just the focus of investigation, but also the nature of the interactionist approach itself. We can trace the changes in terms of a series of challenges that it faced, to which it has adapted in various ways. The first serious challenge was, of course, to establish itself in a field that was largely dominated by psychological approaches imbued with positivistic ideas about scientific method. In setting out from rather different assumptions, stressing the need to get to grips with the cultures of schooling, rather than from a narrowly conceived methodological rigour, it was criticized for ignoring the need to engage in reliable measurement and generalization, for producing impressionistic accounts of teachers' attitudes and behaviour, and for speculating about the causes and consequences of these. It was helped in overcoming this challenge by being part of a broader movement that attacked scientism and questioned older approaches to the study of society. And, over time, the value of ethnography, and of qualitative work generally, has come to be widely recognized. Initially, it was seen as a useful complement to more 'rigorous' approaches. Later, it came to be treated as an approach that was valuable in its own terms – to the point where there were some even on the qualitative side who thought that the pendulum had swung too far (Hammersley, 1985 and 1987; but see Woods, 1987).

In this initial period, we find Peter Woods engaging with the methodological issues that divided the older approaches from the newer ones. In a contribution to the Open University course E202 Schooling and Society, whose predecessor (E282 School and Society) had played a key role in publicizing and developing the new sociology, Woods outlined the nature of an ethnographic approach and the rationale for it. He was to return to this theme many times later, notably in his books *Inside Schools* and *Researching the Art of Teaching*. Also at this time he founded the St Hilda's Conference, which became a focus for the development of ethnographic work on education.

The second challenge to interactionist ethnography came soon after it had started to gain ground against psychological approaches. Its source was one of the other main strands in the new sociology of education, that influenced by Marxism and 'critical' theory. Increasing emphasis came to be placed by some writers on the constraints operating on teachers, constraints that prevented change occurring. This led some to adopt reproduction theories, which explained the source of these constraints as lying in the needs of the capitalist system. Particularly influential here was the work of Althusser (1971) and Bowles and Gintis (1976). These reproduction theories were at odds with the guiding assumptions of interactionist ethnography in some important respects: they were not grounded in the analysis of ethnographic data, but were the product of theoretical work and/or aggregate data analysis; and they tended to downplay the significance of the perspectives and interpretations of the actors involved in the education system. In short, these theories implied a rather deterministic view of the way in which schools operated, as against the interactionist emphasis on agency and contingency.

The challenge from Marxist work forced interactionist ethnographers to pay more attention to the structural forces that shaped what went on in schools and classrooms. Much emphasis was given to 'linking micro and macro'. In Woods' case this took the form of a concern with bureaucracy rather than with the effects of capitalism *per se* (Woods 1979); though, of course, for those of a Weberian turn of mind there is a close link between the two. At the same time, reproduction theories soon came to be criticized even from the Marxist side, in particular because they seemed to carry pessimistic implications for the possibilities of educational change; indeed, because they themselves threatened to play a role in reinforcing the status quo. This led many who were concerned primarily with the political aspects of education to emphasize the relative autonomy of schools and teachers, in a way that was analogous to the approach of interactionists. The result was a process of mutual accommodation, though without complete integration. Woods' recent work on creative teaching provides an illustration of this, being concerned with the way in which teachers use what scope there is in their increasingly constrained situation today to promote critical learning experiences and educational change.

Another early challenge came from developments in the field of educational evaluation, notably the emergence of an emphasis on the teacher-as-researcher and on democratic evaluation. Here, the criticism was that interactionist ethnography, and other work in the sociology of education, was too academic, too remote from the practical educational concerns of teachers. Furthermore, it was criticized for an unethical approach in its dealings with informants: collecting data for its own purposes, instead of recognizing the right of the people being studied to exercise control over the use of the data they provided. Over time, this attack developed into a broader critique of the very distinction between educational researchers and teachers and its institutionalization (Rudduck, 1987; Elliott, 1988 and 1991).[2] The response of interactionist ethnographers to these developments was to give rather more attention to ethical issues than had been done previously, but also in some cases to adopt a more collaborative role towards the people being studied, and to give more attention to the contribution that sociological work could make to practice and policy (Woods and Pollard, 1988). Again, Peter Woods was in the forefront of these developments.

A third challenge came from feminism. Feminists criticized sociological and educational research, including interactionist ethnography, for either neglecting girls and women or for assuming that despite studying only boys and men they could make claims about pupils and teachers in general (see Acker, 1981). Moreover, it was argued that in doing this they had ignored the ways in which schools discriminate against girls, and thereby themselves contribute to the reproduction of the sexual division of labour (see Deem, 1980). Of course, feminists not only criticized previous work but also produced a large number of studies themselves, many of these ethnographic in character: they focused on the experiences of girls in school, and on teacher–pupil interaction, analysing these from the point of view of gender discrimination. The effect of this development was to broaden still further the already wide range of issues that interactionist ethnographers were concerned with, as well as to emphasize the general relevance of the gender dimension. Like others, Woods has taken increasing account of gender differences in his research. He also initiated a collection of ethnographic articles dealing with gender and ethnicity (Woods and Hammersley, 1993).

The impact of feminism highlighted the importance of reflexivity, of the ways in which analysis could involve presuppositions that the analyst was unaware of, which significantly shaped the account produced. In addition, it raised questions about the ethics of ethnographic work, particularly about the proper relationship between researcher and researched. One element of this has been to reinforce the pressure towards involving the people studied, or at least some of them, in the research process. As noted earlier, Woods's approach to ethnography has changed over the years in this respect, though without abandoning the key role of the researcher.

The fourth challenge to interactionist ethnography is rather more recent, and is much less straightforward in its implications than earlier ones. This is what has been referred to as postmodernism. In one respect this influence simply underlined the political criticism of deterministic system theories, mentioned earlier. Here, postmodernism was compatible with interactionism. It led, for example, to studies of the trajectory of education policies, from their formation through to their impact in schools, in which the contingency of the outcome, and the role of local social contexts, was emphasized (see Bowe, Ball and Gold, 1992; Ball, 1994). However, in addition, under this influence conceptions of the macro context changed, taking account not just of older notions about the intensification of work, but also of ideas about postmodern society: about, for example, the effects of globalization, the compression of time and space, the increasingly central role of knowledge production, and the blurring of cultural and social boundaries (see, for example, Hargreaves, 1994). Also complementary to interactionism was the concern of postmodernism with the role of narrative and discourse, reinforcing the earlier influence of ethnomethodology. And, closely associated with this, was a reaction against overly cognitive conceptions of human beings, stimulating sociological work on the body and the emotions, which has started to filter through into research on education – as some of the papers included in this volume illustrate.

However, there were also aspects of postmodernism which, while not necessarily incompatible with interactionism's principles, nevertheless raised questions about its practice. Most obvious here is the way in which some postmodernist literature challenges the idea that research can provide objective representations of the world; indeed, it questions the desirability of attempting to produce these. In the process it draws attention to the rhetorical means employed by ethnographers in the texts they produce. In some quarters this postmodernist emphasis on textuality has led to dramatic changes in writing, such as the use of multivocal forms, collage and poetry. British ethnographers have not, for the most part, gone very far in this direction. Woods' attitude is characteristic here, seeing the 'new techniques and approaches as enriching our existing research methods armoury, rather than replacing it' (Woods, 1996, p. 77). The book from which this quotation comes displays the effects of postmodernism and of the other challenges discussed here, but it does so in a way that is concerned with consolidation and development rather than with beginning again from scratch. And, ironically, it could be argued that this is more in the spirit of postmodernism than is modernist textual experimentation.

The final challenge to interactionist ethnography is even more recent than that from postmodernism, and is very different in kind; though in a curious way it underlines the postmodernists' rejection of assumptions about linear progress, and their sympathy for more cyclical notions of social change. It is a challenge to educational research generally, but one whose implications are especially threatening for interactionist ethnography. At root it involves a reversion to a preference for the kind of work that dominated the study of teaching and learning before interactionism arrived on the scene in the 1970s. Current educational research has been criticized for failing to build a cumulative body of theoretical knowledge that could provide a sound basis for effective pedagogical practice (Hargreaves, 1996). What is demanded is research that can tell teachers which of various techniques is the most effective. And, necessarily, this requires the measurement of teaching and learning, and perhaps even the use of experimental methods to investigate the relationship between them. This critique has been taken up by influential government agencies like Ofsted (Office for Standards in Education), the TTA (Teacher Training Agency) and even the DfEE (Department for Education and Employment) itself. As a result, it is likely to have consequences for the future funding of educational research, in terms of constraints on what sort of work can be done. How serious a threat it poses to the kind of research represented in this book remains to be seen.

As this brief history indicates, whatever homogeneity interactionist ethnography may have possessed in the early 1970s – and it was by no means entirely uniform even then – by the 1990s it had been shaped by internal and external forces to such an extent that it is no longer marked off so clearly from other approaches as it once was. But, in many respects, this also reflects its success in influencing work right across the field of education, not just in sociology but also in curriculum studies, administration and management, and even psychology. And it continues to be a thriving tradition, as the articles in this book show: it has a great deal to offer anyone concerned with the nature of teaching and learning in educational institutions. Above all, it raises questions about the goals of pedagogy and how these are viewed differently by the various participants, about the contingent processes involved in teaching and learning, and about the ways in which those processes are shaped by education policy and by other aspects of their social and political context.

A Resumé of the Chapters

In the first contribution, Jennifer Nias argues that many primary school headteachers continue to identify as teachers, not just as managers or leaders. She employs ethnographic evidence from 10 English primary schools to analyse the strategies that these headteachers used in school assembly, in order to reach staff as well as children. Direct teaching methods were linked to the implicit assertion of positional and personal authority, and to the explicit statement of values. Indirect methods were intended to influence others to think and behave in ways consistent with those values. Heads also used assemblies to teach curriculum skills, processes and content, and to develop a 'whole school' curriculum in the minds of all members of the school community.

In the second chapter, Geoff Troman sets out to show how interactionist studies reveal the complex and contradictory character of teachers' responses to government-sponsored restructuring policies. He draws on his recent investigation of an English primary school, examining the way in which one of the teachers in the school, who was also a 'subject manager', adjusts to the new demands placed upon her. These demands lead to both positive and negative reactions on her part, and Troman uses this case to reflect on the ambivalence or liminality experienced by many primary school teachers today and their responses to it – processes in which national policy gets reconstructed at micro level.

In 'Side-stepping the Substantial Self', Bob Jeffrey provides a parallel analysis to that of Troman, extending the work he carried out with Peter Woods and others on the way in which primary school teachers have responded to changes in education policy. He uses a case study approach, focusing on one reception class teacher in their sample whom they had categorized as complying with recent education policy changes. He outlines the challenge posed to her by the new audit accountability, and the way she adapted to this. He documents the emotional costs of her compliance, resulting from the fact that the new regime is premised on assumptions about education that are at odds with her own. She has adapted her behaviour, but retains her commitment to a more child-centred approach.

In the following chapter, Bethan Marshall and Stephen Ball portray similar processes of teacher adaptation, but this time in secondary schools. Through a close analysis of the language that four teachers use to talk about their experience of the new demands, the authors show how these are at odds with the teachers' substantial selves. One of the themes threading through what the teachers say is a sense of loss, in relation to both the quality of teaching that could be done in the past and the quality of their relationships with students. Closely related is a feeling of being at the mercy of changes beyond their control. As part of this, there is a heightened sense of conflict with school management, so that teachers experience decisions as simply imposed, and see meaningful teaching being replaced by the demands of accountability. The consequences for teachers of recent education reform, and some of the reasons for the current low morale within the profession, are revealed.

In Chapter 5, Andy Hargreaves focuses on the psychic rewards that teachers experience in their work, and more broadly on the character of their emotional relationships with children and young people. He draws on three studies involving interviews with elementary and secondary teachers in Canada, comparing his data with those reported by Dan Lortie in the classic study *Schoolteacher*. Hargreaves argues that there seems to have been a change in the extent to which pupils express gratitude to teachers when they are in school, rather than deferring this until they leave. He also points to differences between elementary and secondary teachers in the language used to talk about pupils: a language of love and care versus one of respect and acknowledgment. Finally, he points out that elementary school teachers in his sample seemed to experience greater negative as well as positive emotions towards their pupils. And he relates this to their exercise of power, noting that this factor has sometimes been neglected in accounts of elementary and primary school teaching.

In the next chapter Pat Sikes emphasizes the importance of understanding teachers' life experience, and the contribution that life history work can make to this. Having reviewed the advantages of this approach, and some of the problems surrounding its use, she illustrates its value through a discussion of her own recent work. This looks at the effects of parenthood on teachers' perspectives and pedagogical strategies. Her research shows that if we are to understand what goes on in the classroom, we cannot ignore what happens in the personal lives of teachers outside of it.

In 'Representing Teachers', Ivor Goodson assesses the current emphasis within educational research on teachers' stories and narratives. He notes that, ironically, this has occurred at a time when teachers' work is being technicized and narrowed: more and more central edicts and demands impinge on the teacher's world, squeezing out the space for reflection. He argues that, in this context, the elicitation of stories and narratives can draw attention away from the forces that are shaping teachers' lives, divorcing the teacher from knowledge of political and micro-political realities. He underlines the need for research using teachers' stories and narratives to locate these in terms of wider historical and political discourses and structures.

In Chapter 8, Alex Moore provides an overview of the different discourses that have informed, and continue to shape, initial teacher education. He sees these as focusing on the *competent practitioner*, the *reflective practitioner*, and the *charismatic subject*. He carries out a critical assessment of these paradigms, and argues a case for the inclusion and development of an additional one, based on reflexivity and on a recognition and celebration of the idiosyncratic, contingent aspects of teaching and learning. This paradigm, which re-emphasizes the significance of intra- as well as interpersonal relationships in classroom practice, encourages teachers to explore critically their own classroom behaviours and those of their pupils against the background of the wider social context.

In the next chapter, Andrew Pollard and Ann Filer review and illustrate the major findings from their Identity and Learning research programme, a series of ethnographic case-studies following pupils through primary and on to secondary school. They relate these findings to the declared aims of current government policy. The conclusion they reach is that the thinking behind this policy underplays the influence of social factors on the development and learning of children, and even more importantly underestimates the children's active role in their own education. The authors set out to show how ethnography can illuminate the relationship between the presuppositions of education policy and its impact.

In 'Looking Back at the Boys', Lynda Measor returns to some of the data she collected on pupils transferring from middle to secondary school in a project carried out with Peter Woods in the 1980s. She outlines recent developments in feminist thinking about gender, and especially about masculinity, and considers what light this can throw on the attitudes and behaviour of the pupils in that study. In particular, she examines the form that the boys' concern with masculinity takes, and its consequences for them, for their teachers, and for girls.

In the final chapter Martyn Denscombe explores aspects of the personal experience of young people that might serve as critical incidents in shaping their attitudes towards health risks, such as those involved in smoking, the use of alcohol and substance abuse. He does this on the basis of questionnaire and focus-group data from 15–16-year-olds. He comes to the conclusion that what is crucial in this process is not the nature of the experiences themselves but rather how the young people interpret these experiences. In the spirit of interactionist ethnography, their perceptions take centre stage in his analysis.

As I have made clear, all the other chapters also partake of this spirit. We hope they form a fitting tribute to the work of Peter Woods.

Notes

1 Both Hargreaves and Lacey had worked in boys' schools, but study of a girls' school had been included in the Manchester programme: see Lambart, 1976, 1982 and 1997.
2 Some versions of action research also drew on Marxism, indicating the continuing overlaps between the new approaches to the study of education that had developed in the early 1970s (see Carr and Kemmis, 1986).

References

Acker, S. (1981) 'No woman's land: British sociology of education 1960–79', *Sociological Review*, **29**, pp. 77–104.

Althusser, L. (1971) 'Ideology and the state', in Althusser, L., *Lenin and Philosophy and Other Essays*, London: New Left Books.

Atkinson, P., Delamont, S. and Hammersley, M. (1993) 'Qualitative research traditions', in Hammersley, M. (ed.) *Educational Research: Current Issues*, London: Paul Chapman.

Ball, S.J. (1994) *Education Reform: A Critical and Post-structural Analysis*, Buckingham: Open University Press.

Bowe, R., Ball, S.J., with Gold, A. (1992) *Reforming Education and Changing Schools: Case Studies in Policy Sociology*, London: Routledge.

Bowles, S. and Gintis, H. (1976) *Schooling in Capitalist America*, London: Routledge and Kegan Paul.

Carr, W. and Kemmis, S. (1986) *Becoming Critical*, London: Falmer Press.

Deem. R. (ed.) (1980) *Schooling for Women's Work*, London: Routledge.

Elliott, J. (1988) 'Educational research and outsider–insider relations', *Qualitative Studies in Education*, **1**, 2, pp. 155–66.

Elliott, J. (1991) 'Changing contexts for educational evaluation: the challenge for methodology', *Studies in Educational Evaluation*, **17**, 2, pp. 215–38.

Hammersley, M. (1985) 'From ethnography to theory', *Sociology*, **19**, pp. 244–59.

Hammersley, M. (1987) 'Ethnography and the cumulative development of theory', *British Educational Research Journal*, **13**, 3, pp. 283–96

Hargreaves, A. (1994) *Changing Teachers, Changing Times: Teachers' Work and Culture in the Postmodern World*, London: Cassell.

Hargreaves, D. (1967) *Social Relations in a Secondary School*, London: Routledge and Kegan Paul.

Hargreaves, D. (1996) *Teaching as a Research-based Profession: Possibilities and Prospects*, London: Teacher Training Agency.

Lacey, C. (1970) *Hightown Grammar*, Manchester: Manchester University Press.

Lambart, A. (1976) 'The sisterhood', in Hammersley, M., and Woods, P. (eds) *The Process of Schooling*, London: Routledge and Kegan Paul.

Lambart, A. (1982) 'Expulsion in context: a school as a system in action', in Frankenberg, R. (ed.) *Custom and Conflict in British Society*, Manchester: Manchester University Press.

Lambart, A. (1997) 'Mereside: a grammar school for girls in the 1960s', *Gender and Education*, **9**, 4, pp. 441–56.

Morrison, A. and McIntyre, D. (1969) *Teachers and Teaching*, Harmondsworth: Penguin.

Morrison, A. and McIntyre, D. (1971) *Schools and Socialisation*, Harmondsworth: Penguin.

Rudduck, J. (1987) 'Teacher research, action research, teacher inquiry: what's in a name?', in Rudduck, J., Hopkins, D., Sanger, J. and Lincoln, P., *Collaborative Inquiry and Information Skills*, British Library Research Paper 16, Boston Spa: British Library.

Woods, P. (1987) 'Ethnography at the crossroads: a reply to Hammersley', *British Educational Research Journal*, **13**, 3, pp. 297–307.

Woods, P. (1996) *Researching the Art of Teaching*, London: Routledge.

Woods, P. and Hammersley, M. (eds) (1993) *Gender and Ethnicity in Schools: Ethnographic Accounts*, London: Routledge.

Woods, P. and Pollard, A. (eds) (1988) *Sociology and Teaching*, London: Croom Helm.

1   Primary Heads as Teachers: Educating the School through Assemblies

Jennifer Nias

It was fashionable in the 1980s and early 1990s to see primary headteachers as managers. Their preparation and their work were frequently discussed in these terms, and it was in this capacity that they featured in many books and government publications (Bell, 1988; Dean, 1987; Department of Education and Science, 1990; Webb and Vulliamy, 1996). More recently, attention has switched to their role as leaders (Teacher Training Agency, 1998). Both views are important. Both are partial. Neither does justice to the fact that many primary heads continue to identify themselves as teachers (Southworth, 1995). They do not regard themselves solely as managers or leaders, but still willingly retain strong connection with their pedagogical roots. In their own eyes, they are educators who have moved into a different milieu but who continue to teach.[1]

In this chapter, I argue that primary heads' long-standing self-identification as teachers carries through into their new role and shapes the ways in which they interpret it. From many possible aspects of their educational activity, I have chosen to focus upon their conduct of school assemblies. These events – that is, those occasions when all the children in a school, except those who are exempt, and the teaching staff are expected to be present – offer heads a unique opportunity to exercise their pedagogical skills in a public forum and to show their commitment to their educational ideals. Assemblies are also more accessible to the researcher as an educative activity than, for example, staff meetings or informal conversations among individual staff members. I make a distinction between the direct and indirect strategies that heads use in their teaching, suggesting that direct methods are linked to the implicit assertion of authority and the explicit statement of values, while indirect methods are a way of influencing others to think and behave in ways consistent with those values. Taken together, the strategies that they employ make many school assemblies into vibrant occasions that hold the attention and increase the learning of adults and children.

I first became aware that many heads continued to think of themselves as teachers when, more than 20 years ago, I interviewed several individuals who reported how much they missed the warm, affective relationship and sense of belonging that they had built up with particular classes (Nias, 1989a). Further, they often felt deprived of the opportunity to exercise the classroom skills they had spent many years acquiring. Of course, there is a substantial minority of teaching heads in England and Wales and many of these find their double role burdensome (Hayes, 1996). But in general, even the busiest heads seek opportunities to work with children and take pleasure from helping them learn.

However, except in the taxing role of teaching head, heads cannot remain teachers in the conventional sense. They have, by definition, chosen to move into a new career phase, in which their personal concerns (Fuller, 1969) are not so much with their own sense of pedagogical competence but with their capacity to exert influence over a wider sphere than the classroom (Nias, 1989a). 'My class' has, for most heads without a regular teaching commitment, become 'my school'. Teaching has become a pervasive educative activity aimed at fostering the development of every child in the school and, for some heads, of every teacher as well. For those heads who have a vision of the school they wish to create, educating also means attempting to persuade all its members to adopt, and act in accordance with, the values that determine its culture and the nature of the education offered within it. In two linked research projects (Primary School Staff Relationships Project, Nias, Southworth and Campbell, 1989; Whole School Curriculum Development Project, Nias, Southworth and Campbell, 1992) we drew attention to the fact that the heads of the 10 participating schools were skilled and resourceful educators who used every possible occasion to promote the learning of both children and adults. Further, they were committed to their own professional growth as well as to that of their staffs. It was clear that transplantation to a new setting had not severed their pedagogical taproots. It was in part as teachers that they continued to think, act and grow.

Their school-wide teaching took many forms (Nias et al., 1992). For all heads, however, assemblies have several unique characteristics. They are legally required as part of schools' daily routines and are therefore proof against many of the normal vicissitudes of primary school life. The conditions under which they take place are sufficiently formal and ritualized to encourage a sense of the seriousness of the occasion, but also informal and comfortable enough to encourage the sustained attention of both adults and children. Sometimes ancillary staff, parents and governors are present, in addition to children and teachers. 'Showing' or 'sharing' assemblies enable teachers and pupils to show the headteacher, and one another, a cross-section of the work that is going on in classrooms, and so to inform one another of the nature of teaching and learning throughout the school. They also give everyone insights into the practical implications of agreed school policies. In short, assemblies regularly provide heads with a large 'class', in conditions particularly conducive to all its members' teaching and learning.

Teachers are, however, deeply concerned about control as well as about learning. They expect and are expected by others to be in control – of themselves, of their pupils, and of the latter's learning; and they generally hold that a respect for the authority of the teachers or for the subject matter is a necessary condition for learning (Nias, 1997). Consequently, heads too are mindful of the need to establish and maintain their right and capacity to control others, though in a wider arena than the classroom (Southworth, 1995). Like their staffs, they are therefore also concerned about legitimation, since the exercise of unlegitimated power does not in the long term result in productive learning or the creation of harmonious communities. Legitimation comes, in schools, from two sources. For heads in particular it flows from their position, that is from the formal, legal authority which is an intrinsic part of their role. But it also grows from their personal qualities and skills, as these are shown to children, to teachers and, often, to governors and parents as well. This means, among other things, that heads need to demonstrate publicly their ability to relate constructively to children, to show a good level of pedagogical expertise and an understanding of their staffs' jobs and working lives. In this context, too, assemblies provide unique opportunities for the emphasis of positional authority and the building and maintenance of personal authority.

Heads' desire and ability to exploit the educational potential of assemblies have received very little attention in the sparse literature on them. Studies of secondary schools stress the symbolic importance of these gatherings in affirming the status quo, and emphasize their ritualistic and conservative nature (Burgess, 1983; King, 1983; Woods, 1979). Similarly, Pollard (1985) and Nias (1989b) see primary school assemblies as playing a key role in establishing and maintaining the 'institutional bias' (Pollard, 1985) or 'culture' (Nias et al., 1989) of individual schools. None of these studies interprets the tacit and often overt emphasis in assemblies upon control as an aspect of heads' educative role.

As far as I am aware, Nias et al. (1992) is the first study to draw attention to the active ways in which assemblies could contribute to teacher and pupil learning, and to curriculum change. In that research we were repeatedly struck by the energizing nature of the assemblies that we observed. They were occasions when adults and children came purposefully together, learnt from one another, and enjoyed their shared participation in a whole school gathering. They clearly deserved closer study, not as the daily 'acts of collective worship' required by the 1989 Education Act, but because of their rich educational potential.

Background Information

I have drawn the argument presented in this chapter from data collected in 10 primary, infant or first schools. Details of the schools are given in Nias

et al. (1989 and 1992). They were part of the Primary School Staff
Relationships (PSSR) and Whole School Curriculum Development
(WSCD) projects. Briefly, they all had heads without regular teaching
commitments, and between 5 and 11 full-time teachers; but in all other
respects they differed widely from one another. There were also considerable differences in the nature and organization of assemblies. A summary
of these differences is given in Table 1.1, except for times of day which
varied so much within and between schools that even a summary would be
confusing. Suffice it to say that schools did not always begin the day with
assembly. Common alternative times were immediately before and after
morning break, and Friday afternoons.

Similarly, schools varied in their arrangements for the days on which
there was no gathering for all the children together. In some, class assemblies took place instead; in others, children were grouped in various other
ways (e.g. Years 1 and 2 and Years 5 and 6).

Parents and governors were welcome at all assemblies and often attended
'showing' or 'sharing' assemblies. In all the schools, the ancillary staff who
worked directly with the children were frequently present, while other staff
(e.g. caretaker, cook, secretary) attended on special occasions. Assemblies
lasted from 15 minutes to an hour or longer, and ranged in form from the
traditional story, hymn and prayer to multimedia presentations. In some
schools, children and staff waited in silence for assembly to begin; in
others, quiet talking was allowed. Occasionally, children could sit where

Table 1.1 School assemblies in project schools

School	Times in week all children present	Times in week all teachers present	Times in week head took assembly (excl. hymn practice)	'Sharing' or 'showing' assemblies
PSSR Project				
Greenfields	5	5	Head present: staff took assembly in turns	Yes
Hutton	5	4	4	No
Lavender Way	3	1 (alternate weeks, 2)	1	Alternate weeks
Lowmeadow	5	5	3	Yes
Sedgemoor	5	5	3	Yes
WSCD Project				
Carey	5	3	3	Yes
Fenton	3	3	3	Yes
Ingham	3	3	2	Yes
Orchard	1	1	1	Yes
Upper Norton	4	3	2	Yes

they liked; in most schools they entered, sat, and left with their classes. Sometimes staff had set places, at others they sat wherever there was a space. Nor did staff and children always sit in rows; common alternatives were informal groupings or a broad horseshoe.

Whatever the nature of the spatial and organizational arrangements, headteachers made every effort to ensure that assemblies were pleasant occasions. The school halls were kept clean, and in cold weather they were warm. They were decorated, wherever physically possible, with attractive, well presented children's work and, sometimes, with flowers or plants. When visual aids were used (e.g. for displaying the words of a hymn) they normally functioned satisfactorily, though acoustics were poor in a few halls. Staff and pupils usually entered and left to music, played on good quality apparatus, and the music itself varied: from folk-songs to Bach, from Pink Floyd to Hindemith. The atmosphere was quiet, relaxed and unhurried; when children were allowed to talk to one another at the start and end of assembly, they were encouraged to use soft voices. In none of the schools did we ever hear a raised voice during assembly, nor as the children came in and left. When individual pupils became restless they were quietly restrained by the nearest teacher. Laughter was common, the atmosphere friendly. The youngest children often sat on teachers' knees, older and younger children sometimes entered or left holding hands.

One other feature was common to all but one of the schools, though there were differences in detail among them in this respect too. With the exception of Hutton, every school 'shared' or 'showed' children's work on a regular basis (usually once a week). In most schools, there was a rota, allotting one class (or, occasionally, a pair of classes) to take responsibility for organizing an assembly; this by convention was based upon, and incorporated, their recent work across many curricular areas. However, in Upper Norton and Fenton the weekly 'showing' assembly normally consisted of class teachers and small groups of children sharing work-in-progress. Whereas the more formal 'showing' assemblies required considerable prior organization and rehearsal, this type of 'sharing' assembly was normally arranged in a few minutes and as a result of *ad hoc* consultation between teachers and their children.

Direct Teaching Strategies

When headteachers chose to teach the school directly – that is, to instruct, inform or demonstrate – they acted in a manner that emphasized their legal and moral responsibility for the learning of children throughout the school, and therefore their implicit right to control and guide it. Viewed this way, their use of direct teaching strategies served two ends at the same time: it conveyed strong messages to the school community about approved educational aims, attitudes and actions; and it underlined the authority of the person from whom these messages came. By drawing attention to their formal role, and by giving ritual force to the beliefs and values that they articulated and exemplified, these headteachers emphasized their controlling interest in the education of the adults and children in 'their' schools.

They were also aware that much of their personal authority stemmed from their ability to show the teachers that 'I can do their job' (Head, Fenton). So, they regularly demonstrated their practical competence in assemblies. In particular, they communicated skilfully with large groups of children of mixed ages and abilities, and related sensitively to individuals within this context. Of course, their pedagogical scope was limited by the size and format of assemblies. However, they often practised with very great skill the art of story-telling, for example holding a mixed-age audience of more than 200 spellbound and attentive for 20 minutes or more. In all the schools, teachers learnt to respect the effect that assemblies had upon children's ability to listen:

> I think the listening is very good. With the best will in the world it's hard for class teachers to provide a time when children sit and listen as they do when they go into assembly. Every child does this and it's expected of them and they do it.
>
> (Lowmeadow)

Heads also demonstrated more active teaching methods and the use of a wide range of curricular resources. Sometimes they did this through the medium of a new curriculum area, showing staff and children how to work with drama, clay or water-colour, for example. More often, they did it as part of the school's programme of social, moral or religious education. They strove to make their assemblies interesting, created opportunities for the children to be involved and, whenever possible, provided them with direct experience. Here are two brief examples:

> In one assembly on Spring, the head read a poem and then with the aid of the caretaker, who had been waiting in the next room, introduced into the hall the two new lambs from the school's mini-farm.
>
> (Hutton)

> Assembly was compelling, the children hung on her every word (and so did I), as we followed Handel through the second half of his life, listening to extracts from the *Water Music*, *Music for the Royal Fireworks* and *The Messiah*. As usual, the staff as well as the children were invited to respond during the story.
>
> (Lowmeadow)

Assemblies were also a time when heads demonstrated their own commitment to high standards of craft performance. In particular, they were punctilious about preparation and presentation. For example:

Everything is arranged before the children come into the hall and Evelyne is always there waiting for them. This morning she had a covered table, a chair, four daffodils in a vase, the overhead projector and screen.

(Ingham)

The prayer was so apposite that later on I asked Dorothy if she had made it up. She said, no, she'd got if out of a book but had altered the words in advance. She showed me where she had pencilled in her own words, before assembly.

(Upper Norton)

In addition, several of the heads were ready to intervene when they were conscious that children were accidentally being presented with inaccurate information (e.g. at Upper Norton when a teacher confused the use of 'dominant' in referring first to genes and then to eyes; at Carey when the teacher of Year 2 children suggested that leaves stayed on deciduous trees for a year).

Heads also used demonstration in another way: they deliberately modelled the kinds of relationships that they wished to promote in their schools and tried to exemplify the values of which they spoke. Our descriptions of assemblies are full of instances of headteachers behaving towards children and staff, as well as to visitors and parents, with consideration, patience, respect, courtesy, kindness and understanding. Although the heads were firm in their dealings with boisterous or disruptive children, and could be very stern when they judged it appropriate, we never observed harsh or punitive behaviour. Rather, for example, the head of Sedgemoor consciously eschewed in assembly a loud or dominating stance that would lead parents or children 'to a view of teachers as "them"'; and when the head of Upper Norton arrived in the school she consciously set out to demonstrate to some of her staff what she meant by 'discipline which is based on emphasizing the positive rather than the negative in children's behaviour'. Two instances from among many illustrate the ways in which headteachers modelled the kinds of relationship which they wanted to encourage:

Catherine tells them quietly about the icy slide which children had made in the playground, points out that she had previously asked them not to slide and gives reasons why they shouldn't use it – e.g. a child had cut her chin. She tells them 'they will have to stop using it or they are all going to have to stay in'. But it's done with a tone of sweet reasonableness. There is a clear message throughout assembly: You are the type of children who we can reason with and you'll see the sense of our arguments.

(Lavender Way)

As soon as they were seated one of the youngest children began crying loudly. Simon said, 'Whatever's the matter, Anna?' She replied, 'I want my Mummy'. He said, 'Well, you'll have to put up with me', and waded in amongst the children to lift her up and cuddle her. Then he said, generally, 'Who wants her?' She said she wanted her teacher and Simon passed her across to the class teacher whose knee she sat on for the rest of assembly.

(Fenton)

Heads also used assemblies to make explicit their ethical and social expectations for teachers and children. For example, at Upper Norton the head said:

I use assemblies to establish a code of conduct. They are a chance to reward certain kinds of behaviour and to remind the children about standards of discipline.

Fieldnotes record part of such an assembly taken by this head:

She sat in front of them on her own chair with a book on her knee, very still, with an apparent severity which was relieved only when she smiled, which she did relatively seldom, but with warmth.

She talked about selfishness, with illustrations from her own experience over half-term . . . She read a story . . . Then we sang a hymn. She stopped us after the first verse and said, 'Look at the words of that. We chose a hymn today with an easy tune so you could all sing it. Now let's sing.' . . . She showed concern for the children who said they had not enjoyed half-term, but at the end she also quietly but sharply reprimanded P, who had misbehaved throughout.

On other occasions, she made clear in assembly the importance that she attached to consideration for and cooperation with others, honesty, perseverance, courage and hard work. Other heads conveyed in similarly direct and effective ways their belief in the importance of values and qualities such as kindness, generosity, care for the environment and for personal property, helpfulness, self-discipline, trustworthiness.

In stressing the content of the school's social and moral curriculum, heads often implicitly addressed adults as well as children. Teachers knew that this was happening. As one said:

Ethics are presented in assembly and developed in the classroom . . . It enables children to see the whole policy through the school . . . After a while they get the message in assembly from the others round them. They see a still picture rather than a moving one. And we also learn what's expected of us.

(Lowmeadow)

The heads also encouraged in assembly a sense among teachers, ancillary staff and children that they were engaged in a joint educational venture. In the schools belonging to the WSCD project, in particular, they drew attention to curricular themes that were common to more than one class and to ways in which children in one age group could enhance the learning of those in another. In so doing, they made explicit their belief that the learning of all children was everyone's concern.

Indirect Teaching Strategies

When heads taught the school directly, their words and actions were often aimed primarily at the children. By contrast, when they used more oblique methods, their main target was usually the adults, especially teachers; they consciously sought to promote the professional learning of their staff by creating opportunities for individuals to lead, by guiding them when they did so through the use of suggestion, questioning and selective praise, and by encouraging them to teach one another. In addition, in staff-led assemblies, especially 'showing' or 'sharing' assemblies, teachers could see one another in action, something very difficult to achieve in most primary schools. In other words, through the mutual exposure of regular staff-led assemblies, teachers and children learnt what others were doing, the standards they had reached, the pedagogy that was used and how the curriculum had been interpreted. Also, as teachers publicly shared their work, they stimulated one another in ways that promoted both emulation and self-evaluation; and as they perceived links between the work they were doing and that of their other teachers and age groups, they became more aware of the school-wide nature of the curriculum. Finally, heads used such assemblies to collect information about and monitor the work of teachers and children so they could more sensitively and productively facilitate their future learning.

Although all the teachers in these schools felt 'showing' assemblies to be professionally valuable, some – especially those who lacked confidence – found them threatening. As a teacher at Carey explained: 'This isn't because we compete . . .'. Rather, 'when a feeling of dread' existed, it was because individuals felt that standards of professional competence in the school were so high that they might easily fall short of them. The data suggest that such feelings of inadequacy need to be repeatedly counter-balanced by positive reinforcement and open expressions of praise by both heads and colleagues, if 'showing' assemblies are to make the powerful contribution to staff learning and to the acceptance of common standards and practices that headteachers believe is possible. As the long-standing head of Sedgemoor said:

> I've seen people's assemblies change quite dramatically as they've gained confidence. They've become involved and much more prepared

to have a go at things when they realize that other people are not sitting there critically.

Teachers to whom responsibility for assembly had been delegated often tried to provide an example of 'good curriculum practice' (that is, practice that reflected the head's aspirations for the school as a whole). During these assemblies, heads took a back seat, but by their presence and their openly expressed approval they legitimated the attitudes and actions of the teacher in charge. We noted deputies cast in this role of 'leading professional' in six of the ten schools; and in the WSCD Project schools there were many instances of subject coordinators taking assemblies in which they deliberately led the learning of their colleagues in particular curriculum areas. We saw assemblies that demonstrated 'good practice' in every National Curriculum subject except history and geography, and also in cross-curricular themes such as multiculturalism. In addition, teachers were encouraged to use 'showing' assemblies to show one another, and the headteacher, what they had learnt on INSET courses. Two from among many instances of delegated leadership are illustrated:

> Several children from Rob's (deputy) class shared some CDT work – working models of a waving hand . . . Rob told the children that other models were on display in the classroom and that they were welcome to go and look at them and make them work as long as they treated them carefully.
>
> (Fenton)

> This morning it was Naomi's (Science coordinator and Year 2 teacher) assembly which was on light and colour. She told us that the work had begun when they'd been putting up the Christmas lights in their classroom. This had prompted them to think about light. She showed us some experiments they had done with coloured acetates held in front of torches. She talked about light travelling in straight lines, and demonstrated that if you put a mirror at different angles in front of it, it was reflected in different directions. She talked about prisms and the colours of the rainbow. Considering the colours of the rainbow had led them on to colour mixing . . .
>
> (Carey)

Heads did not leave to chance the learning that might result from such assemblies. Instead, they interacted at the time with class teacher and pupils and/or they offered praise and constructive criticism after the event. Their staffs realized that in acting in these ways their heads were reinforcing and underscoring their beliefs about and standards for the education of the children in the school. As one said,

He sort of allows a standard to be set by praising, but not praising anything he doesn't like. I think he sets quite a high standard through that means. You can see that in 'showing' assembly, in that he will only praise what he thinks is good.

(Orchard)

Fieldnotes at the same school record:

The third year were showing us their work. Ron (head) sat next to Sarah (Year head) and from time to time they chatted, obviously about the work, he smiling, nodding, very supportive, giving many clear signals to Sarah, to the children and perhaps to other staff of his approval of either individual children's efforts or the nature of the work itself.

(Orchard)

In this school the head was adamant that children should be helped to understand their work and not simply to produce it. This came across very clearly in the ways in which he interacted with them in 'showing' assemblies. A typical fieldnote reads:

Throughout the whole proceedings, Ron asked questions of the children: . . . Just once or twice when none of the children could provide the answers, he would ask the other children in the school and even less often he might ask for clarification from Dave . . . Yet he rarely pressed the children if they didn't know the answer. He would nod and then sometimes take that as a cue to ask some of the other children. Nor did he ever ask a child to do anything the child didn't want to. 'Are you going to read us this piece of writing' he said to one, showing his picture. 'No', said the child. Ron nodded, replying, 'Fine', and carried on.

(Orchard)

The knowledge that the head would repeatedly question a class during their assembly, even if he did not put pressure on individual children, had an effect upon the staff who realized, as one said, that 'It's Ron's way of finding out exactly how much these children know.' Fieldnotes confirm this. As one teacher said:

I think he does have quite a bit of influence on the staff in his subtle way. I think most people are just a little bit nervous of him, as I am. He knows exactly what he wants, the sort of approach he wants the staff to take towards the children . . . And his questions in assembly reflect this. 'Why did you do this? Do you know why that happened?' . . . I think he likes all the work presented exceptionally well too, and every child to try their very best.

Another Orchard teacher summed up a view that was expressed in one way or another in all the schools: 'I think that a lot of the time "showing" assemblies are for the teachers rather than the benefit of the children' (Orchard).

Teachers in all the schools were certain that they did learn from these colleague-led assemblies. Examples of their comments include:

> I think it's this communication again throughout the school, knowing what other units are doing. It helps to keep other members of staff involved with what is going on.
>
> (Orchard)

> I think there's a rubbing off process. Once one person says 'Look, this is what we've been looking at', somebody else thinks 'Oh yes, maybe we ought to think about it.'
>
> (Sedgemoor)

> Always on Friday it sparks off discussion and it goes on during playtime and lunchtime, about what the children have been doing and sometimes it carries over and people go and visit and have a look. People go into other classrooms. People always find things for other members of staff after the Friday. 'You're doing something on —, would you like this book?' or whatever. Assembly is informative to staff and I would hate to see it go. The children really enjoy each other's input too.
>
> (Upper Norton)

> That has been the success: People are aware of what other people are doing and are sharing ideas. We don't have the opportunity to brainstorm in a team like you would in a two-form entry (school), but we've got assembly.
>
> (Headteacher, Upper Norton)

Further, assemblies were a powerful incentive to individual self-evaluation. They provided an opportunity and reason for teachers to 'reassess what you've been doing with the children. You look at what you've been doing, when you're trying to piece it together, and you realise . . .' (Teacher, Sedgemoor); and to reflect upon their own standards. For instance:

> A very high standard is set for all assemblies . . . That's good. That's much better than going somewhere where it's a low standard and you can just do any old thing . . . I'm quite often amazed at how Evelyne does wonderful assemblies, but not just her – everybody. So you have to fit in with that . . . It doesn't have to be terribly elaborate, but what you

set out to do you have to achieve . . . because people have set a high standard.

(Ingham)

Heads also used staff-led assemblies to make or emphasize links between different aspects of the curriculum, in order to help children and adults make greater sense of learning throughout the school. For example, they encouraged interaction between age groups over similar topics, so implicitly highlighting for teachers and children the existence of progression in learning.

Sometimes their role was facilitative; they encouraged staff to share particular aspects of their classes' work, created time during which this could happen ('showing' assemblies could sometimes take an hour or more, but we seldom detected any sign of restlessness among the children), or invited participation from others in the school whom they knew had relevant experience to contribute. For example:

Miss B encourages you to pick up quite a lot of the content of assembly as a focus for storytime or written work.

(Lowmeadow)

So great was the other children's interest in the animation machines that, with Ron's approval, the Year 5s came round the units later in the day to show others the constructions they'd made.

(Orchard)

Dorothy had suggested beforehand to Katherine and Gina that when the Year 5 children 'showed' the paintings they had done with the advisory teacher, Gina should encourage the Reception and Year 1 children to come out and give their opinions on them.

(Upper Norton)

Occasionally heads' intervention was more overt. For instance:

She looked at the star-shaped Christmas decorations hanging in the hall which had been constructed from nonagons and linked this with all the other work they'd done on nine.

(Upper Norton)

Dorothy [head] noticed the interest that Year 3 and 4 children were displaying in the model drawbridges that Year 5 had made and were explaining. She said: 'You're on second lunch today, aren't you? Could you be in the library corner at lunchtime and demonstrate to people who're interested how your drawbridges work?' They all enthusiastically said that they would.

(Upper Norton)

A typical comment from the staff at this school was:

> It's only through sharing in assembly on a Friday that I find out what other classes are doing and how the work that I'm doing ties in with theirs.
>
> (Upper Norton)

The same finding emerges from the data from other schools. The ways in which heads used 'showing' and 'sharing' assemblies were of fundamental importance in letting teachers and ancillaries see what was happening in other classes and in helping them to discern coherence in it.

These kinds of assemblies also prompted teachers to become more aware of progression in children's learning. One teacher said:

> To a certain extent you are conscious the whole time, of the rest of the school, because whatever number work I'm doing with my class is being built upon and extended throughout the rest of the school . . . Often this is pinpointed in our sharing assemblies. Something that one class does comes up in another class in a completely different form, but the basic is still there.
>
> (Upper Norton)

Another commented that 'showing assemblies' were important 'in order to provide continuity throughout the school' (Orchard).

Teachers in several schools said that the children themselves enjoyed the chance to 'come together' (Lowmeadow), 'feel together' (Sedgemoor), or 'pull everything together and explain it' (Orchard). They claimed, and our data confirm, that children became aware, through assembly, that they were not isolated in their learning and that there were similarities and connections between the work of different classes. Typically:

> It's looking at the children's reaction when they sit in sharing assemblies. They listen and they watch the children who are sharing and you can see it going through their minds. 'We've done something like that.' They will often look at each other, often look because they are also seeing a link, 'We've done that haven't we?', 'We're going on to do such and such.'
>
> (Upper Norton)

Lastly, as experienced teachers, the heads also took advantage of all assemblies to collect information about the nature and quality of the learning and teaching that was going on in their schools, so as to build upon it in the future. For instance, at Fenton, the head commented on the progress being made by the newly appointed music coordinator towards her self-defined priority that the children would get 'better at sitting quietly and listening when there's music playing'; and the head of Greenfields noted the improved relationship between older and younger children as they entered the hall. As the head of Lavender Way said, 'Weekly forecasts are how I learn what teachers are doing. Assemblies are how I know what children are doing.'

Conclusion

I have presented data from two qualitative research projects to suggest that primary heads, despite their distance from the classroom and their change in role, still choose to be teachers, albeit working with much larger numbers, with adults as well as children, and with broader, school-wide aims in view. I have focused upon school assemblies because these gatherings can be viewed not just as 'collective acts of worship', but also as educational opportunities during which heads revealed the range and subtlety of their pedagogical interest and behaviour.

Sometimes, and most obviously, these headteachers used direct methods, especially story-telling, stating, informing and demonstrating, to teach parts of the schools' curricula, particularly but not exclusively those relating to religious and ethical education. In taking a central role in the transmission of ideas, information and skills, they set before children, staff, and sometimes parents and governors, an unambiguous statement of their moral, social and educational beliefs and values, and a clear picture, reinforced by their own behaviour, of what these might look like in practice. Their choice of content and of the ways in which they presented it also indicated to children and adults that the curriculum was a collective as well as an individual concern. They employed these formal approaches to teaching in settings and in a manner that reinforced their positional authority, and therefore their right to exercise control over education in 'their' schools. In addition, by displaying their pedagogical competence, they established their professional credibility. This in turn helped to sustain their personal authority.

It was less obvious that heads were teaching when they delegated leadership of assemblies to others. Nevertheless, their words and behaviour indicated that they were doing so, albeit obliquely and often quite subtly. Their indirect teaching strategies consisted of watching and listening, and then suggesting, questioning, giving encouragement and selective praise. The effectiveness of their actions depended not so much on the manner or setting in which the latter took place as upon the willingness of staff and children to perceive and interpret them correctly. Their success was, then, a measure of the heads' ability to influence rather than to control their mixed-age 'pupils'.

Heads relied heavily upon influence in promoting the professional development of their staff. This was particularly evident in relation to 'showing' assemblies, control of which was completely delegated to teachers, but which were subject to intervention and constructive comment by the heads. For their part, teachers understood that their heads were using these assemblies to show selective approval, to reinforce their aims and priorities and to emphasize the school-wide nature of the curriculum. Notwithstanding this, they generally enjoyed them and found them professionally useful and stimulating. Children also learnt from them and participated actively in them.

Although I have distinguished between heads' direct and indirect teaching approaches, they treated them not as alternatives but as mutually complementary. They pursued their educational aims through assemblies in as many ways as possible, combining instruction with gentle guidance, leadership with delegation, demonstration with encouragement of others, statement with questioning, admonition with praise, order with spontaneity.

The argument presented in this chapter qualifies or challenges existing studies of assemblies in two ways. First, there is the question of control. Our data support the established view that one function of school assemblies is to reinforce the authority of the head and so to underscore the role of the school as an instrument of social control. However, this interpretation overlooks the related facts that headteachers continue to identify as practitioners and that, to teachers, control is a necessary means to an educational end. I suggest that the heads in these schools organized and ran their assemblies in ways that emphasized their authority because they wished to use them for pedagogical purposes. From their perspective, school assemblies were classes on a grand scale, available to be educated. For this to be possible, the 'class' must be quiet and orderly and its members receptive. Viewed this way, heads' tacit and overt emphasis on social control was intended to be facilitative rather than repressive.

Second, our data differ from those presented in other studies. Teachers in these schools did not perceive assemblies as interruptions to classroom time (Rutter, Maughan, Mortimore and Ouston, 1979), to be equated as 'low-priority, intrusive events' (Rosenholtz, 1985, p. 371), with loudspeaker announcements and paperwork. Rather, they welcomed them and often enjoyed their attendance at them. This was not only because assemblies enabled them to see and communicate, albeit non-verbally, with their colleagues, but also because they felt that these occasions promoted their own knowledge and expertise and the motivation and understanding of their pupils. In particular, 'showing' assemblies provided a rare opportunity for mutual professional observation and learning.

It is clear from the evidence presented here that primary school assemblies offer headteachers a tool of powerful pedagogical and curricular potential. They provide a focused arena for the display of heads' teaching skills and the demonstration of curriculum practice. They enable heads publicly to reveal, reaffirm and exemplify their educational and moral goals; and to guide, instruct and encourage both staff and pupils. They give adults and children a chance to learn from and interact with one another, and they allow heads to gather information about classroom practice. If we are to take seriously heads' continuing identification as teachers, and their maturing skills as educators, assembly deserves greater attention from researchers than it has so far attracted.

Note

1 In this respect they resemble Peter Woods, who has never, I suggest, lost his instinct to further the learning and the development of those with whom he comes into contact. His capacity to guide and subtly shape the thinking of his students and colleagues has been matched over the years by the generosity with which he has provided them with support, challenge and opportunities for growth. As one who has both learnt from him and greatly benefited from his encouragement, I am glad to be able publicly to recognize his continuing work as an educator and researcher.

References

Bell, L. (1988) *Management Skills in Primary Schools*, London: Routledge.

Burgess, R. (1983) *Becoming Comprehensive: A Study of Bishop Macgregor School*, London: Methuen.

Dean, J. (1987) *Managing the Primary School*, London: Croom Helm.

Department of Education and Science (1990) *Developing School Management: The Way Forward,* a report by the School Management Task Force, London: HMSO.

Fuller, F. (1969) 'Concerns of teachers: a developmental characterization', *American Educational Research Journal*, **6**, pp. 207–26.

Hayes, D. (1996) 'Aspiration, perspiration and reputation: idealism and self-preservation in small school primary headship', *Cambridge Journal of Education*, **26**, 3, pp. 379–390.

King, R. (1983) *The Sociology of School Organisations*, London: Methuen.

Little, J.W. (1988) 'Assessing the prospects for teacher leadership', in Lieberman, A. (ed.) *Building a Professional Culture in Schools*, New York: Teachers' College Press.

Mortimore, P., Sammons, P., Stoll, L., Lewis, D. and Ecob, R. (1988) *School Matters: The Junior Years*, London: Open Books.

Nias, J. (1989a) *Primary Teachers Talking: A Study of Teaching as Work*, London: Routledge.

Nias, J. (1989b) 'The symbolic importance of school assemblies in schools with collaborative cultures', Paper presented to Annual Conference of American Educational Research Association, San Franscisco.

Nias, J. (1997) 'Responsibility and partnership in the primary school', in Taylor, P. and Miller, S. (eds) *The Primary Professional*, Birmingham: Educational Partners.

Nias, J., Southworth, G. and Yeomaus, R. (1989) *Staff Relationships in Primary Schools: A Study of Organisational Cultures*, London: Cassell.

Nias, J., Southworth, G. and Campbell, P. (1992) *Whole School Curriculum Development in Primary Schools*, London: Falmer Press.

Pollard, A. (1985) *The Social World of the Primary School*, London: Cassell.

Rosenholtz, S. (1985) 'Effective schools: interpreting the evidence', *American Journal of Education*, **93**, pp. 352–88.

Rutter, M., Maughan, B., Mortimore, P. and Ouston, J. (1979) *15,000 Hours: Secondary Schools and Their Effects on Children*, London: Open Books.

Southworth, G. (1995) *Looking into Primary Headship*, London: Falmer Press.

Teacher Training Agency (1998) *Leadership Programme for Serving Heads*, London: TTA.

Webb, R. and Vulliamy, G. (1996) *Roles and Responsibilities in the Primary School: Changing Demands, Changing Practices*, Buckingham: Open University Press.

Woods, P. (1979) *The Divided School*, London: Routledge.

2 Researching Primary Teachers' Work: Examining Theory, Policy and Practice through Interactionist Ethnography

Geoff Troman

In discussing the research agenda following the 1988 Education Reform Act (ERA), Pollard predicted that the 'core sociological issue of the relationship of the individual to society, of agency and constraint, control and order – will achieve an enhanced place at the centre of studies in primary education' (Pollard, 1992, p. 119). And he saw interactionist ethnography as being central to this.

Of course, this approach has been criticized for failing to link macro and micro levels of analysis. When applied to educational research – owing to its emphasis on subjectivity, agency, the social construction of reality and the everyday life of participants – symbolic interactionism has been accused of 'empiricism' (Hammersley, 1980); of eschewing macro-theory; and of 'macro-blindness' or the neglect of constraints on social life that have their origins in social structure (Power, 1996; Sharp, 1982; Troyna, 1994; Whitty, 1974). However, as Woods argues, while the symbolic interactionist focus is on 'the everyday', neglecting social structure and the constraints it places upon actors is 'not an essential feature of the approach' (Woods, 1996, p. 48). Characteristically, Woods recognizes interactionism's potential to 'approach society and social structure from below':

> by monitoring the attribution of meanings as well as how these sustain situations and processes, and how people define and redefine each other's and their own perspectives, patterns may be identified that exhibit both personal creativity and external constraint.
>
> *(ibid.,* p. 49)

My own work has followed this approach, attempting to chart the impact of education policy on teachers in a primary school, enabling a link to be established between policy generated at the macro (societal) level, and how it impacts at the meso (organizational) and micro (personal) levels (Troman, 1997). In this way, connections were sought between structural and situational factors. These have not been easy to make in the past. Now, owing to legislative initiatives designed to bring education more in line with economic imperatives, the strands of control from centre to periphery are much more visible. In forming links between macro, meso and micro levels, the Education Reform Act of 1988, and subsequent legislation, have provided an opportunity to study the 'interconnections between political frameworks and school and classroom structure and processes' (Woods, 1996, p. 75). Studying these interconnections helps to cultivate the 'sociological imagination' (Mills, 1959).

Arguably, what are needed are detailed studies, informed by symbolic interactionist theory, of what happens when policy reforms are introduced 'into the realm of individual institutions' (Gillborn, 1994, p. 147) in order to discover 'what is going on' (Mac an Ghaill, 1996a). Furthermore, we need to understand the implications the reforms have for teachers and how they are experienced at the meso (organizational) and micro (personal) levels (Reay, 1996). Policy can be more completely understood by looking at its micro aspects to find out more about practitioners and to look at policy with an 'inside-out perspective' (Ball, 1987). Ozga (1990) sees policy analysis as bringing together macro and micro levels of analysis to ensure that the integration of policy analysis with analysis of actors' perspectives provides a 'bigger picture'.

There is a growing tendency in policy theory and research to move from a straightforward conception of policy towards more complex models (Vanegas, 1996). Traditionally, policy was seen as a facticity handed down by the powerful and implemented, unproblematically, by the less powerful. Ball characterizes this simplistic linear model as follows:

> Policies as texts 'conjure up' pristine and magical thought worlds of practice – ideal settings in which the intentions of policy makers enter smoothly and unhindered into the minds and actions of the practitioners.
>
> (Ball, 1996, p. 9)

In this view of policy, little attempt is made to understand the social processes involved or the perspectives and experiences of those who implement the policy (Vanegas, 1996). Recently, new and more complex ways of conceptualizing policy have arisen. For instance, there have been calls to focus policy research on the sites of implementation (Bowe, Ball and Gold, 1992; Elmore, 1996; Fitz, Halpin and Power, 1994; Halpin and Troyna, 1994; Raab, 1994). Bowe et al. (1992), who are very critical of top-down models, have argued that 'policy formation does not end with the legislative moment, . . . it includes the implementation' (Vanegas, 1996, p. 3). Ball argues that policy is an

> economy of power, a set of technologies and practices which are realised and struggled over in local settings. Policy is both text and action, words and deeds, it is what is enacted as well as what is

intended. Policies are always incomplete insofar as they relate to or map on to the 'wild profusion' of local practice. Policies are inevitably crude and simple. Practice is sophisticated, contingent, complex and unstable. Policy as practice is 'created' on a trialectic of dominance, resistance and chaos/freedom; that is requirements, prohibitions or incentives, responses and interpretations, and a great deal of 'other' action which is not directly related to policy at all.

(Ball, 1996, p. 3)

Policy sociology considers policy as a cyclical process and aims to provide an analysis of it in the various phases of the cycle. It offers, too, a means of bridging the macro–micro gap (Hargreaves, 1985), since a study focused on the impact of a range of policies in the 'zone of implementation' (Bowe et al., 1992) will tend to expose the constraints and 'influences of wider societal factors on what teachers do' (Woods, 1996, p. 48). Given the lack of studies of primary schools as organizations, it seemed timely and appropriate to utilize a policy sociology approach in order to view the impact of a range of recent policies on them.

My research approach was underpinned by the 'loose body' (Woods, 1996) of symbolic interactionist theory. Symbolic interactionism is seen by some as the polar opposite of functionalist and conflict theories (Worsley, 1970), in that it rejects determinism and views social order as the outcome of interaction among members of society. While Mead (1934) certainly stresses the importance of socialization as a shaping force to produce internalized norms of conduct, the individual 'may always act impulsively and creatively in ways that have not been learned from society' (Worsley, 1970, p. 545). Emphasis is on the construction and maintenance of the self (Woods, 1996). The socialized individual is capable of thought, invention and self-determination (Strauss, 1959). Symbolic interactionists therefore concern themselves with the subjective meanings and experiences of individuals (Hitchcock and Hughes, 1989). Blumer (1976) argued that social researchers guided by the theoretical framework of symbolic inter-actionism would necessarily need to focus on actors' meanings, motiva-tions and interpretations. Like Blumer, Woods stresses the importance of the 'empirical social world', that is:

the minute-by-minute, day-to-day social life of individuals as they interact together, as they develop understandings and meanings, as they engage in joint action and respond to each other, as they adapt to situations, and as they encounter and move to resolve problems that arise through their circumstances.

(Woods, 1996, p. 37)

Of course, detailed ethnographic studies of schooling have often pointed to the inadequacy of macro perspectives as explanations of the social processes of schooling. Marxist correspondence theory of schooling, for example, was undermined by studies showing that, far from schools producing a docile workforce for capitalism, they actually were a site for resistance and rebellion (Willis, 1977; see Woods, 1996). Similarly, teacher responses cannot be merely read off from the restructuring policies themselves (Ball, 1994). Teachers in the past have proved to be extremely resistant to imposed change. They have, for instance, deflected and subverted policies rather than implementing them unproblematically (Simons, 1988). On the evidence of other empirical studies of the impact of innovation, patterns of implementation can be expected to be varied and complex (Bowe et al., 1992; Grace, 1995; Pollard, Broadfoot, Croll, Osborn and Abbot, 1994). The changes have to be mediated through the teachers' professional ideologies (Broadfoot and Osborn, 1988) and in the context of their existing work cultures (Mac an Ghaill, 1992). Although the changes are, in the main, legislated, teachers may still have room for 'negotiating' them at school level. How these negotiations are played out is a central concern of this chapter.

I provide a case study of one subject manager, derived from a larger primary school ethnography (Troman, 1997). I develop a description and analysis of her perspective, in order to illustrate the approach adopted in my study and to stress the capacity of interactionist ethnography to illuminate the policy process at the implementation stage. I am, therefore, attempting to realize one of the 'promises' of symbolic interactionism detailed by Woods (1996).

Methods

This case study is based on data collected during 18 months of fieldwork in a primary school. The school, Meadowfields, is located on the outskirts of an English South Midlands market town and had 450 pupils with a staff of 17 teachers. Access to the school to carry out the research was granted by the headteacher and senior management team, following negotiation. While usually being in the role of researcher, I sometimes had to adopt other roles in the school. For example, I occasionally stood in for teachers in some classes or worked with small groups of children on specific projects. The data were derived from informal conversations, interviews, observations and school documents (curriculum policy statements, governors' meeting minutes, school development plan, and so on). Data collection took place in a variety of contexts including staffroom, staff meetings, senior management team meetings, headteacher's office, and in-service education and training days for the teachers. Tape recordings of conversations, meetings and interviews were transcribed and analysed and observations recorded in fieldnotes. Ongoing analysis of verbal data and observational notes informed subsequent data collection and enabled 'progressive focusing' (Glaser and Strauss, 1967) and 'spiralling insights' (Lacey, 1976) to develop.

Though the case study reported here focuses on a subject manager's responses to the impact of several educational policies, the wider study was concerned with the restructuring of teachers' work and the impact of this on their professional and personal identities and on their occupational cultures. By concentrating on a single case I realize that claims of generalizability, or of proof with respect to theory, would be inappropriate (Gomm, Foster and Hammersley, 1998; Hammersley, Gomm and Foster, 1998). I seek merely to explore macro–micro links and to illuminate the policy implementation process. The power of the single case should not be underestimated (Wolcott, 1995).

The Subject Manager's Work

Bowe et al. (1992) argue that the intensification of work in the secondary school has produced conflict through the separation of managers and teachers. In this situation, those teachers who are senior managers but also members of the teaching staff – for example, deputy headteachers and members of the senior management team – are caught between management and workers, and experience considerable frustration and conflict owing to this role. They 'now stand in a dual relation to the staff and to senior management. [They] "understand" both parties, stand between and inhabit their two worlds, but feel unable to secure a permanent reconciliation' (Bowe et al., 1992, p. 149). This kind of tension is likely to be experienced more acutely in the primary school where, in the new role of subject manager, the boundaries between management and teachers might be expected to be less clearly demarcated than in secondary schools.[1] Indeed, new managerial roles in the primary school provide opportunities for teachers and offer a range of new professional identities, but the adoption of these is proving problematical (MacLure, 1993). Some aspects of the new teacher role provide opportunities for role enhancement, while others threaten to deskill teachers. The new role of subject manager has a potential for role tension and conflict. Although Woods, Jeffrey, Troman and Boyle (1997) argue that the primary teacher's traditional role as generalist class teacher was diffuse and inherently conflictual, recent research indicates that these features have been exacerbated in the subject manager role (Webb and Vulliamy, 1995). Those teachers who are subject managers – and they form the majority of the profession (Troman, 1996) – are likely to experience heightened conflicts and role tensions for the following reasons:

- The introduction of market principles and management-led reform into primary schools is potentially at odds with the existing dominant ideologies of teaching (Ball, 1994).
- The unceasing drive to raise educational standards has ensured greatly

raised expectations of the subject manager role (Webb and Vulliamy, 1995).

- Official role expectations for the subject manager are now clearly specified. More explicit job descriptions now embody policy maker and headteacher definitions of that role (Troman, 1996).
- Accountability procedures, such as school inspections, now focus in a major way on the subject manager role (Webb and Vulliamy, 1996).
- The changes in teachers' work has involved 'galloping role inflation' (Campbell and Neill, 1994). Apart from their considerable managerial role, the subject managers are also class teachers having to implement the National Curriculum, assessment and testing.
- With the growth of school development planning, the work of subject managers is linked more clearly with specific development targets (Webb and Vulliamy, 1996).
- With the demise of advisory teachers (Webb and Vulliamy, 1996), and the decline of LEA-provided INSET, many subject managers may be solely responsible for the school-based development of their subject.
- Changes in organization and role are taking place in a context marked by contradictions. For, though top-down managerialism is evident and the power and authority of the primary headteacher is undiminished, they coexist alongside the discourses and practices of devolved management, flattened hierarchies, participative decision-making, collaborative work cultures, shared professional learning and teacher empowerment (Grace, 1995).
- The traditional factors of low levels of time, authority and resources operating on the coordinator's role seem likely to remain (Kinder and Harland, 1991).
- Role expectations are now being transformed into role obligations and role tensions are becoming constraints (Woods et al., 1997).

In the following section I explore the perceptions of Elizabeth, the maths coordinator at Meadowfields. Her perspective, revealed through conversations, illuminates the changing nature of her work as a subject manager and her interpretation of the official version of the subject manager role. It exposes the ambiguities of intensification, and the conflicts and tensions in the new role. Before I undertake this analysis, though, I will provide some contextualization.

Background

All the teachers at the school, with the exception of the newly qualified, had a curriculum responsibility that included the supervision and monitoring of the work of their colleagues. However, it was Elizabeth who, in my estimation, approximated most closely to the official model of the 'good teacher' (Troman, 1996). Elizabeth is 50 years old and has been in teaching for approximately 30 years. She spent a short time in secondary schools before moving to the primary sector, where she has worked for the major part of her career. As a subject manager she had not received any management training. At Meadowfields a general pattern seemed to be for the teachers to acquire additional management responsibilities as their careers progressed in the school. A key time in the allocation of these responsibilities had been in the aftermath of an inspection by HMI, who instructed the school to formulate a new school development plan, which 'should include the redefinition of staff roles and responsibilities'. Coordinators of subjects that had been most criticized by HMI were replaced. Elizabeth had been appointed by the headteacher following ERA as a change agent to facilitate his restructuring of the school, and in this role he described her as the 'first chisel in the rock'.

She was a member of the senior management team and, like her colleagues, was a full-time class teacher. She and other subject managers were, of course, heavily involved in implementing all of the measures of the ERA, measures that in terms of policy had been the subject of constant changes since 1988. As subject manager for mathematics, she was responsible for developing the subject throughout the school, and this involved leading a large programme of school-based INSET. Additionally, she was responsible for the teacher appraisal scheme and the ordering, purchase and allocation of resources for all subjects. She was highly thought of by all of the other teachers I had conversations with. When asked to recall concrete incidents when a subject coordinator had helped them with professional development, they frequently mentioned her name.

While her teaching commitment, managerial responsibilities and membership of the senior management team led me to identify her as a subject manager, her perspective on herself, her work and the social relations of the school, as shown through analysis of conversations, showed ambivalence towards the new role. She might be considered, therefore, as a partial, or even reluctant, teacher/manager. Although she was seen as successful in the new managerial role, she felt uncomfortable with many aspects of her new expanded and intensified work. She would also reflect critically on the impact of managerialism on her and the school. There was, therefore, evidence of role conflict in her perspective. She was not completely 'caught' (Ball, 1994) by the new managerialism, and still felt drawn to her former role as a creative and relatively autonomous generalist class teacher (Woods, 1995). Her feelings about the subject manager role were, therefore, suggestive of an 'ambivalent enhancement'. Her positive feelings related to greater expertise, ownership and control. These appeared to meet her personal needs. Negative feelings were associated with the intensification of work, and reduced ownership and control in some key areas. I shall examine each of these aspects in turn.

Positive Feelings

Greater Expertise

Elizabeth appeared to enjoy her role when helping other teachers by giving advice informally. She had produced a voluminous resource pack for teachers to draw on in their teaching. In the INSET sessions she led she demonstrated her expertise by enthusiastically communicating her views about and methods of teaching mathematics through investigations. She felt that this method of teaching, although requiring more skill, should be adopted throughout the school. However, many of the teachers resisted this approach and continued using published Maths schemes. Elizabeth's involvement in planning was not restricted to topic and lesson planning. As a member of the senior management team, she was closely involved with school development planning and the formulation of school policy. Indeed one of her first managerial tasks at the school, following ERA, was to formulate a maths policy. In previous posts, she 'really hadn't been aware of school policy', and certainly hadn't written one, but at this school she showed a measure of pride in having done it:

> I think the first thing I did when I came here was write the school's maths policy. There were no guidelines, real sort of clear guidelines. So I went on an Open University Maths diploma course which was a great help. I worked with a couple of other people to get some ideas together but it's one of those things, it was best working on your own though it was supposed to be involving everybody and everyone's ideas to make the whole thing work. It really wasn't feasible because there was no time to do it in school. It had to be done at home. So, it's pretty much my document and now, of course, that's totally out of date.

While feeling proud of using new knowledge and skills in maths teaching in order to write policy, Elizabeth seemed to recognize here that the new managerialism should be accomplished collaboratively, rather than individually. She was almost apologetic in her admission that this managerial task was accomplished alone, even though intensification of work had forced the situation; and she recognized that, in some tasks, solitary working may be superior to collegial effort (Hargreaves, 1994).

Ownership and Control

Elizabeth obviously enjoyed some parts of her work as a manager and seemed to possess some 'natural' management skills:

> It's nice to have a say in what goes on in school, and I think I've been here long enough to know how things happen, how people tick and

what's accepted and what's not, and how to get around people, or talk to people or whatever. I just like to be in the know as well.

Of course, she recognized that management roles, while providing opportunities for being in control, can contribute to further intensification of work:

> . . . enjoyable, I suppose you could use that word. If I wasn't doing it, like if I wasn't doing maths in that coordinator's role, I'd be very irritated by perhaps what another coordinator would do, and that sort of feeling. I'd feel that I wanted to be in charge of it, even though sometimes the workload is heavy. But, I think sometimes I could do without bits of the management role.

As a teacher governor, she was unsure about potential managerial domination by the lay governors, but did see that there could be benefits:

> Governors have got better management skills than we have. They're more aware of budgeting than we are. Perhaps we can palm off some of these jobs onto them and let us control what happens in school and the education side of it.

Elizabeth felt that there was a collaborative culture in the school, and that she gained from it. She not only gave advice but also received it:

> I think the collaboration here is very good. I feel I can go and talk to most people in a very casual way and get ideas. They're very forthcoming.

Negative Feelings

Intensification of Work

She clearly recognized the recent intensification of her work and gave many indications of pressure, tension and stress, in phrases such as the following:

> heavy workload . . . being asked to do too much . . . extra jobs . . . no finish/no end to it . . . pressure on you . . . all the time spent trying to do your best . . . now it's two topics a term and it's a nightmare . . . God I haven't done this and I haven't done that and I've got to do that . . . being asked to do too much . . . getting in the way of my private life . . . feeling dizzy/shell-shocked at the end of the day . . . we seem to spend most of our time going round in circles . . . I didn't do half as much work out of school as I do now . . . making me rush things . . . it's taking longer and longer at home to do the stuff, like I say it's lucky

> that my husband is a teacher . . . children aren't being taught what's in the plans in some cases because there isn't time to do it . . . I don't think I'm teaching as well as I used to simply because I'm being asked to do too much . . . it doesn't make for a very smooth, calm person . . . you're fighting against it all the time . . . pressure on you to get things up and running.

Although experiencing intensification of work arising from largely managerial tasks, she still put the children in her class first:

> It's [managerial work] getting in the way of my private life. I think I end up feeling dizzy at the end of the day because so many other things have happened, like some stock will arrive, or somebody'll want to see somebody about something or the Head will want to see you about something, or you're meeting with somebody else, and at the end of the day I feel quite sort of shell-shocked sometimes. But it really doesn't get in the way of what's happening in the class because that's got to come first or else the school falls apart, because you can't cope in the classroom then. I think everybody has days when they're going sort of off the cuff and that can happen any time. You can have a late night, friends call round, but the majority of my time outside school, the extra time, it's taken up, I don't call the extra time for the kids, that's always going to be there, more time's taken up with sort of management coordinating stuff.

In his study of a primary school, Hayes (1994) found some teachers who were reluctant to engage in collaborative whole-school decision-making and assume further managerial responsibilities. This was for the very practical reason that participation would demand extra time commitments which, the teachers believed, would result in their having reduced time for planning and teaching their classes. The teachers were class-focused rather than whole-school focused and, therefore, were 'restricted' rather than 'extended professionals' (Hoyle, 1974). Although this was true of some of the teachers at Meadowfields, Elizabeth seems to have partly resolved the tension between managerial and teacher roles by displacing some of the extra management tasks into her personal life, thereby further increasing intensification. She blamed herself for not 'being as quick as others' to complete tasks and often took work home. She felt fortunate that her teacher husband understood the pressures and did not complain. Some of her female colleagues completed their work at school by staying behind for several hours so that they could avoid feelings of guilt induced by complaints from non-teaching partners about bringing work home.

Elizabeth felt under pressure to fill in many planning sheets:

It's just an extra job. Because Art is part of our topic work, we have to list Light (a Science subject) as part of our topic. So we record it on our Art sheet, Science sheet and Humanities sheet. Now, Art's connected to music, so you're writing things out four or five times.

However, as part of management, she participated in making the decision to have multiple planning sheets. Indeed she required the teachers to submit their maths planning to her and thereby contributed to the intensification of their work:

I'm putting pressure on people. I'm just thinking, well, they're not actually doing much extra work, they're just putting it all on one side of paper and it's building up a scheme of work. But it's asking somebody to do something else.

She notes, too, the artificiality of the system that separates managerial planning from teaching:

You're duplicating planning, and sometimes it has little to do with what you're doing in the classroom, and sometimes it's not needed for what you're doing in the classroom.

Reduced Ownership and Control

Elizabeth previously worked in a private international school in France, which was organized on democratic principles. She now believes that owing to the veneer of democracy and the extent of micro-political activity, Meadowfields has fallen short of genuine and equal participation:

Before I came here I was at an *avant-garde* school. It was brilliant. They didn't have a head, they had a chairperson, who was voted in for two years. Anybody could have been chairperson and everybody had a say in how the school was run. It took a long time to get anything done but at least you felt you were working for the school, not an authority – it was independent. It was a small school. It wouldn't work on a big scale. There was only about 180 kids. No decisions were made at a meeting until you had time to go away and think about it. You weren't bamboozled into saying 'yes' or 'no' straightway. You could come back to the next meeting and vote on it.

If Elizabeth was losing some control in decision-making, this was also occurring in school policy formulation:

The county is saying that two sides of A4 is all you need for your policy documents, but it can't be very clear if it's just two sides. What I wrote wasn't just my ideas, it included a lot of some very clever people's thinking in maths and how it should be taught. I thought that was very valuable – but two sides, that's meaningless. But that's what we're supposed to be doing so that's what we are doing.

Elizabeth's teaching philosophy seems at odds with 'technicist' versions, yet she recognizes that in her teaching now she must on occasions depart from her child-centred approach in order to engage in managerial tasks, such as planning and recording and reaching targets, which have been specified by others. She recognizes that she has lost some ownership of pedagogy, and that bureaucracy has eclipsed teaching and eroded personal relationships:

You could do a topic for a whole term and all the kids do lots of investigative work, and lots of testing out their theories, lots of making stuff to see if it works and really delving quite deeply into a subject, but not just the facts of a subject but to understand how things worked. And that was fine spending a term on a topic. Now it's two a term and it's a nightmare. We've got to do sound and light in seven weeks. You can't do a lot of getting to know what sound is all about and then do any really valuable investigations in that time. You've got to be feeding them information, in a way, to a certain extent you've got to give information. Some kids know because they catch on more quickly and they're making connections, but those little mites at the bottom – you're just shoving stuff at them I feel sometimes.

The main focus was the children and now it seems to have shifted from that a lot on to how you record what you're teaching and how you record what the children are doing and how you plan so far ahead for everything, that you almost forget the kids that are involved in it.

In writing a recent school policy, to accommodate the recent national policy changes, she felt deskilled and frustrated. She expected external 'experts' to eventually reveal the 'perfect' policy:

We've had no training for this, that's why it's so frustrating not know-ing you're doing the right thing. I've spent years and years trying to do it [formulate policy] . . . there's nothing clear from the maths team [LEA maths advisors and advisory teachers] . . . they just give out ideas and you have to work it out yourselves. That's a bit more work. If we're going to have to do it like that why don't they just give us the sheet and say, 'There you are'.

Here the dependency on external 'experts' potentially undermined profes-sional judgment and reduced control.

Elizabeth is also losing control of how she carries out her work as subject manager. Since the inspection, she was expected to undertake classroom observation of colleagues for monitoring and appraisal. HMI had included this strong expectation in their report, and the headteacher had been instructed to include it in the job descriptions of senior management, and to give coordinators the authority to carry it out. A 'floating' Deputy Headteacher form of organization made a small amount of non-contact time available for this task:

> What's meant to happen now is that I'm able to go into different areas to work with people – it's a much more organized set-up. It's actually working in classrooms with people. I worked with their planning but I haven't worked in classrooms with anybody yet and that's part of the brief since the inspection. I don't know how that's going to work – it's going to be a bit delicate I think because I don't want to tread on anyone's toes.

The new managerial role here stands in contrast to older versions of professionalism in which classroom autonomy was central. Elizabeth respected the autonomy of colleagues and gave it priority over monitoring and advisory work. Thus, as in Campbell's (1988) study, 'paradoxically, from the point of view of curriculum development, the concept of the class teacher's "autonomy" in curricular matters was to some extent shared by the [coordinators] themselves, despite the fact that the consequence of their curriculum development activities was to bring such a concept into question' (p. 227). Elizabeth hesitated to enter into classrooms in her advisory role to work alongside colleagues because this might involve her in making evaluations of her colleagues' teaching:

> It's just the way you approach people, isn't it. You work with them rather than showing them this is the way to do it. That's not what you do. You can't go in and say that to a teacher who has been teaching for 'n' number of years and imply that they're not doing it the right way. I must say I haven't solved that problem yet. I haven't actually gone into a classroom yet.

Holding these reservations, yet having to monitor the work of colleagues in her managerial role, she relied on unobtrusive means of evaluation:

> You get their plans and it all seems fine but it's not being done that way, and that came out in the inspectors' report as well, that what is happening in the policy is not happening in the classroom. Not in one but in all classrooms. And then just by – it's almost like being a spy – but it's an accidental spy – so you see things on blackboards or see peoples' worksheets and just think, 'Oh my God that's happening.' And how do you stop it happening?

She was also uncertain how to proceed on the strength of evidence from colleagues' planning:

> I think they know they have got some gaps in their planning and I can go and talk to them about it. But I don't want to go and tread on their toes. It's got to be done very carefully and I haven't put my mind to that yet.

Elizabeth's previous experience of being observed herself by a colleague warned her of the potential falseness of classroom observation:

> I hate people watching the way I teach. You really feel you're being seen with a critical eye and that's got to be avoided really. I remember Frances came and she asked if she could come in and listen to the language that was used. Not just mine, but I think the language in the class. So I said, 'That's alright.' But when she was there I didn't speak the way I do normally at all. It was all totally false, and I thought, 'Well Christ if she thinks that's what it's like all the time?'

Elizabeth can provide a rationalization for the gap between policy and practice in the school, and can sympathize with her colleagues who cut corners because of the intensification of work, their educational values, or their lack of subject confidence and expertise:

> In some cases, children aren't being taught what's on the plans, in some cases because there isn't time to do it, and in other cases because people don't believe that what's on the plans is what the children should be taught. It's over a year now since we had an INSET on this aspect of maths and this sort of thing shouldn't be happening at all. But people forget, and if it's not your subject and you don't feel too confident you fall back on old methods and the things that you did at school. I do that as well.

There was also recognition that the production of documentation that accompanied bureaucracies and managerialist cultures had ascendancy over issues central to teaching and learning:

> . . . as long as you've got your planning in place, and it's all nicely written up, what you get through to the kids is secondary. Partly because you've hardly got time to think about them, you're thinking so much about the planning.

Conclusion

The in-depth analysis of a single case gives insight into the complexity of the changes that are taking place, and the role conflict and stress associated with them. In an important sense what is happening here is that Elizabeth is undergoing reskilling as an education manager. It is also worth noting that gender may be an important factor. In a study of women in the public and private sectors who had recently been promoted to management, Harris noted contradictions in their accounts of the process of becoming a manager (Harris, 1995). She explained these as revealing conflicts or tensions in the roles they occupied, or the circumstances of uncertainty or confusion in which they worked. They experienced disorientation, bafflement or puzzlement as they attempted to adapt to their changing roles (Harrison, Hunter and Marnoch, 1992). She also suggests that her interview material indicates a sense of transition in their personal biographies as they take account of discontinuities, while seeking to retain a continuous sense of self.

Woods (1995) writes of a 'liminal' stage, a kind of betwixt and between in which teachers mourn the loss (Nias, 1991) of some aspects of the old as they struggle to adapt to the new. For Woods, contradictions in teacher accounts can be considered partly as an expression of the teachers' experience of 'liminality'. In conditions of rapid cultural change the production of professional subjectivities is a shifting scene (Mac an Ghaill, 1996b).

Research in education policy studies has, for too long, ignored the empirical reality of policy implementation in the primary school (Pollard, 1992). The 'rich underlife of social processes attending the recontextualization of policy' (Ball, 1994, p. 19) has been neglected. This chapter has sought to address this neglect. In doing so, my method has been 'bottom up'. I have tried, through the experiences and perspective of one teacher, to chart the 'effects' (rather than outcomes) of policy in the school, and to understand 'what takes place' – from the inside (Fitz et al., 1994, p. 64). I have shown how official policy is interpreted by a teacher, at school level. Policy goals are not directly translated into action, but are transformed when they are recontextualized (Ball, 1994). I have exposed some of the struggles over the implementation of policy. In focusing on how the subject manager dealt with the problems that policies raised for her, I have shown something of the impact that the policies have on her consciousness and sense of self. Through interactionist ethnography we come to understand more of the implementation process and of teachers' responses to it. These responses indicate 'creative social action not robotic reactivity' (Ball, 1994, p. 19).

Note

1 A large proportion of the policy document 'Primary Matters' (Ofsted, 1994) is devoted to rehearsing solutions designed to rectify the failure to implement the National Curriculum more fully. One cause identified was poor curriculum management and what was recommended was more and better management of teachers' work. The key to this was seen to be, as in previous reports, to promote the importance of the management aspects of the role of the curriculum

coordinators. These were renamed as 'subject managers' because 'coordinators [was] too limited a description' (*ibid.*, p. 9, para. 37), as it certainly was if all of the likely elements of the coordinator's role which emerged in the 1992 discussion paper (Department of Education and Science, 1992) were included in it.

References

Ball, S.J. (1987) *The Micro-Politics of the School: Towards a Theory of School Organisation*, London: Methuen.

Ball, S.J. (1994) *Education Reform: A Critical and Post-structural Approach*, Buckingham: Open University Press.

Ball, S.J. (1996) 'Recreating policy through qualitative research: a trajectory analysis', unpublished.

Blumer, H. (1976) 'The methodological position of symbolic interactionism', in Hammersley, M. and Woods, P. (eds) *The Process of Schooling*, London: Routledge and Kegan Paul.

Bowe, R., Ball, S.J. with Gold, A. (1992) *Reforming Education and Changing Schools: Case Studies in Policy Sociology*, London: Routledge.

Broadfoot, P. and Osborn, M. (1988) 'What professional responsibility means to teachers: national contexts and classroom constants', *British Journal of Sociology of Education*, **9**, 3, pp. 265–88.

Campbell, R.J. (1988) 'Conflict and strain in the postholder's role', in Glatter, R., Preedy, M., Riches, C. and Masterson, M. (eds) *Understanding School Management,* Milton Keynes: Open University Press.

Campbell, R.J. and St. J. Neill, S.R. (1994) *Curriculum Reform at Key Stage 1: Teacher Commitment and Policy Failure*, Harlow: Longman.

Department of Education and Science (1992) *Curriculum Organisation and Classroom Practice in Primary Schools: A Discussion Paper*, London: DES Information Branch.

Elmore, R.F. (1996) 'School reform, teaching and learning', *Journal of Education Policy*, **11**, 4, pp. 1–10.

Fitz, J., Halpin, D. and Power, S. (1994) 'Implementation research and education policy: practice and prospects', *British Journal of Educational Studies* **42**, 1, pp. 53–69.

Gillborn, D. (1994) 'The micro-politics of macro reform', *British Journal of Sociology of Education*, **15**, 2, pp. 147–64.

Glaser, B.G. and Strauss, A.L. (1967) *The Discovery of Grounded Theory*, Chicago: Aldine.

Gomm, R., Foster, P. and Hammersley, M. (1998) 'Case study and generalisation', Paper presented to the Case Study Research in Education Conference, CEDAR, University of Warwick, March.

Grace, G. (1995) *School Leadership: Beyond Education Management, An Essay in Policy Scholarship*, London: Falmer Press.

Halpin, D. and Troyna, B. (eds) (1994) *Researching Education Policy: Ethical and Methodological Issues,* London: Falmer Press.

Hammersley, M. (1980) 'On interactionist empiricism', in Woods, P. (ed) *Pupil Strategies: Explorations in the Sociology of the School*, London: Croom Helm.

Hammersley, M., Gomm, R. and Foster, P. (1998) 'Case study and theory', Paper presented to the Case Study Research in Education Conference, CEDAR, University of Warwick, March.

Hargreaves, A. (1985) 'The micro–macro problem in the sociology of education', in Burgess, R.G. (ed.) *Issues in Educational Research: Qualitative Methods*, Lewes: Falmer Press.

Hargreaves, A. (1994) *Changing Teachers, Changing Times: Teachers' Work and Culture in the Postmodern World*, London: Cassell.

Harris, P. (1995) 'Learning to manage: changing jobs, changing selves?', Paper presented at the Annual Labour Process Conference, Blackpool, April.

Harrison, S., Hunter, D. and Marnoch, G. (1992) *Just Managing: Power and Culture in the National Health Service*, Basingstoke: Macmillan.

Hayes, D (1994) 'Teachers' involvement in decision-making: a case study of a primary school at a time of rapid change', unpublished Ph.D. thesis, University of Plymouth.

Hitchcock, G. and Hughes, D. (1989) *Research and the Teacher: A Qualitative Introduction to School-based Research*, London: Routledge.

Hoyle, E. (1974) 'Professionalility, professionalism and control in teaching', *London Educational Review*, **3**, 2, pp. 15–17. Also in Houghton, V., McHugh, R. and Morgan, C. (eds) (1975) *Management in Education: The Management of Organizations and Individuals*, London: Ward Lock Educational in Association with the Open University Press.

Kinder, K. and Harland, J. (1991) *The Impact of INSET: The Case of Primary Science*, Slough: NFER.

Lacey, C. (1976) 'Problems of sociological fieldwork: a review of the methodology of "Hightown Grammar"', in Hammersley, M. and Woods, P. (eds) *The Process of Schooling*, London: Routledge and Kegan Paul.

Mac an Ghaill, M. (1992) 'Teachers' work: curriculum restructuring, culture, power and comprehensive schooling', *British Journal of Sociology of Education*, **13**, 2, pp. 177–200.

Mac an Ghaill, M. (1996a) 'Manufacturing identities? Work, self and the primary school', Paper presented at the British Educational Research Association Conference, University of Lancaster, September.

Mac an Ghaill, M. (1996b) 'Sociology of education, state schooling and social class: beyond critiques of the New Right hegemony', *British Journal of Sociology of Education*, **17**, 2, pp. 163–76.

MacLure, M. (1993) 'Arguing for your self: identity as an organising principle in teachers' jobs and lives', *British Educational Research Journal*, **19**, 4, pp. 311–22.

Mead, G.H. (1934) *Mind, Self and Society*, Chicago: University of Chicago Press.

Mills, C.W. (1959) *The Sociological Imagination*, New York: Oxford University Press.

Nias, J. (1991) 'Changing times, changing identities: grieving for a lost self', in Burgess, R.G. (ed.) *Educational Research and Evaluation*, London: Falmer Press.

Ofsted (1994) *Primary Matters: A Discussion on Teaching and Learning in Primary Schools*, London, Ofsted.

Ozga, J. (1990) 'Policy research and policy theory: a comment on Fitz and Halpin', *Journal of Education Policy*, **5**, 4, pp. 359–62.

Pollard, A. (1992) 'Teachers' responses to the reshaping of primary education', in Arnot, M. and Barton, L. (eds) *Voicing Concerns: Sociological Perspectives on Contemporary Education Reforms*, Wallingford: Triangle Books.

Pollard, A., Broadfoot, P., Croll, P., Osborn, M. and Abbot, D. (1994) *Changing English Primary Schools: The Impact of the Education Reform Act at Key Stage One*, London: Cassell.

Power, S. (1996) *The Pastoral and the Academic: Conflict and Contradiction in the Curriculum*, London: Cassell.

Raab, C.D. (1994) 'Where are we now?: reflections on the sociology of education policy', in Halpin, D. and Troyna, B. (eds) *Researching Education Policy*, London: Falmer Press.

Reay, D. (1996) 'Micro-politics in the 1990s: staff relationships in secondary schooling', Paper presented at the British Educational Research Association Conference, University of Lancaster, September.

Sharp, R. (1982) 'Self-contained ethnography or a science of phenomenal forms and inner relations', *Boston University Journal of Education*, **164**, 1, pp. 48–63.

Simons, H. (1988) 'Teacher professionalism and the National Curriculum', in Lawton, D. and Chitty, C. (eds) *Bedford Way Papers 33*, Institute of Education, University of London.

Strauss, A.L. (1959) *Mirrors and Masks: The Search for Identity*, Glencoe, IL: Free Press.

Troman, G. (1996) 'Models of the good teacher: defining and redefining teacher quality', in Woods, P. (ed.) *Contemporary Issues in Teaching and Learning*, Buckingham: Open University Press.

Troman, G. (1997) 'The effects of restructuring on primary teachers' work: a sociological analysis', unpublished Ph.D. thesis, The Open University.

Troyna, B. (1994) 'The everyday world of teachers?: deracialised discourses in the sociology of teachers and the teaching profession', *British Journal of Sociology of Education,* **15**, 3, pp. 325–39.

Vanegas, P. (1996) 'An exploration of the educational policy process: teachers in Columbia', Paper presented at the British Educational Research Association *Conference, University of Lancaster, September.*

Webb, R. and Vulliamy, G. (1995) 'The changing role of the primary school curriculum coordinator', *Curriculum Journal*, **6**, 1, pp. 29–45.

Webb, R. and Vulliamy, G. (1996) *Roles and Responsibilities in the Primary School: Changing Demands, Changing Practices*, Buckingham: Open University Press.

Whitty, G. (1974) 'Sociology and the problem of radical educational change: towards a reconceptualization of the 'new' sociology of education', in Flude, M. and Ahier, J. (eds) *Educability Schools and Ideology*, London: Croom Helm.

Willis, P. (1977) *Learning to Labour*, Farnborough: Saxon House.

Wolcott, H.F. (1995) *The Art of Fieldwork*, London: Altamira.

Woods, P. (1995) *Creative Teachers in Primary Schools*, Buckingham: Open University Press.

Woods, P. (1996) *Researching the Art of Teaching: Ethnography for Educational Use*, London: Routledge.

Woods, P., Jeffrey, B., Troman, G. and Boyle, M. (1997) *Restructuring Schools, Reconstructing Teachers: Responding to Change in the Primary School*, Buckingham: Open University Press.

Worsley, P. (ed.) (1970) *Introducing Sociology*, 2nd edn, Harmondsworth: Penguin.

3 Side-stepping the Substantial Self: The Fragmentation of Primary Teachers' Professionality through Audit Accountability

Bob Jeffrey

From research spanning three projects, Woods and colleagues established a typology of teacher reactions to the intensification of primary teachers' work: enhanced teachers, compliant teachers, non-compliant teachers, and diminished teachers (Woods et al., 1997). The 'compliant teacher' category was the largest: 29 teachers from a sample of 64. This chapter investigates, in more detail, the effects of audit accountability on the professional identity of one of those teachers.

Professional Responsiveness and Audit Accountability

Accountability can be seen as a means of ensuring responsiveness: the willingness of an institution – or indeed of individuals – to respond to outside pressures and new ideas. There can be different kinds of account-ability. Professional accountability, according to Kogan, is the control of education by teachers and professional administrators (Kogan, 1989; see also Eraut, 1992). It involves obligations:

- to serve the interests of clients;
- to self-monitor and periodically review the effectiveness of one's practice;
- to expand one's repertoire, to reflect on experience and to develop one's expertise;
- to contribute to the quality of the organization in which one works; and
- to reflect on and contribute to discussions about the changing role of the profession in the wider society.

A rather different form of accountability, which can be referred to as 'market accountability', came to be emphasized in the 1980s under the Conservative government. So, for example, schools were exhorted to respond to the needs of the community through competing with each other for clients (Ball, 1990; Gewirtz, 1996). From this perspective, professional accountability was regarded as a producer-orientated system, with teachers' main interest lying in perpetuating their status and in some cases using their position to advance value-based beliefs (Hatcher, 1994; Troman, 1997). By restructuring the system of accountability towards the market model, those supporting this approach sought to constrain the power of providers in favour of the 'consumer' (Lawler, 1997). However, since this amounted to the creation of *quasi*-markets, rather than privatization of the state education system, in practice it involved a rather different kind of accountability: audit accountability.

This 'heavy duty accountability' (Woods and Jeffrey, 1996a), in the form of the specification of policy guidelines and targets plus regular audits, has taken different forms in various parts of the private and public sectors. However, there is a common thread: the use of bureaucratic procedures to verify compliance. As such, it is not only a technical practice, but articulates values with rationalizing and reinforcing public images of control. At school level this has been translated into managerial approaches that use concepts such as 'goal definition, efficient resource allocation, financial performance, competition, economy, efficiency and effectiveness' (Power, 1994). As Power notes:

> audits generally act indirectly upon systems of control rather than directly upon first order activities. [. . .] Audit has thereby become the 'control of control', where what is being assured is the quality of control systems rather than the quality of first order operations. In such a context, accountability is discharged by demonstrating the existence of systems of control rather than by demonstrating good teaching, caring, manufacturing, banking etc.
>
> (Power, 1994, p. 19)

The primary teachers in our research accepted the principle of public accountability. As one of them said: 'I think you have to be accountable. I don't object at all to accountability. I think that it's a good thing.' However, many were concerned about the kind of accountability regime under which they now had to labour (Troman, 1994). Alongside the introduction of the National Curriculum, the associated national standardized testing, and public disclosure of results, schools have been set in competition with one another. Added to this are Ofsted (Office for Standards in Education) inspections, subjecting what goes on *inside* schools to audit, testing teachers' compliance in delivering the National Curriculum and examining evidence of planning and record-keeping. These developments have marginalized professional accountability, as many primary school teachers see it (Jeffrey and Woods, 1998; Woods and Jeffrey, 1996b); and from their point of view, schools have become less responsive to the needs of children and their parents. These developments have also intensified primary teachers' work (Troman, 1997; Woods et al., 1997).

Intensification and Accountability

Besides the audit explosion, other macro elements are connected with changes in teachers' experience of work: notably, crumbling social structures and globalization. The more that traditional structures lose their hold, and the more that daily life is recast in terms of a dialectical interplay of local and global, the more individuals are forced to negotiate lifestyle choices among a diversity of options. According to Giddens, trust can no longer be anchored in criteria outside the relationship itself, 'such as criteria of kinship, social duty or traditional obligation' (Giddens, 1991, p. 6), or, in the case of teachers, in forms of professionalism. For primary teachers the downgrading of the notion of professional responsiveness – albeit idealized and bounded (Nias, 1989) – results, together with a disconnection between responsiveness and accountability, in a reduction of the trust that previously secured their confidence and professional identity. As another teacher commented:

> There's got to be a sense of trust. If you've been appointed and been given a job, there's got to be a sense of trust. If you feel that the powers-that-be just don't trust you, don't trust you to do the job properly, and then they home in here like some kind of old-fashioned police, it's awful, it's really horrible. And you just sit there thinking, 'are all jobs like this now, or is it just teaching that is being put through this?' You wonder are there any jobs left where you're trusted to do it. It's awful.

According to Giddens, as the significance of place is removed from 'time and space', abstract systems are produced to replace outmoded social structures such as status passage and religion (Giddens, 1991). Abstract systems can be split into two sorts: symbolic token and expert systems. The first of these is a medium of exchange involving the standardization of value across a plurality of contexts. The most obvious example is money. The expert system, on the other hand, brackets time and space through employing technical knowledge. Validity is established independently of practitioners and clients, for example by the counsellor and the therapist. In the school context a standardized inspection system seems to combine both kinds of abstract system. It is intended to ensure that the value of schools can be ascertained and compared in standardized terms. The inspectors are also considered to be experts in applying technical knowledge to the grading of schools and teachers, independently of practitioners' and clients' insights and involvement in the judgments that are recorded. For abstract systems to be valued by the practitioners and clients, they must be trusted by the individual in the same way as traditional social structures were once trusted.

How these developments have affected what we referred to as the 'compliant' group of primary teachers is the subject of this chapter. To a large extent, the work of English primary teachers is characterized by direct engagement with their pupils as people, and an exploration of the curriculum as a means of understanding and engaging with the world (Woods, 1995; Woods and Jeffrey, 1996b). These engagements are based on primary teachers' wider educational beliefs, pedagogic knowledge and experience. And many English primary teachers have been imbued with the values of a holistic and child-centred pedagogy, emanating from educational academic institutions in the 1960s and from the influential Plowden Report (Plowden, 1967; see also Darling, 1994; Siraj-Blatchford and Siraj-Blatchford 1995). In spite of recent criticism of these values and practices (Alexander et al., 1992), older primary teachers have been concerned to maintain these principles pragmatically within the contemporary context of a National Curriculum (Woods and Jeffrey, 1996b). These teachers have a '"substantial self", a set of self-defining beliefs, values and attitudes [which] develops alongside [their] situational selves and is highly resistant to change' (Nias, 1989, p. 203).

Carol is an example of this kind of primary teacher. She is 44, single, and lives alone in a large metropolis; her relations live approximately 100 miles away. They cannot understand why she chooses to work in a deprived area far from her family, but she is committed to the children she teaches. She works in an Early Years department and is imbued with the theory and practice of the sort of child development theories and practices that were prevalent in the 1960s and 1970s, based on the work of Dewey (1929) and Bruner (1986). She has responsibility for language throughout her school and attends courses regularly to keep up with curricular and pedagogic developments. She has been described as a 'disturbed conformist' (Woods et al., 1997), and we can get a clearer sense of what is meant by this category through an examination of the tension felt by her as a result of the imposition of audit accountability.

New Clothes

An Unsuitable Fitting

Carol initially tried to incorporate her own child-centred approach into the new technical framework, but she found this increasingly difficult; the pressure on her grew as the Ofsted inspection approached:

> I'm quite happy to make a list of things that go on in the classroom, but then you've got to look it up in the National Curriculum and put it under certain headings. I'm finding it exceedingly difficult to do. For

example, you have to write down the fact that the children in the 'role play' areas and the 'puppet theatre' are 'presenting to audiences'. You have to make all these incredible lists, about what dramatic areas it comes under. I can't think like that, I can make a list of the things I am providing, but that isn't enough. There is a lot of language and vocabulary going on in the play corner because there are two telephones in there, but knowing that isn't enough anymore. I have to detail the educational experiences. I just can't write all that down.

Prioritizing 'control of control' (Power, 1994) reduced her engagement with the classroom work:

I've taken this group on a visit around the school and introduced them to different parts of the school. In retrospect I shall do a lesson plan on geography and actually say that that's a geographical skill and that this is the geography work that I've done. But to me it seems a waste of time in a sense. I have set up the structure, which is where the evidence is. If you are aware of what your aims and objectives are, and you have set up the structures and access to equipment, you have done the thing that is so important for young children. However, the most important thing seems to be to keep this blessed paper work up to date.

Carol felt that the forms for recording 'control of control' assumed a radically different classroom context from the one that she felt was most appropriate:

It's harder for the early years because they [Ofsted] are already talking about 45-minute lessons, and they will be in the classroom watching how many reception kids stick at something for 45 minutes, in a directed lesson. Usually I would suggest that they get the construction equipment out and make something and if it grabs them they will be there for half an hour, if not they will finish in five minutes. The secondary school orientation came over, although the emphasis was very subtle. They queried why timetables and weekly plans were not available earlier. Our weekly plans were done as close to the actual inspection as possible, because they were referenced to what happened the week before, we did them in context. I just thought that as long as I'm seen to be vaguely in control I assumed I wouldn't get a low mark.

However, her control over the classroom operation was not the main focus for the audit; instead, it was the bureaucratic means by which this could be established. A professional judgment based on an educational body of knowledge or that of an experienced practitioner was no longer seen as enough:

> I reckon that if you know about Early Years you can actually get a feel about whether the kids are on task and are productive. I think you can do that just by walking into a class. I agree there's more to it, but I still think you can get a general flavour of whether it's a class where the children are all well occupied or where they are just killing time.

Trust that teachers and the school are doing their best for pupils has been eroded, along with the decline in social institutions. In adopting an audit form of accountability it is essential for Ofsted that judgments can be standardized across a large sample, irrespective of place. Any judgment based on an extensive body of knowledge would require a specialist, highly trained inspector. Not only might these be in short supply, but any national conclusions would be open to criticism over validity. Consequently, the measurement of the control mechanisms used by the teachers – their plans and records – takes priority, for these are easier to assess. In this way, what is being measured may appear to be the same thing right across the country. Statistical outcomes based in quantifiable judgments are employed, rather than qualitative judgment:

> I hate this thing about statistics, it just makes me really angry that people start looking at these graphs and saying, 'Oh well, you didn't do very well in reading that year.' That really makes me very cross because I think of the kids as individuals and the way they progress here. I cannot prove it by statistics, but since we've worked this developmental approach to reading, we have a lot of very confident, enthusiastic readers going throughout the whole school, but that doesn't come over in raw statistics.

According to Carol, this narrow focus does not reflect the full range of competencies and capabilities of her pupils. She was also concerned that the narrow criteria used to examine her 'delivery' of the curriculum would not uncover the underlying reasons for her decision-making. 'What looks like bad practice can actually be exceedingly good practice, for example there may be a good reason for walking around ignoring a child.' She felt that she employed a wide range of aims and objectives, together with subtle processes that were not easily amenable to marking procedures.

She was encouraged to plan her teaching programme well in advance, so that the assessors could make a judgment as to whether she was complying with the overall National Curriculum programme, which made it difficult for her to vary the pace of the learning engagement:

> It takes the less capable and the second language users that haven't got a very wide vocabulary about a week and a half for them to fall into what we're doing. Fitting into this formula where I have to keep to a predetermined plan isn't the way I work. It's unreal.

At a curriculum level the same applied as far as she was concerned. When a friend of the school asked if they had a scheme of work for language:

> I went into a major panic mode and said, 'No I hadn't', and he said, 'Of course you have' and he listed some of the things that we'd actually been doing. That is my worry, that I'll actually say no to things that are going on in this school, that I'll think, 'Oh no, no, we're definitely not doing that', and we are doing it. The policy statements that we've got are very much linked to what goes on in this school but I just don't think like 'management'. I'm never likely to ever ever be promoted because I don't think in those terms.

Furthermore, *delivery* of the curriculum was prioritized over individual interest and process:

> I can't really explain it, but all the things that I've been good at for the last 20 years I've been told I can't do them any more. That's not right, I've got to formulate things a certain way. I've always had a structure but I've always worked on what the kids have got interested in and involved in. I've always drawn from the children and I've always gone off at tangents if it's got really interesting. So I'm finding it difficult now. We're doing a project on shape at the moment and the plan was to look at a different shape each week but the kids got so wrapped up in it that we were doing circles for about three weeks. We're still doing triangles now and they're so enthusiastic about it that it seems point-less to actually suddenly decide artificially to move on to squares.

Delivery becomes a driving force because of the way in which the assessment is directed at measurable judgments about whether the National Curriculum has been 'covered'. The quality of the engagements, as this relates to Carol's educational philosophy, is not considered.

The new clothes bring new terminology. Carol is steeped in her own value-based child-centred discourse. The new form of audit accountability discourse not only challenges her working practices, but in order to main-tain her working life Carol has to start using its mode of language and way of thinking. But this is not so easy. Just as it was difficult trying to fit her value-based working patterns into a technical grid of examination and assessment, it is difficult for her to talk a new language. The 'terminologies' constitute new jargon that Carol must begin to use if she is to communicate with her colleagues and Ofsted inspectors:

> I find it very hard to think in the terminology that's grown up in the last two to three years. If somebody else is talking to me about it, I understand it; it's not a complete mystery to me. It's just that I find it quite difficult to think that way and half of me resents it in some sense

because in some way I see no need for it; it's almost like setting up jargon just to make it more complex than it really is. I obviously can't speak for other members of staff, but I think there is a similar feeling that, because we've been teaching the length of time we have, it's probably harder for us in some ways than it is for the less experienced.

The language of this audit discourse is outlined in Jeffrey and Woods's (1998) description of the Ofsted Handbook:

> Measurable factors predominate as they affect such matters as attainment, progress, strengths and weaknesses, effective and ineffective teaching, needs, management, resources, objectives, assessment, use time, competence, planning, skill. The model of the teacher and the learning situation provided in the handbook is essentially a transmissional one in which information is passed to pupils, and pupils are seen as developing through the manifest technical skills of the teacher. Phrases like 'contribution to pupils' attainment and progress', 'overall strengths and weaknesses in different subjects', 'effective teaching', 'the extent to which teaching promotes learning', 'secure knowledge and understanding of subjects', 'employs methods and organisational strategies which match curricular objectives', 'needs of pupils', 'manages pupils well', 'achieves high standards of discipline', 'assesses pupils' work thoroughly', 'uses assessments to inform teaching', 'uses homework effectively to reinforce and or extend what is learnt at school' illustrate the model that Ofsted prefers.
>
> In this model, the child is seen as a pupil (rather than 'child'), in need of managing and disciplining and needing to learn certain prescribed things in order to be able to survive in a competitive market. The teacher is seen as someone who has to impart knowledge and understanding of a set curriculum, who supplements deficiencies, assesses and evaluates pupils' efforts from an hierarchical position, rather than one who removes obstacles to learning and works with children.

(p. 57)

The introduction of new language forms acts as symbolic power (Bourdieu and Wacquant, 1992). 'Getting done' becomes the overriding imperative (Apple, 1986). And less time on classroom activities means less depth of engagement:

> I don't think I'm sinking, but I don't think I'm doing anything to any depth because there just isn't any time. You just seem to lurch from one thing to something else to something else to something else and you don't really get time to spend on getting that depth. We're supposed to be doing something on buildings and the kids have all brought me bits

of paper with the age of their house on. We're going to stick it on the timeline because I thought buildings were quite a good thing to link in, but have I had time to get that up there, no I haven't.

More initiatives and demands continually dominate teachers' time. This has been recognized by the Chief Inspector of Schools, the Secretary of State for Education, and by a leading right-wing polemicist (Lawler, 1997), who all argue for a reduction in paperwork and meetings. However, it is the new audit accountability system which they advocate that demands this attention to systems of control. The new ill-fitting clothes challenge Carol's identity.

Altered Identities

Carol feels that audit accountability marginalizes her experience, promotes loss and increases an emphasis on performance.

Marginalization of Experience

As the system of control impinges on schools, teacher experience and expertise are marginalized as the accounting takes over:

> In the past I put the structures in place, for example I had a list of things I planned to introduce them to in the first month. I felt that was enough. Whereas now I feel obliged to account for myself in much more detail. It's as though we haven't been trying to do it for the past 20 years and trying to get it right, as though we've just been messing about and having a good time and not trying to teach the kids to read.

This process is underpinned by a value-system based on continually rising levels of achievement, albeit in a much narrower definition of children's achievement than that to which Carol subscribes. However, the technology of its operation dominates, for two major reasons. First, 'control of control' is easier to evaluate in a standardized form than qualitative judgments of teaching and learning of teachers operating in specific locations. Secondly, a technical appearance implies a rational and non-subjective approach that appears to simplify the process of teaching and learning, and make it more amenable to control.

The extra work of providing written evidence of the process of teaching not only marginalizes the attention given to the teaching itself, but undermines teacher confidence; since the system requires that teachers chart the minute detail of their work. The details are recorded and filed in a similar way to the collection of the detail about a mentally ill person's life for examination in the asylum (Goffman, 1961). The detail of a teacher's work, in terms of accountability, might well be a legitimate subject of enquiry.

However, if the technology of the process involves examination of the work by a distanced hierarchical process, then it constitutes a major shift in power to 'overseers' (Power, 1994, p. 47). It is the audit nature of the process that raises anxiety, for it means that written accounts will be judged by someone at a distance rather than there being an engagement with the teacher about purposes and strategies.

Loss

There is also a loss of control, enjoyment, confidence, role, creativity and commitment. Carol resents the inevitability of the process and compares it to the intense experience of her mother dying:

> It's part of the same process as a death isn't it, that things are not going to be as they were and it's quite a hollow feeling isn't it? Whatever Ofsted was, we had to work hard for it and we had to focus on that and nothing else. It's something that's completely out of your control. There are two issues involved, there is the lack of control and the realization of what is taking over and the stress level in itself is like coping with a death because you are so worn down. The stress level I felt was as high in some ways as when I watched my mother slowly die. It was a horrible, horrible experience to go through. It was one of these horrendous experiences where she was in hospital just deteriorating slowly and slowly and slowly, and the build-up to the inspection was similar. There was the terrible pressure of visiting her and guilt if you didn't go. It builds up and everything was outside that experience. It became unreal in some ways, and that was what Ofsted was like.

The loss of control felt by Carol is due to her not being involved in the judgment process in the way that she would be in the context of combined professional responsiveness and accountability. There is also a loss of control over the direct engagement with her work, due to the prioritization of 'control of control' and the separation of responsiveness from accountability.

A loss of enjoyment is also experienced:

> When they [the children] first came into school, it was just such a happy time to be with them. I just used to really enjoy it. Maybe that was a bad thing, maybe I enjoyed it too much. I'd just be in there playing with them and sitting down in the book corner and reading with them; I really got a lot out of that. So I don't have the job satisfaction I once had working with young kids because I feel every time I do something I just feel guilty about it. Is this right? Am I doing this the right way? Does this cover what I am supposed to be covering? Should I be doing something else? Should I be more structured?

Should I have this in place? Should I have done this? You start to query everything that you are doing – there's a kind of guilt in teaching at the moment really.

Fun in primary teaching means that the person is subjectively engaged with the learning process; and that process is often extremely productive when engaging the emotions (Drummond, 1991; Bonnett, 1994; Woods, 1993; Woods and Jeffrey, 1996b). The power of the teacher to engage children, excite them and be creative does not fit easily within an 'audit' conception: 'I could go into any class in this school and get them fairly well motivated but that seems to not be important any more.' There is a sense of 'grieving' (Nias, 1993) as feelings and emotions are marginalized.

Indeed, audit accountability shifts the emotions towards persecutory guilt:

> Persecutory guilt is the kind of guilt that leads many teachers to concentrate on covering the required content, rather than ignoring it or subverting it to develop more interesting materials and approaches of their own. It is the guilt that inhibits innovation in 'basic' subjects for fear of prejudicing the test scores by which one is ultimately held accountable.
>
> (Hargreaves, 1994, p. 143).

Andy Hargreaves was referring in this quotation to primary teachers in Canada and the United States, but much the same applies here. Confidence is a key element in teaching and this has to be based on teachers believing that what they are doing is appropriate, and that it has a solid value-base with which they concur, for this is also moral work (Hargreaves, 1994). After a gruelling inspection Carol finds that:

> getting back to normal is actually quite hard in lots of ways. I can't quite analyse this but it's something to do with having all the stuffing knocked out of you, all your confidence going. You think that as it's all over, I can do this, that and the other, but when it comes down to it you're not quite sure really what you want to do. It's just a bit dis-orientating. You don't have any belief in yourself. Whereas before the inspection you'd think to yourself, 'Oh yes I must do this and that now', I question everything in such depth that I feel a bit insecure.

She also suffers a little from depressive guilt, which according to Hargreaves may be rooted in childhood and the psychological self:

> I suppose in some ways I'm not a particularly confident person, so I'd always throw myself into things to prove that I was of value and that's actually not enough now, is it? I'm sure that this is insecurity on my

part. Wherever I land up working, I always have mountains of jobs to do. I'm always quite willing and I'm sure that that is insecurity, that if I say that I've got lots of things to do I must be worthwhile because that makes me feel quite important. I'm more a doer than a thinker, but you've got to lock into these bloody terminologies now or you've had it, haven't you? You've got to think certain ways and that's quite hard.

The loss of confidence triggers the depressive guilt, and the two together can contribute to a downward spiral. She is conscious of this loss of role on the part of her headteacher:

I think one of the problems with Victor was that he lost his role through the Ofsted inspection. He didn't quite know what to do for us. He's always been there in the background, he's always been there for us and he didn't know what to do for us this time. He couldn't get us out of what we had to go through. It was out of his control in a lot of ways and he lost his role, he didn't know what to do. We just had to go through this. He couldn't make it easier or better for us even if he wanted to.

After the inspection her headteacher took on a different role, one dominated by the new form of accountability:

There's also a tremendous amount of pressure on me to monitor in other classes from Victor, but not really from Victor, from on high. We're supposed to be monitoring what goes on in the other classes because we were told to do that by Ofsted. The focus at the moment is language, so there's more pressure on me to start the process because I'm the postholder.

Other teachers have extended themselves in this process (Woods et al., 1997), but for Carol this route was not possible.

Increased Performances

Carol resented the move towards increased performances:

No, I don't really want to do a performance because in actual fact I'll fail abysmally at that because it's just so alien to me. I'm almost better to be myself and not actually achieve at a high level, but at least I shall have some degree of pride and credibility when I come through it.

So the maintenance of the value-based self becomes the overriding concern at the expense of being accredited by the accounting process. In the event she had to perform for the inspection and she did not enjoy it:

It was a horrible experience and I knew that whatever I did, I'd never look good in an Ofsted inspection. I just don't perform well when I'm on show to start with and the formula is just one that's almost certain to make me look bad.

However, Carol, like most of the teachers in our sample, were compliers (Woods et al., 1997). How did she manage the new design and her altered identity?

Wearing It In

Carol was resigned to the new situation:

There's just no escape is there, really? There is no way you can say 'I don't agree with this'; you've got to do it. I suppose that really sunk in after two meetings. They were saying they had got a remit, they work it, and leave; and it's just tough whether we like it or not, there really was no room for argument or debate about it.

She had the same feeling about the schemes of work:

Obviously things are escalating. We've got all these schemes of work to put in place. I mean it's just got to be done, even if you hate it, it's got to be done.

However, she was also practical. She needed to secure an income as a single person. And she still needed an identity, which she established by drawing on her humanity towards other people. Individuals now need to adopt a lifestyle to replace the disappearance of identity-giving social structures (Giddens, 1991). In Carol's case she created her own sense of place. The humanistic emphasis of her teaching is also part of who she is:

I am resigned but I think it's due to my nature, because I am the kind of person that fits in. If I feel that I can make things smooth for other people, then I feel as if I've got a place in life, that's just me, isn't it? It's the way I cope as well. It's the way I manage to get through.

She faced up to the circumstances. The inspection process was almost like a cauterizing of her past teaching practice, and an event that propelled her into a new world:

I finally had to face up to change just as I did when my mother died. I'd conveniently not faced up to what was going on. I knew that I had to deliver all these things and prepare all these things but I hadn't really faced up to it. If I'd had any illusions before, they went when the

> Ofsted inspection came and all the things that we had to do for it. I
> knew I couldn't carry on the way that I wanted to.

For Carol, the new forms of accountability are not ones with which she
could engage authentically, for they were part of an alternative value
system based on technology. Jennifer Nias suggests that because primary
teachers' selves are incorporated within their teaching practices, any policy
change will only be successful if their values are altered (Nias, 1989).
However, it appears that there is another strategy: that of marginalizing
values through the introduction of a new discourse that emphasizes technology, in this case via audit accountability:

> If you say to Veronica and myself 'that's how it's got to be' then we're
> not the people that we were before. It's almost like telling us to change
> our personalities, the thing that has actually made us what we were
> over the last 24 years. To suddenly turn round and say to somebody,
> 'you can't do that any more' is completely and utterly demoralizing.
> It's not just a case of taking on something new, it's just something
> that's so alien to the way we work.

Nevertheless, she engages with the new form. In her responsive mode she
not only agrees to take on a new responsibility after the inspection, but
finds herself leading a series of in-service training sessions for other staff.
However, her control of the subject-matter and her relations with staff alter
as she takes up a more managerial role:

> I've also agreed (like a twit) to be the IT coordinator and we've got new
> computers in the school so all the staff meetings this term had me
> fronting them on IT and language. It was announced in the staff
> meeting without a by-your-leave. I think the poor staff got fed up
> with the sound of my voice. I don't think they wanted to hear anything
> from me ever again! I began to feel awful about delivering anything. I
> began to feel really bad about it.

She has introduced innovatory practices into the school in the past, but her
approach then contrasted with the current one:

> The reason it was accepted was something to do with the fact that
> people weren't coerced into doing things. They weren't made to feel
> bad about what they were doing. Instead of being told that they had to
> do things that were alien to them, it was a slow, gradual process and
> I'm just not the kind of personality that goes around telling people
> what they've got to do. I think the reason it was successful is because
> people didn't feel threatened by it.

Still, under the new regime, she also mediates and moderates as far as she can:

> I've moderated this wonderful system. I actually write down what I'm doing and then when I feel a bit weak in the head I go through and look the activity up in the National Curriculum and what the learning objectives are. I might do it a month afterwards and then I add the possible learning outcomes in later on. If I feel like doing something different I do it and then I write it down afterwards! I don't know whether I'm telling management that but I'm telling you!

When it comes to monitoring, she devises her own way of doing it:

> My definition of monitoring is going into someone else's class just to find out what they're doing that's good. It might as well be for our own ends. We suggested that less experienced teachers, like Corrine for example, might come into a class and see how groups were organised.

One of her colleagues, the deputy head, has made it her business to become familiar with the 'jargon', so Carol uses her to mediate the new discourse:

> I'm quite happy to give them [inspectors] a long honest spiel about why certain things are in place and why children are being asked to do that, but when I actually sit down to write it I find it less easy to do using the new jargon. I go and ask the deputy head if I've written it down in the right way because I'm not very good at the jargon. I explain to Toni, the kind of things that have gone on in the classroom. She then translates it and says 'well you've done this and you've done that' but I don't see it in those kinds of terms.

Carol also tries to maintain a connection with those discourses that reflect her values. She relishes listening to speakers like Michael Rosen (a respected author and reviewer of children's literature) because 'We could really do with somebody coming in, firing us up and making us feel good about ourselves again.' They are in tune with her past professional life:

> It's been wonderful for me. I got on a course for looking at bilingual learners in mainstream education and how you accommodate them. It's running at the Centre for Language in Primary Education for 10 weeks and it's brilliant. They are wonderful people that run it.

But she still doesn't want to join the accredited management career paths, a feature of the new managerialism:

> It's been fun. We've done some quite heavy stuff but at the same time it's been really interesting. We've had kind of all sorts of lectures and that's done me a lot of good. I don't do all the homework, but I'm not choosing to get accredited by the University, which I could do if I wanted to. It's just a case of getting some ideas about supporting children.

At the same time as being resigned, facing up, engaging, mediating and seeking out familiar discourse, she analyses the current context. Carol is not resentful of inspectors themselves, but of the process, for she is a person who sees the humanity in all people. She has worked with some of the inspectors who carried out the Ofsted inspection on the school:

> I just thought 'well that's their job, they've been told that that's what they've got to do and that's what they are going to do'. What they were trying to tell us is that they have got to do this job. They didn't actually say they agreed with it, it's just a job they've got to do. They didn't actually say what they thought about it at all, they just said how it was going to be administered because that was how they have been told to do it.

A Tighter Fit

Although the process of audit accountability involves a distancing in the operation of 'control of control', it has not remained at a distance from affecting pedagogy, since audit practices 'strongly influence the environments in which they operate' (Power, 1994, p. 48). As audit is largely concerned with 'control of control' and is a dominant form of accountability, this 'results in a preoccupation with the auditable process rather than the substance of activities' (*ibid.*). Following the introduction of inspections, the government has introduced prescriptive programmes into schools, which are amenable to standardized audit assessment. Carol attended a course for the new prescribed Literacy Hour and found that control over her pedagogy had diminished further, even though she was not totally alienated by the content of the programmes:

> Some of it was excellent. A lot of the suggestions were good. They talked about phonics not being taught if it was not appropriate, grammar not being taught effectively by marking children's work and children looking at their mistakes. All those kind of things were really quite interesting and, you know, there was some very, very valuable stuff came out of it, but at the same time it was very much a formula.

It was not only formulaic and prescriptive, but the presentational style and tone was very hierarchical:

Every time he was asked questions he started fielding queries, they were very nicely deflected. It was a bit fascistic in a way because you were not allowed to query things. They're very nice about it, but it was 'oh well we'll get back to that later'. They'd got the patter for deflecting us to something else. Part of me felt it was like an evangelical American drive to sell this 'wonderful way'. I loathed it on that level because I thought it was quite impersonal.

First, the audit accountability approach demanded attention to forms of control. Secondly, the inspection took an examination role using narrow criteria. Thirdly, a prescriptive pedagogic innovation was introduced, which further separated Carol from her work in spite of her appreciation of some of it:

We have to have the whole class work on a text and then you have to have grouped reading sessions, but you've got to choose ability groups. Now I don't think staff are going to like that. If there's a degree of flexibility, we'll be OK with it, but if we have to stick to these structured ability groups I think it may come a cropper in the end.

The Literacy Hour's prescriptive nature and its lack of flexibility diminished Carol's responsiveness to this particular innovation. It reinforced her experience of the change that had taken place: 'I'm quite happy to go along with new things but I have realized that I can't go off on my own tack any more. I've lost control of my work.' She sums up her sense of loss as follows: 'We seem to land up jumping through hoops when really there's no need, but we'll never go back, will we? That's the problem.'

Conclusion

In Carol's experience, the evaluation of primary teaching under audit accountability is one in which:

- the teacher becomes increasingly separated from direct involvement with her work;
- monitoring abstract systems becomes the focus for assessing accountability;
- place is removed as a factor in describing and defining pupils' educational reality;
- the professional perspectives of the teacher become marginalized;
- the teacher loses considerable control over the curriculum and over pedagogy.

Michael Power (1994, p. 8) identifies opposing models of control and accountability: see Table 3.1.

Table 3.1 Modes of control and accountability

Style A	Style B
Quantitative	Qualitative
Single Measure	Multiple Measures
External Agencies	Internal Agencies
Long Distance Methods	Local Methods
Low Trust	High Trust
Discipline	Autonomy
Ex Post Control	Real Time Control
Private Experts	Public Dialogue

Audit accountability in schools displays many of the features of Style A. First, it examines the 'control of control' mechanisms as indicators of good practice. Secondly, it assesses individual pupils in terms of achievement scores from standardized tests and extrapolates from these to levels of achievement for the school. Thirdly, inspectors assess the extent to which the curriculum is being delivered. While some of the evaluative processes used involve qualitative judgment, the recorded outcomes are quantitative ones based on the use of single measures for each operation, and are carried out by external agencies using methods that do not engage the teacher. A low level of trust is involved, discipline is exerted and the assessors take on the role of experts, as Giddens (1991) described.

However, this situation did not result in Carol either becoming 'deprofessionalized or reprofessionalized', as in Troman's study (1997). Her solution was to hop between the discourses. She was resentful as well as being resigned and amenable; but she nevertheless maintained professional responsiveness and kept in touch with her values. Her professional identity as a member of a valued and recognized profession had been damaged by its marginalization. The meso structure of professional knowledge and educational values, which assisted her construction of identity, had been removed. Her 'sense of place', in terms of educational values, had been undermined. She attempted to regain a sense of place by drawing on her own feelings for the people she works with, and to do this she engaged with them at times in implementing the new programme. But she also maintained as many links to her 'substantial self' as possible. She did not lose her past, but she did lose control over her present. She may never be able to 'go back', but she can draw on the past again if, along with others, she is able to re-establish 'place' as a determinant of identity and professionalism.

At present, Carol is living a fragmented professional life hopping between discourses and straddling them. She experiences the conflict between the discourses of technicization and value-based working practices, and she engages with the conflicts and contradictions within both. If abstract systems are to be successful, they must gain people's trust

(Giddens, 1991, p. 15), or individuals may maintain alternative perspectives and beliefs in the hope that they can reassert them as expressions of 'place' in another 'time and space'.

References

Alexander, R., Rose, J. and Woodhead, C. (1992) *Curriculum Organisation and Classroom Practice in Primary Schools: A Discussion Paper*, London: HMSO.

Apple, M. (1986) *Teachers and Texts*, London: Routledge.

Ball, S. (1990) *Politics and Policy Making in Education: Explorations in Policy Sociology*, London: Routledge.

Bonnett, M. (1994) *Children's Thinking: Promoting Understanding in the Primary School*, London: Cassell.

Bourdieu, P. and Wacquant, L.J.D. (1992) *An Invitation to Reflexive Sociology*, Cambridge: Polity Press.

Bruner, J. (1986) *Actual Minds, Possible Worlds*, London: Harvard University Press.

Darling, J. (1994) *Child Centred Education and Its Critics*, London: Paul Chapman.

Dewey, J. (1929) *The Quest for Certainty: A Study of the Relation of Knowledge and Action*, New York: Minton, Balch.

Drummond, M.J. (1991) 'The child and the primary curriculum – from policy to practice', *Curriculum Journal*, **2**, *2*, pp. 115–24.

Eraut, M. (1992) *Developing the Professions: Training, Quality and Accountability*, University of Sussex Professorial Lecture, Brighton. Sussex.

Gewirtz, S. (1996) 'Post-welfarism and the reconstruction of teachers' work', Paper given at the British Educational Research Association Conference, Lancaster.

Giddens, A. (1991) *Modernity and Self-Identity*, Cambridge: Polity Press.

Goffman, E. (1961) *Asylums*, Harmondsworth: Penguin.

Hargreaves, A. (1994) *Changing Teachers, Changing Times – Teacher's Work and Culture in the Postmodern Age*, London: Cassell.

Hatcher, R. (1994) 'Market relationships and the management of teachers', *British Journal of Sociology of Education*, **15**, 1, pp. 41–62.

Jeffrey, B. and Woods P. (1998) *Testing Teachers: The Effects of School Inspections on Primary Teachers*, London: Falmer Press.

Kogan, M. (1989) 'Normative models of accountability', in Glatter, R., Preedy, M., Riches, C. and Masterson, M., *Understanding School Management*, Milton Keynes: Open University Press, pp. 139–53.

Lawler, S. (1997) 'Teachers are the victims of the state and bureaucracy', *Times Educational Supplement*, London: **22**, 24 October.

Nias, J. (1989) *Primary Teachers Talking*, London: Routledge.

Nias, J. (1993) 'Changing times, changing identities: grieving for a lost self', in Burgess, R.G. (ed.) *Educational Research and Evaluation*, London: Falmer Press.

Plowden (1967) *Children and Their Primary Schools*, London: HMSO, Central Advisory Council for Education in England.

Power, M. (1994) *The Audit Explosion*, London: Demos.

Siraj-Blatchford, J. and Siraj-Blatchford I. (1995) *Educating the Whole Child: Cross Curricula Skills, Themes and Dimensions*, Buckingham: Open University Press.

Troman, G. (1994) 'Auditing the educators: technologies of accountability and the primary school', unpublished analytic memo, 7 June.

Troman, G. (1997) 'The effects of restructuring on primary teachers' work: a sociological analysis', unpublished Ph.D. thesis, Open University.

Woods, P. (1993) *Critical Events in Teaching and Learning*, London: Falmer Press.

Woods, P. (1995) *Creative Teachers in Primary Schools*, Buckingham: Open University Press.

Woods, P. and Jeffrey, B. (1996a) 'A new professional discourse? Adjusting to managerialism', in Woods, P. (ed.) *Contemporary Issues in Education*, London: Routledge.

Woods, P. and Jeffrey, B. (1996b) *Teachable Moments: The Art of Creative Teaching in Primary Schools*, Buckingham: Open University Press.

Woods, P., Jeffrey, B., Troman, G. and Boyle, M. (1997) *Restructuring Schools, Reconstructing Teachers*, Buckingham: Open University Press.

**Tales of Fear and Loathing:
Teachers' Work and Recent
Educational Reform**

Bethan Marshall and Stephen J. Ball

> What is under-theorised in education is the emotional, the irra-
> tional, the fear, and the guilt that always accompanies any attempt
> to understand.
>
> (Orner, 1998, pp. 278–9)[1]

There is a moment in the 1970s remake of the film *The Invasion of the Body
Snatchers* in which the husband describes to his wife, the film's heroine, the
benefits of giving in. From the other side, he argues, you can't understand
what all the fuss is about. He is no longer the slob who watches sport, he is
courteous and tidy. To desire to retain the messiness of his former but
authentic existence seems on the surface perverse. Indeed, she used to
complain about it. But it is this very transition that has alerted her to the
fact that he is not himself. He is inhuman. The fight to remain human, to
remain authentic against the appeal of apparent but threatening content-
ment, is impossible; and our heroine is eventually exposed by a former
friend and ally.

Although the original 1950s film was in part an allegory about
McCarthyism, there is a sense in which the 1970s version echoes wider
concerns about the pressure to conform, to give in to power; about the
difficulty of resisting the *zeitgeist* and the attraction of internalizing the
values that you have doubted. Woods et al.'s analysis of primary school
teachers' experience of educational reform addresses this dilemma. The
study explores the relationships between teachers' sense of self and work
identities, and the requirements and effects on them of the reform process
in English schools in the 1990s. It draws primarily upon teachers' perceptions of what their role has been, what it might be and what it has now
become (Woods, Jeffrey, Troman and Boyle, 1997).

In this chapter, using aspects of Woods et al.'s framework, we pursue the
issue of change and the self in the secondary sector, drawing on data from
an ESRC-funded study of value change in four metropolitan schools (three
comprehensive, one grant maintained).[2] In that study a cross-section of

staff were interviewed in each school (118 interviews in all) between 1994 and 1997. Here we employ just a tiny proportion of that data, related to the theme of change and the 'teacher self'. Our aim is to point up, in a preliminary way, some of the values and emotional dimensions of educational reform, and to use this perspective to consider resulting changes in 'what it means to be a teacher'. We try to do this by listening closely to what teachers say, taking what Woods calls a 'warm hearted approach' (Woods, 1990). Material is presented and discussed from interviews with just four teachers from three of the schools. They are: Martineau (Mr Wolfitt), Fletcher (Mrs Austen), and John Ruskin (Mr Gainsborough and Mrs Truffaut). Martineau is a grant maintained girls' school situated in an LEA that has pursued policies to encourage the development of market relations. The school was created by an amalgamation in 1985 and has moved over 10 years from having a poor reputation to being over-subscribed. Fletcher is an over-subscribed school in an LEA that remains strongly committed to comprehensive education, and no schools have opted-out. However, Fletcher's recruitment is odd insofar as it fails to recruit significant numbers of students from its immediate, very middle-class, surroundings. John Ruskin is situated in a socially diverse inner-city LEA and 'presents' itself as a comprehensive school – 'we believe we're a local neighbourhood-based comprehensive' (Head of John Ruskin) – but it has a high proportion of middle-class students and is heavily over-subscribed.

The contrast that we portray, between a possible 'then' and a very real 'now', counterpoints two distinct 'structures of feeling' and two opposed discourses. The contrast is grounded in careful attention paid to the language and emotions of the teachers quoted, although these are clearly related to changes in objective conditions of work. The validity of our interpretation rests upon the extent to which our 'indicators' of change, as perceived and described by the teachers, stand up to scrutiny as systematically distinct *and* adequately capture substantively different constructions of 'what it means to be a teacher'.

Loss

The language that these teachers use to describe their view of their changing roles and their investment of self in those roles in part echoes the heroine's sense of loss in *The Invasion of the Body Snatchers*. Mr Gainsborough, the Head of Art at Ruskin school, describes himself 30 years ago:

> To be honest I really enjoyed my teaching in the late sixties and early seventies. It was a very hopeful period, very exciting period, and I felt very much that we were teaching . . . the students were producing some very gutsy work, which was not so much exam-oriented and was not so

much art school. . . . So I felt it was a very meaningful period, and through art we could reach out, create relationships, and also create the atmosphere where we could see students grow within our relationships with them.

The human touch of 'then' with its 'enjoyment, hope and excitement' is contrasted with education now. 'A little bit more artificial now, it's all based on paperwork and how well students perform in examinations.' If the present is 'artificial', the past has authenticity. It was 'meaningful'. By implication, the examinations create this artificiality. The lack of an exam-orientated culture in the past allowed 'gutsy work' to be produced. There is a hint of non-conformity in the word 'gutsy', echoing as it does the aesthetic approbation of the critic Hazlitt, who coined the term 'gusto' to reflect the dissenting spirit within art (Paulin, 1998). Perhaps most significantly, Mr Gainsborough says: 'I felt very much that we were teaching', suggesting that whatever it is he does now, it is no longer 'teaching'.

A further part of the contrast between 'then and now' is the possibility of 'relationships' over and against the requirements of the 'impersonal system'. Relationships have been replaced by the demands of 'performance' (Ball, 1998b). Mr Gainsborough goes on to say, 'I'm part of the system I'm afraid, I haven't stepped out of it. I thought, well, I'll join them now.' What is interesting is his use of the phrase 'I'm afraid'. Dependent on where the comma is placed, he is apologizing either for being part of the system or for failing to step out of it. But with either interpretation there is a strong sense of weakness, even guilt, in his decision to 'join them', an unease at his compliance.

The idea of 'joining the system' acts as a leitmotif throughout the interview. It is a tension Mr Gainsborough clearly finds difficult to resolve. 'We all get brainwashed, falling into the trap to a certain extent. . . . I feel some people say, "Why haven't you tried to change it?"' His emotive description of ensnarement and brainwashing not only suggests the lack of his own sense of control but the unsympathetic face of the system itself. The externalized question acts more as a prompt to himself, to find a justification for his actions. He answers himself in his next sentence. 'Because it's a different world now, it's a different era, it's a different way of working.' The rhythmic repetition of the word 'different', which has an almost musing effect, only serves to reinforce the break between the past and the present, the old world and the new. This is a theme to which he returns,

> I'm also saying that the system is such that – I can't change it, and part of it I'm perpetrating in a way – I can't suddenly change the system within the school even. How could I? So it's disappointing in many ways, that we have joined the rat race.

His use of 'we' here, and in the earlier comment on brainwashing, is interesting. Although he is ostensibly talking about himself, his own struggles, he includes everyone in his dilemma. This is not simply because, as he comments earlier, 'a type of Thatcherism, I feel, has permeated the education system whether we like it or not', but because, as this remark in itself suggests, he does not view the change as organic, a natural development. The word 'permeates' resonates with his central image of change: the system – a phrase that connotes both its all-encompassing, invasive nature and something alien, imposed from the outside – being an irresistible force, like the body snatchers. Thus, the 'system' and conformity to it stands against individuality and authenticity, against the possibility of 'teaching' or its meaningfulness.

Deal (1990, p. 130) argues that loss is a generic feature of organizational change, and can have profound implications for individual and institutional capability. There is, he argues, a 'deep sense of individual and collective loss and grief that lurks below the surface of cultural change. Death or life without meaning are fundamental fears of the human species.' More specifically in relation to teaching, he goes on to say that 'In its wake the decades of change, improvement and reform have left many educators – consciously or otherwise – confused, exhausted and disillusioned' (p. 131).

Bearing this in mind, one way of thinking about the processes of educational reform over the past decade, in the UK and elsewhere, is in terms of a shift in the locus of commitment and control. Essentially, the logics and disciplines of reform have come to articulate and animate schools in terms of 'competition and standards' (see Ball, 1997; Ball, 1998a; Ball and Gewirtz, 1997). Control has shifted from a primary emphasis on professional decision-making to a primary emphasis on accountability, from self to 'the system'. Hence the sense of loss, of alienation. Again, as Deal (1990) comments: 'Accountability pressures have often equated education with achievement test scores. But test scores are not values and high test scores (or low ones) are not substitutes for a shared sense of mission and meaning' (p. 137). This is not simply a change in the technologies of accountability: it is a change in the meaning of education itself and what it means to be educated. (Clearly, however, there will be teachers, perhaps especially among those appointed post-1988, who find satisfaction in their achievements within the logics of performativity. Indeed, in part, the success of the new regime relies on this.) Interestingly, several commentaries and studies examining the architecture and technologies of recent educational reform have begun to argue that there is no clear relationship or mechanism – often assumed by reformers – linking systems of school-based management, or devolved budgets or competition between schools, to the processes of teaching and learning (e.g. Levacic, Hardman and Woods, 1998).

Let us return to Mr Gainsborough. In the context above, the word 'permeates' carries with it a sense of infringement, almost infection, and locates the source of change within schools as beyond their control: 'whether we like it or not'. Mr Gainsborough's unease does not arise only from a frustration at his own working conditions. Lurking beneath the surface is the sense that what he is being asked to do is not right – that his job, like the institution, has become impersonal and even distorted. 'My teaching did involve that sort of compassion to help students who needed that particular help.' 'Now it is oriented towards the students who are talented.' Again he links this with the system:

> However, I'm, I'm seeing deep down that the system is failing students, sort of failing those students who need that help. I think if you look in the broad sense, country-wise I mean, that's why you find so many people who opt out, who are disappointed at education, who are not achieving and feeling frustrated and lost.

Management

Mr Wolfitt (Head of the Arts Faculty) at Martineau school echoes these concerns, describing the potential and current 'disaffection' of pupils who find themselves in the bottom sets. Yet unlike Mr Gainsborough, while acknowledging the external pressures that have brought about new constraints on his practice, he more readily locates the generation of these within the school as much as outside it; in particular, he sees them as emanating from the school's senior management. Since he identifies himself with the middle management, this allows him both to separate himself from the source of change and yet feel its constraints more clearly. If Mr Gainsborough faced an amorphous system that has devalued his work, Mr Wolfitt is confronted by people who are affecting his job and his sense of what is right.

Threaded through his interview is the language of conflict, the language of 'us and them'. He talks of having to 'argue', of having to 'fight quite hard for the area'; he describes the way in which 'people are fighting it out'. Departments are 'pushed' into adopting setting; the school has to 'fight for students'. Although this latter comment suggests that the pressures are also external, this competitive ethos exists within the institution as well. Mr Wolfitt talks of the way in which his school is divided into clusters, which he describes as 'almost competing companies'. He adds: 'The awards evenings, they're cluster-based, so it's like . . . that's another competitive thing.' This internal market detracts, he feels, from a sense of working for the whole school. 'There's nothing that's whole school.' Instead 'it's all about power building'. 'The teams are deliberately held up against each other.' Again we might interpret this as a loss of attachment (Deal, 1990, p. 134).

Significantly, all this allows the senior management to float free of these cluster teams, even though in theory they are each linked to one. 'It's a very nice senior management team but they don't actually have much to do with anything.' This seems to compound the sense of 'us and them'. Here the language is suffused with a sense of abruptness. 'The senior team suddenly decided'; 'we were really sort of called in quite quickly . . . just like that'; 'I mean things like that suddenly happened, and even though they're not on the plan'; 'They suddenly have little things like'; 'They made a very snap decision.'

This sense of abruptness is compounded by the feeling that decisions are imposed. 'Well I think they decided it earlier but they suddenly sprang it on us.' Policy comes from 'on high'. Here the issue of consultation becomes important. 'Now what they haven't done is consulted all the people on the decision.' Even when consultation has taken place, for Mr Wolfitt it is often only a veneer (see Reay, 1998):

> There was a pink paper about setting, but then it was already . . . you see, she's [the headteacher] made it quite clear from the beginning that there was going to be setting, so really there wasn't that much you could do against it, you could only say how you were going to implement it.

It is possible that his comments are influenced by the fact that the Arts cluster alone have not had to introduce setting. Nevertheless, what is fascinating is the way in which Mr Wolfitt interprets the conflict. Instead of challenging the principles that underpin the senior management's decision to introduce setting, a principle with which he disagrees, it becomes more of a debate about management style than about setting itself. He does begin by describing 'the debate about setting which they [the senior management] refuse to acknowledge'. And later he says 'they haven't really looked at the implications of setting'. But this relates more to staffing. 'They didn't look at the implications on staffing' and the dangers of introducing policy without thinking it through. 'I think they're bad at looking at decisions for even quite small decisions, and then having to reverse them because they haven't done that.'

This is characteristic of the way in which he accommodates the principles of new management systems and only questions their shortcomings through the way in which they are implemented. 'I mean we're doing all this TQM stuff, but to be honest I think it's a total waste of time. I didn't think so originally but I can see it's not been taken on board . . . by the senior team.' Yet at a certain fundamental level the new modes of working do conflict with his view of his role as a teacher and his sense of what a school should be about:

> The problem with teaching . . . it's not about management . . . people say they're teachers, they don't say they're managers . . . All [TQM] has got to say is all the structures around what's going on in the classroom, so in a sense it's missing the point of the whole institution . . . it hasn't got anything to say about that.

He goes on to say:

> because of all the changes, we're not getting the input that we used to
> have in terms of what's going on in the classroom, new teaching
> strategies, new ideas . . . how you can develop this aspect of the
> Art curriculum and do exciting things with Renaissance paintings,
> all that sort of thing . . . Nobody has the time to do it after school all
> those groups, support groups have collapsed, and we're not getting
> the money to do it, to go on courses to do it, it's all being spent on
> TQM.

In all this there is a strong sense of the shifting focus of commitment
and potential disappearance of meaning from the classroom and from
relationships, between teachers as teachers, and between teachers and
their students. Indeed, in the world of educational reform and new
school organizations, 'teaching' is almost an epiphenomenon. For Mr
Gainsborough it is 'the system', for Mr Wolfitt 'management', and for Mrs
Austen (Head of English at Fletcher school, who makes a similar point and
is discussed later) it is the Senior Management Team that is the focus of the
production of values and meaning; all these locations are outside of or
'other' to them, to their selves. And in this dislocation even the space that
once existed for contest, debate and consultation has been closed down –
'silenced': 'you can only say how you are going to implement it'. The
possibilities of professional discourse have been replaced by compliance
or retreat – 'so many people opt out' (Mr Gainsborough).

> I think the head had on his agenda when he came to the school, was
> that he came to a school with a very very active staff association, active
> people in the unions . . . very vociferous people. I think his main
> agenda when he came in was to try and silence that and to sort of
> keep people more in check, which I think the structure of meetings is
> very much designed to do . . .
>
> (Mrs Austen)

Like Mr Gainsborough, Mr Wolfitt is also concerned that his practice is
reorientated by the requirements of 'performativity' and the role of 'performance' in 'representing' the schools to its 'audiences':

> it is a problem with performance, the public performance in education,
> although it's educationally beneficial, vary for those students involved,
> it is inevitably selective, and what you're doing is concentrating on the
> able students . . . at the expense, well you haven't got the time to spend
> so much on others.
>
> (Mr Wolfitt)

A key dilemma for teachers, the distribution of their time and energy across the student body, is pre-empted. As Woods et al. (1997) put it: 'A foreshortening of choice for the teacher in resolving dilemmas' produces 'tension', and 'where there was felt to be very little choice at all' there is 'constraint' (p. x). The former is 'the product of trying to accommodate two or more opposing courses of action where choice is limited or circum-scribed' (p. 21). The latter is 'structural', in the sense that the dilemmas are beyond personal resolution within the immediate context. 'Constraint implies compulsion, force, repression of natural feelings' (p. 21). What these teachers are saying is that they are now in a position of adopting pedagogies and making decisions about their use of time that go against their professional judgments about best practice; and these constraints are not simply practical, but also constitute what Woods et al. (1997) call an 'assault on values' (p. 84). Furthermore, in three of the four examples discussed here, the value concerns of the teachers are related, in particular, to the reorientation of their practice towards the needs and interests of the 'high achieving' students and away from others.

Trust

Mrs Austen at Fletcher displays aspects of both Mr Gainsborough's sense of loss and Mr Wolfitt's suspicion of his senior management team. These two combine in her analysis of her changing role, one with which she, like Mr Gainsborough, is distinctly ill at ease:

> I think that one of the biggest mistakes that ever came in was the introduction of this awful terminology of senior management team. Which came in, what, about 7–8 years ago. It's very isolationist and I know that people cringe when they hear it, when you hear about the senior management team *will* do this.

Without the label the school was more of 'a cohesive team' with 'much more a sense of people working together towards a common goal'. Identify-ing one group as different from the rest becomes 'isolationist', and with this comes the sense that decisions are imposed: '*will* do this'. The imperative is italicized to indicate the force with which Mrs Austen delivered the word in the interview. The 'isolationism' might also be placed against the 'cohesive team' and 'common goal' – the sense, also experienced by Mr Wolfitt, of a loss of collective endeavour, of purposefulness.[3] This is indicative, perhaps, of the inroads of 'performativity' (Ball 1998a), with its individualizing technologies of surveillance and comparison, as well as the dissolution of arenas of debate within which collective meanings could be explored.[4]

The term 'Senior Management Team' makes people 'cringe'. It is alien to the way in which Mrs Austen views both her role and her vision of the school. This is not seen as an organic development, but one that is imposed from the outside, an industrial model that does not fit. It is the way in which it manifests itself within the school that is problematic:

> Once you've got the introduction and the sort of terminology from industry and those sort of applications, it created sort of boundaries that weren't there before. I mean it tended to be the Head Teacher and the rest of the school.

For Mrs Austen the language itself 'creates a sense of "us and them" which people feel quite strongly' – not least because 'by referring to themselves as such' they become a target for the rest of the staff. Yet, for Mrs Austen, conflict does not reside only in her sense of 'us and them', but in the tension between individuality and conformity. Part of her explanation for this seems straightforward: 'I don't know, maybe it's the sort of imposition of something from above which doesn't allow for as much individuality as schools used to.' The National Curriculum, which she has 'fought against for such a long time about being prescriptive of the kind of literature you've got to study' has now arrived and has to be implemented, even though she believes it has robbed her of her professional judgment. 'You know, we're actually sort of saying which poems you read, which novels you read, when you read them, how – you know?'

Here the change in locus of control over selection of curriculum materials is closely identified with her conception, not just of her professionalism, but of the expression of individuality. On the surface she separates those imposing from above from the schools, by creating a noun out of government actions. It's the 'imposition' that 'doesn't allow for as much individuality as the schools used to'. Without the 'imposition', schools would potentially still allow for individuality. And yet she hesitates, 'I don't know, maybe' and in her next comment brings the changes closer to home. 'And I think possibly it's the nature of all the schools now that it doesn't allow for individualism the way it used to.' Now it is the schools themselves that don't allow for individuality. There is still some hesitation, however, because she separates schools from their 'nature'. The 'it' refers to the nature, not to the schools. This implies a more fundamental shift than simple changes to the English curriculum. It broadens the scope of the discussion. Perhaps what is signalled in Mrs Austen's sense of dissonance is the 'steering' effects achieved by linking institutional autonomy to the requirements of performance and competition and a national curriculum – centralized decentralization (Ball, 1994). She goes on to say:

> And that people have to conform much more to fulfilling, you know, requirements of the National Curriculum – not just the National Curriculum, Heads of Year have got, you know, statistics to try and make sure that, you know, percentages of attendance are all right as

well. So maybe it's just that the education system doesn't allow for that kind of maverick any more.

This last comment is perhaps the most significant, as it acts as a kind of coda to the progression of her thoughts. The changes go beyond the simple imposition of the National Curriculum, and here for the first time she introduces the word 'conform'. Now they do not simply have to conform to the National Curriculum, they have to conform to the requirements of the school. The possibility of a 'maverick' teacher, which she values, is now untenable. She describes an environment of statistics and percentages. Juxtaposed as these are with her concern for literature and poetry, the conflict becomes more redolent of the utilitarian Gradgrind and the imaginative circus people. We have returned via another route to the alienating language of industry: to facts and figures. The school becomes an extension of the factory gate. We are back also to the issue of authenticity – poetry versus statistics – and to the place of 'teaching' in the new world of 'imposition'.

The reader might well want to interject at this point, perhaps with some justification, that what is being recorded here is simply a set of 'nostalgic anachronisms who hunker down and cling to the past' (Deal, 1990, p. 145). These are teachers who are unable to come to grips with the necessities of change and, as Deal suggests, 'struggling with transition is a central feature of life in any organisation' (p. 144). We have two responses to make to that point. First, these teachers are not simply and unthinkingly defending the past – as we shall see, they do recognize the benefits of change or more accurately some kinds of change, to themselves and to their students. In some respects, as Woods et al. (1997) put it: 'there appear to be contrary tendencies occurring at the same time leading to a diminished profession-alism on the one hand, but enhanced on the other' (p. 145). Second, we are suggesting here that these teachers' sense of loss and confusion and guilt relate to something of value – an authenticity of 'teaching' that lies at the heart of the educational enterprise and that generates the commitments and meaning that underpin the efficacy of practice.

To take the first point, Mrs Truffaut (Head of Modern Languages at John Ruskin school), for example, is clear that the National Curriculum, or more precisely the Dearing-revised National Curriculum, is a valuable necessity:

> the National Curriculum was the first attempt at making sense of complete and total anarchy. I personally like the National Curriculum very much because it tells me very good practice[s] of teaching and learning and assessing . . .

She is concerned about what might be seen as the 'other side of indivi-duality' (there may be issues related to subcultural subject difference here):

Everybody doing what the hell they wanted, teaching what topic they wanted, somebody was going to do the perfect tense in Year 8 because they thought kids should know it, others would never teach a verb. So the planning and having to go through a policy decided by you and checked by an adviser or an inspector has ensured that at least you had some sort of standardization in teaching practices in a department.

Ultimately what is at issue could be taken as the balance between gains and losses, 'impositions' and opportunities, in the ongoing restructuring of teachers' work; although the continuing incitement to discourse on teaching leaves little room for the teachers' voice in public debate. The debate is 'about' teachers, not 'for' them. They have no legitimate place from which to speak. The accounts generated in this and other research offer one of the few possibilities for engaging in a restitutive discourse. Woods et al. (1997) weigh the balance, in the primary sector, as follows:

> among the positive features are a welcome for the order and framework of sound planning, new opportunities for self-development, an increase in ownership and control of one's teaching, the ability to 'engage' with others and greater expertise. The negative features are a mirror image of these: bureaucratic and work overload, diminished selves, loss of ownership and control, distance rather than engagement, and an atrophying of skills. . . . But the balance on the whole strongly favours the negative. (p. 84)

In a sense Woods and colleagues are describing a complex microphysics of power that is both productive and oppressive. The balance referred to earlier can perhaps best be thought of as a set of paradoxes rather than as an equation. The four accounts with which we are concerned here are littered with references to the physical and emotional depredations of reform, what Woods (1996) describes as 'the pain of it all' (p. 102). But they can also be read as testimonies of survival. These are not simple stories of oppression and exclusion, but of a struggle between antagonistic discourses – a struggle over and through meanings and practices. For example:

> I mean there are people who have been treated for depression, you know, colleagues I know in the Consortium, one of the four schools, couldn't stand it, couldn't stand the pressure.
>
> (Mrs Truffaut)

> I think teachers are tired. I think it's part of the culture of teaching at the moment is that people are generally overworked and overloaded with work and don't relish the idea of meetings.
>
> (Mrs Austen)

... the will is there but the actual sort of physical strength to initiate lots of different things isn't always there.

(Mrs Austen)

... it is on everybody's agenda, we're frightened to death about Ofsted [Office for Standards in Education] next year. The Head is just levitating with fear, going around picking [up] litter already, doing absolutely crazy memos to middle managers.

(Mrs Truffaut)

we work ourselves stupid, and we have a workload which is unmanageable . . .

(Mrs Truffaut)

Mrs Austen seems very clear about how reform and its consequences affect her work, and her self. There is a reorientation of effort, a deflection:

I think the sort of relationship between the teacher and the child, you know, the sort of trust relationship that you can build up between them . . . I personally have found that I'm not as close to the children as I used to be . . . I mean you used to see a lot of staff working with children in the lunch times, not on an organized basis but on a, you know, sort of, come in and I'll help you with this, that and the other. That used to happen a lot, it doesn't happen so much any more.

Increasingly, it would appear that teachers' energies, physical and emotional, must be invested not in the work of teaching itself but in accounting for the work of teaching. The second-order requirements of accountability and formality increasingly seem to be of most importance in 'what it means to be a teacher':

with the Head, if he hears there's something good he wants it written up and . . . you know! Oh no! – you know? Leave me alone, just let me do something without having to write about it and put it in writing!

(Mrs Austen)

Perhaps we are back to the issue of authenticity, to the possibility of another discourse of teaching. The sense here and throughout the other interviews is that teaching is no longer worthwhile, no longer valid in its own right, no longer quite real until it is 'accounted for'; but then in its new representation, it may not be 'real' at all, it may signify nothing at all:

Yeah I think once you've committed yourself to paper, you know, I mean I sometimes look at our handbook which looks really glossy and good, and I read through it and I think, gosh did we actually write that?, do I believe that? – you know? I mean it's . . . it's a difficult area.

Conclusion

Writing in more general terms, Hanlon (1998) argues that within and around the professions there is a struggle underway between a social service and a commercialized version of professionalism, what he calls a 'struggle for the soul of professionalism' (p. 50). One of the key issues at stake in this struggle, he suggests, is trust, which is one of the recurrent themes in our teachers' accounts:

> the issue of who is trusted and who is not trusted and how some come to be trusted and others not is of vital importance. As society shifts from a Fordist regime of accumulation to a post-Fordist or flexible regime of accumulation the issue of trust comes clearly into focus. Under Fordism, society was regulated on the basis of the welfare state and this legitimated professionalism which was founded on serving people on the basis of need and citizenship. As we move from Fordism to flexible accumulation such a form of professionalism is under attack because powerful actors – the state and large scale capital – no longer deem it appropriate, i.e. they no longer trust the ethos to deliver what is required, increased profitability and international competitiveness.
>
> (p. 52)

Crudely, we might say that the social agenda of welfare professionalism is being replaced by the economic agenda of technical and entrepreneurial professionalism. While this may not seem to have a direct relevance to the changing role of classroom teachers, our data suggest that it does. Changes in the 'soul of the teacher' or the ethos of schooling (or 'structures of feeling' in education) may be subtle and difficult to measure, but they frame or underpin the meaning, values and morale of the teacher.

A complex of overlapping, agonistic and antagonistic discourses are in play in English education – a discourse of authenticity about the meaning of teaching and a discourse of trust and betrayal. The latter is a public discourse – originating from a variety of sites and agents like the TTA, Ofsted, DfEE (Department for Education and Employment), the media and the organic intellectuals of the right – and is about the betrayal of youth and of nation. The former is a private or submerged discourse about the distrust and betrayal of teachers and the meaninglessness of teaching (and thus the betrayal of youth and of nation). As Foucault would have it, 'discourse can be both an instrument and an effect of power, but also a hindrance, a stumbling block, a point of resistance and a starting point for an opposing strategy' (Dreyfus and Rabinow, 1983, p. 201). Guilt and loss are embedded in the nexus between these discourses – a nexus occupied by the teachers we have quoted. Indeed, Hargreaves (1994) suggests that 'Guilt is a central emotional preoccupation for teachers' (p. 142): both *persecutory* guilt, 'which arises from doing something that is forbidden or failing to do something that is expected by one or more external authorities' (p. 143); and *depressive* guilt, which is 'at its most intense, perhaps, when we may be harming or neglecting those for whom we care, by not meeting their needs or by not giving them sufficient attention' (p. 144).

These two forms are represented in the two teacher subjectivities and sets of practice that are counterpoised through the accounts presented above. One, the 'reformed teacher', is accountable, primarily orientated to performance indicators, competition, comparison, responsiveness and so on. Here, cold calculation and extrinsic values predominate. The other is what we might call the 'authentic teacher', whose teaching involves 'issues of moral purpose, emotional investment and political awareness, adeptness and acuity' (Hargreaves, 1994, p. 6). Authenticity is, as Woods (1996) puts it, about teaching having an 'emotional heart'. Or, as Hargreaves argues, teaching is about desire: 'without desire, teaching becomes arid and empty. It loses its meaning' (Hargreaves, 1994, p. 12). In the current processes of educational reform, political enthusiasm for accountability is perhaps threatening both to destroy the meaningfulness of teaching and to profoundly change what it means 'to teach' and to be a teacher. We may end up getting a lot more and less than was expected when the reform of education was begun.

Notes

1 Peter Woods's work is one of the exceptions to this – see, in particular, Woods, 1996. See also Blackmore, 1996 and Hargreaves, 1994.
2 ESRC Grant no. R000235544. See also Gewirtz, 1996; Gewirtz, 1996; Ball, 1997; Reay, 1998.
3 Hargreaves (1980) comments on the loss of sense of community among teachers in grammar and secondary modern schools being amalgamated into comprehensives, but also describes the culture of teaching as marked by a 'cult of individualism'.
4 A comment made by Mrs Truffaut at John Ruskin draws these themes together. She is talking about the introduction of school-based management and its focus on 'finances and statistics' rather than teachers and teaching:

> because they were looking at the wrong thing. They were not looking where they should have been looking which is [at] staff like me who had been trained, staff like me who really had confidence in their education system, who really were part of it and ready to give their Saturdays and Sundays – we used to go train, we used to actually . . . And suddenly we were told we have to have contracts, that we're going to have appraisals, that people are going to go and check our mark books, and that we were a profession who were a disgrace . . .

All sorts of shifts are indicated here. Teachers move from being an asset to a liability. The idea of training as professional and self-development is sacrificed, trust evaporates and is replaced by monitoring and control, and the profession is now a 'disgrace'. Again we have a catalogue of losses of skill, commitment and confidence; and of public and self-esteem.

References

Ball, S.J. (1994) *Education Reform: A Critical and Post-Structural Approach*, Buckingham: Open University Press.

Ball, S.J. (1997) 'Good school/bad school', *British Journal of Sociology of Education*, **18**, 3, pp. 317–36.

Ball, S.J. (1998a) 'Ethics, self interest and the market form in education', in Cribb, A. (ed.) *Markets, Managers and Public Service? Occasional Paper No. 1*, London: Centre for Public Policy Research, King's College London.

Ball, S.J. (1998b) 'Performativity and fragmentation in "Postmodern Schooling"', in Carter, J. (ed.) *Postmodernity and the Fragmentation of Welfare*, London: Routledge.

Ball, S.J. and Gewirtz, S. (1997) 'Girls and the education market', *Gender and Education*, **9**, 2, pp. 207–22.

Blackmore, J. (1996) 'Doing "emotional labour" in the education market place: stories from the field of women in managment', *Discourse*, **17**, 3, pp. 337–49.

Deal, T.E. (1990) 'Healing our schools: restoring the heart', in Lieberman, A. (ed.) *Schools as Collaborative Cultures: Creating the Future Now*, London: Falmer Press.

Dreyfus, H.L., and Rabinow, P. (1983) *Michel Foucault: Beyond Structuralism and Hermeneutics*, 2nd edn, Chicago: University of Chicago Press.

Gewirtz, S. (1996) 'Post-welfarism and the reconstruction of teachers' work', Paper presented at the BERA Annual Conference, Lancaster, September.

Gewirtz, S. and Ball, S.J. (1996) 'From "welfarism" to "new managerialism": shifting discourse of school leadership in the education quasi-market', Paper presented at the 4th ESRC Quasi-Markets Research Seminar, SPS, University of Bristol.

Hanlon, G. (1998) 'Professionalism as enterprise', *Sociology*, **32**, 1, pp. 43–63.

Hargreaves, A. (1994) *Changing Teachers, Changing Times*, London: Cassell.

Hargreaves, D.H. (1980) 'The occupational culture of teachers', in Woods, P. (ed.) *Teacher Strategies*, London: Croom Helm.

Levacic, R., Hardman, J. and Woods, P. (1998) 'Competition as a spur to Improvement? Differential Improvement in GCSE Examination Results', Paper presented at the International Congress for School Effectiveness and Improvement, Manchester.

Orner, M. (1998) 'School marks: education, domination and female subjectivity', in Popkewitz, T.S. and Brennan, M. (eds.) *Foucault's Challenge: Discourse, Knowledge and Power in Education*, New York: Teachers College Press.

Paulin, T. (1998) *The Day Star of Liberty*, London: Faber and Faber.

Reay, D. (1998) 'Micro-politics in the 1990s: staff relationships in secondary school', *Journal of Education Policy*, **13**, 2, pp. 179–95.

Woods, P. (1990) 'Cold eyes and warm hearts: changing perspectives on teachers' work and careers', *British Journal of Sociology of Education*, **11**, 1, pp. 101–17.

Woods, P. (1996) *Researching the Art of Teaching: Ethnography for Educational Use*, London: Routledge.

Woods, P., Jeffrey, B., Troman, G. and Boyle, M. (1997) *Restructuring Schools, Reconstructing Teachers*, Buckingham: Open University Press.

5 The Psychic Rewards (and Annoyances) of Teaching[1]

Andy Hargreaves

Teachers don't teach for the money. Few say that the holidays keep them in the job, either. Despite impossible workloads, external pressures, unreasonable change agendas and all the other dissatisfactions that plague their work, teachers ultimately do what they do for the children. Children and classroom life are what make teaching worthwhile, providing the prime and sometimes the sole source of teachers' work rewards. This is not just an occupational truism, there is research evidence to support it.

In his seminal study of teachers and teaching conducted in the late 1960s, Dan Lortie (1975) became one of the first writers and researchers to give extensive attention to the affective aspects of teaching. Of the teachers he interviewed, 76 per cent selected psychic rewards as their major source of satisfaction, compared with a mere 12 per cent who nominated extrinsic rewards such as pay, and another 12 per cent who nominated ancillary rewards such as convenient hours that fit the demands of family life (p. 104). These psychic rewards involved 'reaching' pupils and helping them achieve. They derived from the service ethic that drew people into teaching, and from the structure of teaching where teachers could best concentrate their energies where they felt they could make a difference: in the classroom.

The psychic rewards of teaching were of three kinds. First, they involved achieving moral outcomes with pupils – 'trying to make them good citizens', to 'stress good citizenship', to 'prepare them for life' so they are 'ready to live in society' (p. 112). Second, psychic rewards came from connecting children to school and learning, 'to make them like school', 'eager to want to learn things', develop 'a love of learning from within' and 'make them think on their own' (p. 114). Third, psychic rewards accrued from benefiting all pupils, not just a few – 'to get every kid to read as well as he can' or 'get across to all thirty of them', for example (p. 115).

Achievement of psychic rewards among Lortie's teachers was most evident when teachers had spectacular successes in turning around individual pupils (p. 123), when graduates returned and thanked them for their influence (p. 123), and when their work was made visible and acknowledged by others through public displays and presentations (p. 125). In all these cases, when pupils showed affection towards and regard for their teachers, and demonstrated that they were enjoying (or had enjoyed) their learning, this was a source of reward for teachers – receiving that affection, they knew they were achieving their purposes (p. 120). 'Psychic rewards', Lortie concludes, 'rotate around classroom events and relationships with students; the cathexis of classroom life underlies much of what teachers feel about their work' (p. 187). Yet the availability of these rewards can never be presumed, nor are they always plentiful – non-compliance, lack of enthusiasm and failure among pupils serve as constant reminders to teachers that their work is not being accomplished (p. 116).

Elsewhere, in different language, other studies have pointed to the fact that the most important rewards in teaching are gained from pupils in the classroom. This is the place from which teacher satisfaction derives (e.g. Dinham and Scott, 1997; Nias, 1989). Primary teachers, especially, claim not only to have affection for pupils but, in some cases, even to love them (Hargreaves, 1994; Nias, 1989). Teachers feel that their work and their worth are in many respects defined by the pupils they teach – with those who teach successful pupils in middle-class communities generally experiencing more rewards than teachers in urban schools with pupils for whom academic achievement is more often a struggle (McLaughlin and Talbert, 1993).

In one of his studies of primary school teaching, Peter Woods deepens the analysis and exemplification of teachers' psychic rewards by examining how teachers described and valued the emotional aspects of teaching and learning (Woods and Jeffrey, 1996). He illustrates:

> How they work affectively to be more effective in the learning situation. They generate relationships that feature excitement, interest, enthusiasm, inquiry . . . discovery, risk-taking and fun . . . The cognitive 'scaffolding' is held together with emotional bonds.
>
> (p. 71)

Woods and Jeffrey describe how their teachers develop their children as people and not merely as cognitive learners by emphasizing life skills, communication and mutual respect; and they emphasize the importance of establishing emotional connections with their pupils by treating them as people, building relationships and understanding, and attending to the emotional aspects of classroom learning. Their study adds the texture and the richness of primary teachers' voices to the more terse analysis of psychic rewards provided by Lortie.

But are all teachers as emotionally loving and caring as the especially 'creative' primary teachers that Woods and Jeffrey chose to study? Are the psychic rewards of less 'creative' primary teachers configured differently?

Do the psychic rewards of secondary school teachers look different, in emotional terms, from those of their primary/elementary school colleagues? And can we assume that pupils always benefit when teachers experience psychic rewards?

To investigate these issues more deeply, I will now draw on three separate studies of my own in which the emotions of teaching have played an important part – all conducted in Ontario, Canada. The first study interviewed 32 Grade 7 and 8 teachers (the end of elementary school in Canada), across 16 varied schools, who had been identified as having a serious and sustained commitment to implementing common learning outcomes, integrated curriculum and alternative forms of assessment and reporting. The study determined how the teachers interpreted and implemented these educational changes in their classrooms.[2] The significance of how teachers' emotions affected their teaching and proposed changes to that teaching quickly became evident when the data were analysed in a grounded way. The second study involved collecting baseline teacher interview data from a dozen or so teachers in each of four secondary schools involved in a school improvement initiative. One part of the interview focused specifically on how teachers attended to pupils' emotions in their classes and what methods they used to stimulate pupils' achievement. The data from one of these schools are reported here. The third study, which concentrated directly on the emotions of teaching and educational change, was based on a mixed sample of 53 elementary and secondary school teachers. This chapter analyses 30 of the teachers' responses to one of the interview questions, which asked them to describe emotionally positive and negative incidents they had experienced with pupils. Comparing data from these studies helps establish more firmly what commonalities and variations exist in teachers' psychic rewards as a whole between and within primary (elementary) and secondary school communities.

Elementary Emotions

Our analysis of Grade 7 and 8 teachers revealed that educational change affected teachers' emotional responses to the structures, practices, traditions and routines of their working lives. It did this because the change was filtered through teachers' feelings about their pupils. Pupils were at the heart of their teaching, and of why these teachers diverged from the teaching norm. The purposes or goals that teachers had for pupils, and the emotional bonds or relationships that teachers established with them, underpinned virtually everything else teachers did.

The data from the study are reported fully elsewhere (Hargreaves, 1998a; Hargreaves and Earl, in press), so a summary of the key findings will be sufficient here:

- Teachers valued their emotional relationships and connections with pupils – they liked and even loved their pupils, they appreciated those who came back and thanked them for what they had done, and they took great pleasure in helping 'struggling' pupils achieve.
- Teachers had emotional goals for their pupils. They saw themselves as developing citizens and not just cognitive learners. They stressed the importance in their classes and curriculum of multicultural tolerance even in largely all-white schools, of successfully integrating special education pupils into regular classes, and of the benefits of cooperative group work for team-building and collaboration.
- Teachers valued establishing close emotional bonds with all their pupils – what Denzin (1984) calls emotional understanding – as a foundation for successful teaching and learning (and not merely as a way of averting or coping with children's personal crises).
- The emotional goals, bonds and connections that teachers valued in their relationships with pupils permeated everything they did – so too did teachers' own strong needs to feel emotionally engaged in and enlivened by their teaching.
- Teachers' preferences regarding school structures, for example, were strongly influenced by their own emotional orientations. For example, they preferred core-grouping structures (rather than fragmented, specialized teaching), which extended their time and range of curriculum responsibility with their pupils, so they could 'roll' with the projects and 'go with the flow' in their classes, following the momentum of interest and learning. Some also preferred to follow their pupils from one grade to the next 'because you know them so well, you know their moods' and their families, and 'can start right in there with them'.
- Teachers' pedagogical preferences were also emotionally influenced. Teachers employed an extremely wide range of strategies to try to 'reach' their pupils any way they could. Their choice of methods at any moment was also shaped by what they felt their pupils needed emotionally as well as intellectually – involving them actively, making the classroom feel safe and reassuring, creating the basis of security in which risks might more readily be taken, and so on. Importantly, these strategies also included 'traditional' teaching. Few, if any, teachers were shrinking violets, mere 'guides-by-the-side'. They liked to be seen, to be heard, to move. They were not ashamed that they loved to present within the extremely broad teaching repertoires they possessed.
- Teachers planned emotionally as well as rationally. As in the Latin origin of emotion – *emovere* (to move out, to stir up) – they made their planning dynamic, involving pupils and colleagues in developing units of study where ideas were 'piggy-backed' on one another, 'bounced off' people, 'bashed' around, 'spun off' each other in a 'free-for-all' like being 'in a pinball machine'. Teachers remained aware of the rational

aspects of planning, being mindful of and coming back to curriculum targets and outcomes – but they did not let this destroy the energizing improvisation and 'flow' of an effective planning process.

Data from this elementary school study extend the meaning of teachers' claimed psychic rewards beyond clichés, homilies and trite truisms about teaching children, not subjects. Not only did teachers in this study attach great emotional significance to teaching and learning, but also (even more than in Woods and Jeffrey's 1996 study) teachers' emotional goals for and bonds with their students shaped and reshaped everything they did – how they taught, how they planned and what kinds of structures they preferred. Importantly, these teachers seemed to derive their psychic rewards not just from the best and most highly achieving pupils, but from pupils of all backgrounds, dispositions and abilities – even 'the hell kids!', as one teacher called one particular class she had taught.

There were hints elsewhere in these teachers' comments, though, that their own approach to classroom emotions might not have been typical of their colleagues. Some of these were depicted as more self-serving and less pupil-centred in their attitudes to school structure and timetabling; for example, wanting to get out their rulers, block the periods off, and put their subjects back in. Equally, there were worries that secondary school teachers might be less caring than them, less likely to watch out for their pupils' welfare. One of Woods and Jeffrey's (1996, p. 63) teachers contrasted her own emotional practice with her secondary school counterparts who 'don't have someone with that overall view . . . don't have the contact' and where 'a lot of human connection is lost'. And Lortie (1975, p. 119) himself noted how 'elementary teachers tend to use affectively hot terms such as "students adore her" or "students love her" [while] high school teachers . . . employ more restrained language, substituting words like "respect" and "esteem"'. In order to explore such comparisons more thoroughly, I will turn next to our secondary school data.

Secondary Emotions

In an ongoing improvement project with four secondary schools in a large metropolitan district, my colleagues and I collected baseline interview data with up to twelve teachers in each school, which included responses to questions about their sources of satisfaction and how they attended to pupils' emotions in the classroom. One of the schools had once served a small village on the edge of the city, but in recent years had been surrounded by new housing development and the influx of a much more visibly diverse pupil population. The pupils had changed, but the staff had remained largely the same, with a mean age in the late 40s that was reflected in the composition of our sample.

When they were asked generally about sources of satisfaction in their work, teachers in the school confirmed the previous literature on psychic rewards and teacher satisfaction, by saying that they derived their greatest enjoyment from working with pupils. What they particularly enjoyed was 'the response of the pupils', 'working with kids', 'the kids' exuberance and enthusiasm', the fact that in physical education 'kids still want to be active in their life, they want to be fit', 'the ongoing joy of being around young people', 'the contact with the kids [who] are eager to learn, and they're fun and they bring such enthusiasm to life', 'when you *do* motivate and change a student and you see the light go on in their eyes and the concept strikes home', and 'the kids – that's the biggest thing that you've got'. As one teacher commented more extensively:

> I love working with teenagers. I can't imagine doing anything else. I find it really stimulating and interesting. I love to work with pupils and see them come in as Grade 9s and then for the four or five years they're here, mature and become quite responsible people.

In all cases but one, pupils and the positive emotion that many brought to the classroom with them were the strongest, and sometimes virtually the single, source of encouragement in teachers' work.

However, while all our secondary school teachers stated that they attempted to be aware of and responsive to pupils' emotions in the classroom, they did so mainly when it was felt that these emotions might interfere with pupils' learning. Teachers generally tried to make allowances for disturbing and distracting emotions that pupils brought into the classroom. In some cases, these emotions were treated as general psychological dispositions that needed to be managed if the classroom was going to be a workable environment. One teacher referred to pupils who were 'overly exuberant (laughs), emotional and usually it's just a case of asking them to calm down or whatever'. However, she also indicated that it was important to determine whether they 'really are being over-exuberant or whether there's really something wrong and they're acting out, because there's a big, more underlying problem'.

Furthermore, when we dug deeper into our data, rather different patterns emerged within this overall emotional response to pupils, than among our sample of elementary school teachers. For one thing, teachers seemed to derive their greatest psychic rewards from older, graduating, able pupils – the younger, less motivated ones being viewed as more of a challenge. For most teachers, low motivation was seen as externally fixed, not as something that they themselves could or should develop.

Being aware of larger problems that were emotionally disturbing for pupils and that intruded into the classroom was something to which teachers tried to be especially attentive. They sought to be 'aware of (pupils') feelings and . . . help them deal with them in a positive manner'. Other teachers acknowledged that:

I don't think you can teach without taking into account that you are looking at thirty people who have all come from a different emotional morning every day. Some of them come to school after having had a lot of problems at home. Some come to school hungry. Some come to school with other things on their mind so that learning is the last thing they want to think of.

Sometimes you get a feeling that it's just a bad day for them or perhaps they'll come and talk to you right away at the start of class: 'I'm having a really bad day; can I sit and do this?'

Teachers were prepared to make individual allowances and interventions for these emotional disturbances and intrusions:[3]

I suppose it depends on whether we know the student is having a bad day and we know ordinarily they are not that way, in which case we would try and be sympathetic or whatever and/or [recognize that] the student's always like that. I suppose . . . well, we just try to deal with it the best way we can. But, you know, you try to sort of recognize them as individual students, whether this is typical for them or not.

I will encourage students if they have a day where they're definitely out of it, they don't feel good or they didn't sleep well last night or there's a problem that they can tell me at the beginning of the class and I will not engage them in active behaviour as much as I would normally. So they can say this or they can say, 'today I need the day off. I need to just sit. Don't ask me any questions'. And if this happens too often then we obviously have to have a talk about it.

Maybe somebody's having a bad day. It's usually mostly up to the teacher's intuition that they can recognize that.

If there is something going on at home or anything else in their lives, then you say, 'Okay, listen. Let's deal with this later, or now, whatever you like' . . .

These teachers' responses about how they deal with pupils' emotions show an effort to be attentive to pupils' emotional states and engagements on the one hand, while regarding these emotional problems as representing deviations from or disturbances to the classroom norm on the other. Classroom emotions are seen to intrude into learning from the outside – from the family, home and personal life. They are viewed as departures from normal days, normal ages or normal academic levels. These norms are used for constructing emotional understanding (although this may often in practice be emotional misunderstanding) of students.[4] As one teacher observed:

> I'm going to have to know about the age level that you're teaching at, which involves actual emotional and academic level, because then if a kid's having a bad day, you can understand that that is typical of a fourteen-year-old, and that allows you then to adapt your lessons to the individual as well. So you really have to understand the child.

Emotions are noticed when they depart from what is developmentally and academically 'normal'. They are noticeable exceptions, characteristic of 'bad days' or days when students are 'out of it'.

The solutions to these disturbances are to make allowances and adjustments for individuals, try to listen and understand, meet with them individually before or after school or during lunch, not take emotional outbursts personally, 'find a nice little quiet spot . . . to make them feel comfortable', and try to deal with emotional problems outside of the classroom learning situation itself (in a separate quiet room, for example). An invisible, unstated backdrop to these teachers' responses is the regular emotional environment of their classrooms and of the teaching–learning process itself. There seems to be a tacit emotional grammar of secondary school teaching in these responses where emotions are normalized or neutralized to make the pedagogical process as smooth and easy as possible for teachers. Emotions are attended to when they intrude upon this grammar, threatening to disturb the order it represents. Emotions appear to threaten to flood the classroom, or to divert students' capacity to benefit from it – so they have to be tolerated, managed and accommodated.

By and large, classrooms are seen as arenas where pupils' emotions are managed and responded to, not as places that can, do or should actively generate particular kinds of pupil emotion (either positive or negative) in and of themselves. Teachers referred only infrequently to classroom learning and to the school itself as places that were also responsible for creating negative pupil emotion or as places that did and should take responsibility for building positive pupil emotion. Only two teachers acknowledged that emotional problems could arise for pupils as a result of what the school and its teachers did (and not just because of external matters in students' homes or personal lives). A member of the school's school improvement committee argued that many of her colleagues:

> Don't come at [things] from a pupil point of view. In many cases I think they come at it from a teacher point of view, so that if a kid is frustrated, they get frustrated, and I don't think, in some cases, they know how to deal with it.

One of the teacher-librarians acknowledged how 'in a library setting, you have to be really conscious of . . . the pressures these kids are under to get assignments in . . . around exam time'. As a result, 'their emotions are right out there, and maybe we see them more than they show their teachers'.

Those teachers who were more ready to design the emotional climate of their classrooms to be supportive for pupils had exceptional or specialized roles compared to the rest of the sample – roles that tended to draw their attention towards the emotional needs of all their pupils. For example, the special education teacher, who acknowledged that 'I'm not sure some of my colleagues would agree with me', said that he sought to:

> Provide a comfort level for everybody. So that, even if they don't happen to like the subject that they're taking with me, that they can still look forward to coming there . . . that their 45 or 75 minutes of interaction there will be pleasant for them and not something that they have to dread every day. I have started for many years as a preamble to any group who I teach, by saying something to the effect that the pupils are more important to me as individuals than they are as math pupils or science pupils or history pupils or English pupils, that I believe at the end of a semester I have achieved something with these students, that I have seen a positive growth in them as human beings. And I am more concerned with them as human beings than I am with them as pupils.

In general, though, providing extra emotional support for pupils, not as compassionate exceptions but as processes that are built into the routines of how classroom learning is organized, and how pupils' voices are heard, can create problems for teachers who organize their classrooms and relationships with pupils in particular ways. One interviewee commented, in this respect, on how the new administrator's clear focus on pupils and pupils' needs had precipitated difficulties among the school's teachers of just this kind:

> Things have changed in some respects, and I think the administration maybe listens to kids a bit more than they have in the past. I think some teachers feel threatened and feel that they aren't getting the back-up from the administration. They want, you know . . . they want solid rules, and when the rules have to be bent because of a particular situation, they're very unhappy.

Even when teachers were specifically asked how the school promoted positive emotions like exhilaration and enjoyment, everything they mentioned took place *outside* the core processes of teaching and learning in classrooms. One teacher thought the school had not really promoted positive emotion, another felt it did not pay sufficient attention to such matters, and a third was transparently thrown off-balance by the question. The examples to which other teachers pointed all took the form of school-wide awards, ceremonies, sports events, rallies, dance competitions, weekly bulletins and other initiatives such as music in the cafeteria. While rituals, ceremonies and celebrations are certainly an important part of cultivating and celebrating positive emotions in all institutional life – a way that the organization reflects itself back in positive and valued ways to its members – among the teachers we interviewed, they did not appear to take place within the classroom itself.

In short, this sample of secondary school teachers was demonstrably 'compassionate' towards and 'very interested in' pupils, and rarely complained about pupils in the staffroom. Yet, while teachers appeared to be ever ready to make allowances for pupils having personal problems or experiencing bad days, they made little reference to changing their core classroom processes so as to be more responsive to *all* pupils' purposes and needs, or to be able to create positive relationships and engagements with learning and change. Emotions appeared to be regarded as a threat to individual learning and classroom order – dangerous and disturbing influences that spilled over from other areas of pupils' lives and that teachers then had to manage. Redesigning classroom life and classroom learning so that these things could be more emotionally positive for all pupils, and giving greater pride of place to pupils' purposes and pupils' voice (on which positive emotion partly depends) were hardly mentioned at all. This is a very different picture of the psychic rewards of teaching and the emotions of classroom life from that provided by the elementary school teachers discussed earlier.

But could some of these differences be attributed to the fact that the sample of elementary school teachers (like that of Woods and Jeffrey, 1996) is that of a group of highly innovative, leading-edge teachers, whereas the secondary school sample concentrates on a less glamorous group of mid-to-late-career teachers in a more conventional setting? Do the data reveal differences in psychic rewards and emotional responses between conventional and leading-edge teachers, more than between primary and secondary ones? To discriminate between these possibilities, I will now turn to data from a third study of a more wide-ranging and diverse sample of primary and secondary teachers.

Mixed Emotions

In an interview study of 60 primary and secondary teachers across 16 schools in four school districts, we asked teachers to describe recent incidents with students that had positive and negative emotional connotations respectively.[5] About 30 teachers in the sample answered this question directly.[6] On 'negative' incidents, 16 secondary teachers provided usable responses (6 men, 10 women; 6 over 40 years of age, 10 under). On 'positive' incidents, the secondary sample was almost the same with two teachers excluded and two new ones included in the responses (i.e. 4 men,

12 women; 8 over 40, 12 under). In the elementary teachers sample, 14 teachers responded usably to 'negative' incidents (5 men, 9 women; 8 over 40, 6 under), and 15 to 'positive' incidents (5 men, 10 women; 8 over 40, 7 under).[7] For the sake of brevity, their responses are analysed in narrative form here, in preference to providing longer quotations. Two issues will be given particular attention. First, contrasts and continuities with Lortie's (1975) original findings on the psychic rewards of teaching; and, second, the psychic rewards drawn from and emotional responses made to pupils, in elementary and secondary schools respectively.

Psychic Rewards

Lortie pointed to three ways in which teachers gained psychic rewards from working with pupils – gratification from graduates who came back to thank their teachers, public performances and celebrations, and spectacular successes with individual pupils. Only one of these was sustained by my analysis of positive emotion among teachers. Just 2 of 30 incidents that stimulated positive emotion among the study's teachers were cases of gratifying graduates – both of them cited by older male secondary school teachers who referred to pupils who had returned to thank their teachers for their professional and personal help, and for preparing them for university effectively. Other teachers at the secondary level – six of them – mentioned displays of acknowledgment, respect, appreciation and gratitude that were much more direct, and less deferred than in Lortie's study. These teachers appreciated it: when pupils regularly said 'hello' to them in the corridors and showed they liked them; when they thanked teachers and brought them presents for doing something special, like allowing pupils to bake during an English class; when they were respected by senior pupils in another role such as athletics outside the classroom, even when their relationship had been at loggerheads within it; or when pupils spontaneously showed they would miss their departing teachers, for example in posters that communicated the fact. My study's secondary teachers, like Lortie's, framed positive pupil responses more through the relatively distanced language of acknowledgment and respect than the language of loving and liking. But this gratitude was not usually deferred until pupils had left school, being expressed to teachers more directly in the school itself. This indicates that the quality of direct feedback and interaction from pupils to their teachers in secondary schools (and therefore the relationships on which they are based) may well have improved since Lortie's day.

A second source of psychic rewards for Lortie's teachers was public performances and celebrations. These kinds of events were completely absent as sources of positive emotion from the accounts of teachers in my study. Although they might well have been valued by teachers, they were clearly not prominent enough to warrant singling out as incidents that produced especially positive emotion.

Lortie's third example of psychic rewards – that of spectacular individual cases of difficult or demanding pupils they somehow managed to turn around against the odds – continued to be strongly represented among the teachers in my study. Indeed, spectacular cases were easily the most frequently cited source of positive emotion among secondary teachers (half the teacher sample) – who were all women, largely in mid-to-late career. Elementary teachers also referred to seven spectacular cases of this kind. Across the two sectors, these cases included: teaching a very disadvantaged pupil useful lifeskills; helping a difficult pupil through a risky but successful drama production; giving a previously underachieving pupil the rare accolade of a perfect mark; encouraging pupils to take responsibility for solving a major classroom problem and seeing them succeed at it; being perceptive enough to identify a pupil with a learning disability and then successfully modifying their learning for them; watching a diffident pupil spread her wings and decide, after much prevarication, to leave school for university; making a kindergarten child stick at learning to write his name and seeing his pleasure at achieving it; seeing pupils benefit from perseverance; motivating an insecure less able child to achieve in mathematics; and, after considerable consultation with parents and a social worker, successfully incorporating a child who had been sexually abused into a class on sexual abuse – to the point where her mature contribution influenced the rest of the class. As in Lortie's study, it seems that while teachers expend their energies on their classes, they continue to invest their hopes in individuals.

A source of positive emotion in my study that was not so explicit in Lortie's discussion of psychic rewards was the satisfaction that teachers gained from strong and rewarding classroom relationships – especially in elementary schools (seven mentions, compared to three at the secondary level). I will develop the discussion of this issue in the ensuing section on elementary school teachers. The point that should be reaffirmed here is that, especially at the elementary level, within their own classrooms teachers today appear to derive pleasure, positive emotions and psychic rewards from their immediate, not deferred, relationships with their classes (as groups, and not just as individuals), compared to the time of Lortie's study.

Some of the differences between the results of this study and Lortie's, however, could also be due to at least two key differences of methodology, and not just changes over time. First, Lortie deduced the nature of psychic rewards in teaching by asking teachers directly about prideful moments in their teaching. In my own study, however, when asked to name spontaneously the positive emotions they experienced with their pupils, only one in five teachers cited pride. Secondary teachers spoke mainly of feeling grateful, respected, acknowledged and validated; while elementary teachers especially seemed to use a rather generalized, and arguably impoverished, language of positive emotion as expressed in words like 'good', 'great' and 'positive'. Requiring teachers to discuss just one emotion may, in this sense, produce an underestimate of the range of psychic rewards that teachers derive from their work. Second, while most of Lortie's teachers' dissatisfaction seemed to originate from outside the classroom, a strategy of asking teachers directly about negative emotions with students, as in this study, may elicit less guarded and 'professionally correct' responses. Certainly, teachers in my sample had not the least difficulty in identifying and discussing examples of negative emotions arising from incidents with pupils which, at least a few teachers said, happened frequently or all the time. We will see next exactly how the landscape of positive and negative emotion in relationships with pupils is configured among secondary and elementary teachers respectively.

Secondary Emotions

In general, the findings of this study point to secondary school classrooms as places lacking emotional intensity – at least from the teachers' point of view. We have already seen that, as in Lortie's study, teachers were more likely to describe their relationships with pupils in terms of acknowledgment and respect than loving and liking. Other kinds of evidence confirmed this pattern.

For one thing, only secondary teachers (compared to elementary ones) cited seeing pupils in a new light, outside their own classes, as a source of positive emotion (there were three such cases). Reciprocally, of course, this also involved pupils seeing their *teachers* in a new light too. Here are two of the examples:

> I had a student last year who was not particularly motivated as a classroom student. I've been dealing with that student in the last little while as a member of an athletics team. As an athlete, he is a very different person than he is as a classroom student. Interacting with the individual in a different context can be very positive. As a classroom student, the person can be disruptive. As an athlete he can be a very positive individual . . . If a person's priority is not what is going on in your class, it can be very frustrating. You get outside the classroom and deal with the same individual where you are into their field of interest, you can see that in this area, what they are looking for is success in something different, and you see a much more positive light of that individual in the different context.

> In Art class [which this mathematics teacher was covering while the teacher was absent], I showed her how to do the math homework [which she implored the teacher to help her with] . . . A lot of the

times, it's more the interaction with the students outside the classroom
on a one-to-one basis, or in a small group. You see them in the lunch-
room where I don't always have to be their teacher, disciplinarian,
inside the classroom. I can let loose a little and also see them in a
different light.

In these cases, there is a hint that secondary school teachers feel they do
not know or are not known by their pupils in any deep sense – that
secondary school classrooms are not places where teachers develop shared
emotional goals with pupils or have close emotional bonds and connections with them. This means, of course, that teachers do not feel known by
their pupils either, as moral, emotional people, and this is a strong source
of negative emotion for them – the most frequently mentioned one by
secondary teachers in our sample (eight nominations).

In these instances, teachers complained about being misunderstood,
unjustly accused, treated as a stereotype, and not acknowledged. Examples
included overhearing pupils refer to a teacher (incorrectly) as gay because
of his high-pitched laugh; being accused of being a 'rat' when teachers
inadvertently betrayed pupil confidences to other teachers or family
members; being unfairly accused of 'picking on' pupils when teachers
were trying to help them; being accused of racism because of not allowing
a pupil hall passes to be excused from class when the pupil already had a
record of wandering about the school; being expected by pupils to behave
like kindergarten teachers and put answers on the board for them to copy;
being treated not as a committed professional, but as a stereotype of any
teacher, whose efforts merit no special acknowledgment.

All but one of these instances (the purportedly gay man) of not being
known or acknowledged as a person were cited by women teachers. Also,
not one example of failing to be acknowledged, as a cause of negative
emotion, was mentioned by the elementary teachers in our study. In addition to this, while only one elementary teacher referred even remotely to
experiences with pupils outside the classroom being a cause of positive
emotion for them, this was a common pattern (cited six times) among
secondary school teachers, and indeed *all* of the male secondary teachers
in our sample cited experiences outside rather than inside their own classroom as the source of positive emotion in their interaction with pupils.

With Oatley (1991), I have argued that one of the causes of negative
emotions is bad relationships or no relationships. Another is where people's
purposes in these relationships are discrepant. From our evidence, in the
eyes of teachers, secondary school classrooms appear to be places where
such patterns and causes of negative emotions are widespread. Secondary
school teachers often feel not known by their pupils; their emotional
connections with them feel more distant than is true for their elementary
colleagues; and their purposes are often at odds with those of their pupils,
placing an emotional barrier between them. The best chances of break-

through, insight and positive relationship are achieved outside the classroom, where teachers have the chance of seeing their pupils and being seen by them in a new light. Men seem especially more likely to gain their psychic rewards with pupils outside the secondary school classroom, and women are most likely to respond negatively to being misunderstood by their pupils. In addition, academic issues of classroom learning more often give rise to negative rather than positive emotion in the accounts of the teachers we studied.

It is not that secondary teachers do not care for or want to connect emotionally with their pupils. Rather, the problem appears to be that the bureaucratic, specialized organizational pattern of secondary school life makes emotional understanding and connection with large number of pupils exceedingly difficult especially given that contact with them is usually highly fragmented (Hargreaves and Earl, in press). The result is that, compared to elementary classrooms, secondary school ones seem to lack real emotional intensity.

Elementary Emotions

Elementary classrooms come across as being undoubtedly more intense than secondary ones. All the positive emotional incidents cited by the study's elementary teachers were rooted in the classroom. Indeed, relationships with students within the classroom were a strong source of positive emotion among elementary teachers – being cited more frequently than any other factor (seven times). Teachers valued being missed by their pupils when they were absent; being their pupils' favourite teacher; having small groups of older pupils voluntarily accompany them to work with kindergarten classes; being loved by pupils; enjoying humour and informality with them; and creating an overall atmosphere in which they experienced lots of 'warm fuzzies' with their classes!

Yet, if classroom relationships were more valued as a source of positive emotion among elementary teachers, this does not mean that elementary teaching was consistently characterized by care, hope and attentiveness – as popular stereotypes from much of the literature on elementary teachers might lead one to believe (e.g. Elbaz, 1991). Compared to secondary school teachers, elementary teachers in our study came across as not only more emotionally positive in the classroom but also as more emotionally negative as well. Their classrooms are more emotionally intense in both respects. For example, while secondary teachers alone complained of not being acknowledged by their pupils, at least four elementary teachers mentioned times when their pupils actively disliked them. In these instances, pupils lacked courtesy; they mimicked and 'parroted' the teacher's words in front of other children; they publicly lost faith in their teacher's coaching ability; or they boldly told their teacher they hated her.

Because elementary schools are places where there are greater differences between teachers and pupils in age, physical size and strategic sophistication, elementary teachers possess more classroom power than their secondary colleagues, as well as showing more care. This power may not usually be explicit and may linger under the surface much more than in secondary teaching, where pupil behaviour is negotiated more overtly between teachers and pupils. However, despite or perhaps because of its more subterranean nature, teachers' power is a particular insistent feature of elementary school life (see also Hargreaves, 1994).

This is clearly illustrated in our data on anger. Elementary teachers described more incidents of being angry about or with their pupils than secondary teachers did (seven compared to four). They also felt frustrated with their pupils more often (eight incidents compared to five). Elementary teachers got angry with pupils they tried to help but who refused to work hard and cooperate and whose 'attitudes stink'; with a pupil who insisted on doing 'their own thing' and not conforming with classroom rules that applied to the rest; with a pupil who complained that things were boring after all the efforts the teacher had made to take her class to an art gallery; with the pupil who mocked and 'parrotted' the teacher in front of other children; with difficult pupils who 'refuse to do their part' when many teachers are giving their best efforts on their behalf; with a 5-year-old pupil who hated her teacher and said she wished she would die; or with one boy who refused to go to the principal as instructed, with the effect that 'you can't help but get angry and agitated when those kinds of things happen'. Anger, in other words, arose when pupils defied their teachers, showed them up in front of others, or failed to appreciate or respond to their efforts when teachers had gone the extra mile for them.

Contrary to the literature on gender and emotion, which argues that women are less likely to express or articulate anger than men (tending to internalize their anger in depression or self-disappointment instead), women were no less likely than men to express anger regarding their pupils in this study (e.g. Crawford, Kippax, Onyx, Gault and Berton, 1992). This slightly surprising finding may be explained by the fact that while in society as a whole women more usually occupy subordinate positions within relations of power, in elementary school classrooms the opposite is true. In his research on emotions and power, Kemper (1995) showed that anger is more likely when the target of a person's anger is not in a position to threaten them, retaliate or otherwise do them harm – to respond to wrath with vengeance. Compared to their secondary school counterparts, within their classrooms at least, elementary teachers are much more firmly ensconced in this micropolitically superior position. Further empirical support for this argument can be found in the fact that elementary teachers, especially older teachers, were even more likely than their secondary colleagues to express negative emotion in relation to problems of pupil behaviour (11 teachers compared to 7).

Conclusion

The data from these three studies confirm that the psychic or emotional rewards of working with pupils are still extremely important for teachers. As in Lortie's (1975) classic study, teachers still draw great emotional satisfaction from spectacular successes with individual pupils, whose lives and learning they have managed to turn around. They also derive pleasure from pupils who thank them for their efforts – but compared to the time of Lortie's study, teachers do not now have to wait until their pupils have left until this gratitude finally comes their way. Another significant factor is the additional psychic reward that elementary teachers especially mentioned in my study (which was not cited by Lortie) of having strong and rewarding relationships with their pupils as individuals and as classes. These new sources of satisfaction may also explain why teachers did not mention public presentations and celebrations as causes of positive emotion in the studies reported here.[8] In some respects, at least, it seems teaching has moved on emotionally since the time of Lortie's study.

Peter Woods' work on creative, innovative leading-edge teachers, as well as mine reported here, has deepened the understanding of teachers' emotional relationship with their pupils. It has shown how teachers of this kind care deeply for their classes. They value establishing emotional goals for them and bonds with them – and these goals and bonds permeate everything that innovative teachers do in developing broad teaching repertoires, in creating structures that support their relationships with pupils, and in planning emotionally as well as rationally. But the data from other teachers discussed here suggest that the depth of care and the extent of positive emotion that teachers draw from and invest in their teaching relationships with pupils is not so consistently present among teachers as a whole. We should beware, then, of taking the emotional voices of a minority of especially creative or caring teachers to be representative of the emotional voice of teaching in general (Hargreaves, 1996). There is more emotional diversity in teaching than this. Methodologically, the approach adopted here has enabled not only an enriched understanding of teachers' classroom satisfaction, but also exposed their classroom dissatisfactions.

Among secondary teachers, the evidence cited in this chapter suggests that, while teachers are generally compassionate towards their pupils, their classrooms lack emotional intensity. They are concerned to fend off and manage negative emotion that threatens to intrude from the outside, rather than to develop positive emotions in their own right. Secondary teachers gain many of their emotional rewards and build meaningful relationships with pupils outside the classroom, not within it. Inside the classroom, teachers often feel not known or misunderstood by their pupils. Their purposes and agendas are often at odds with those of their pupils. Academic learning is more often a source of negative than positive emotion for them. Secondary schools may not be emotional deserts, but their structures, curriculum, purposes and practices seem to create classroom environments that are more affectively arid than in the primary/elementary domain.

By comparison, elementary school teaching is permeated by greater emotional richness. Teachers place high value on their relationships with pupils as a source of positive emotion, and claim to derive all their positive emotion from classroom-based incidents (Nias, 1989). Yet, elementary teaching is not only more emotionally intense in a positive sense. Unfashionably, and in striking contrast to data drawn exclusively from leading-edge teachers, elementary teaching, even more than secondary teaching, is permeated by the emotions of power as well as those of care. Elementary teachers report incidents of being actively disliked rather than merely not known as a source of negative emotion; and they are far more likely than secondary school teachers to report being angry with their pupils (and this is true of women as much as men). Elementary teaching is not all about love and care; it is about power and control as well.

Emotions are exceptionally important in teaching – that is evident in the works of writers like Lortie and Woods, and in the data reported here. Leading-edge teachers demonstrate how developing emotionally rich relationships with pupils provides a solid foundation for really successful teaching and learning. But, in general, secondary school teaching seems devoid of this emotional intensity. If reformers really care about quality, they would do well to turn their attention away from curriculum consistency, inspection processes, other technologies of control, and accountability measures towards developing structures, purposes and programmes of secondary schooling that will help teachers and pupils build a more solid emotional understanding with each other, on which successful teaching can truly be based (Hargreaves and Earl, in press).

Meanwhile, we must take care not to be seduced into the romantic delusion that because elementary teaching is more explicitly and intensely emotional, all this emotion is necessarily a good thing. Bad adult emotions are dangerous weapons when let loose among the young. As Goleman (1995) argues, in personal terms, emotional intelligence means being able to manage one's emotions as well as express them, so that they do not get out of control – primary/elementary teacher development programmes would do well to pay attention to this. More politically, there may even be more reform work to be done to redistribute power in primary/elementary classrooms, to make pupils more responsible for their own learning, so that caring yet also ultimately controlling teachers who want to organize everything themselves do not feel unduly outraged when unmotivated pupils fail to appreciate their efforts 'after all they have done' for them.

Notes

1 A substantial part of this chapter draws on a research project on 'The emotions of teaching and educational change', funded by the Social Science and Humanities Research Council of Canada.
2 For further methodological empirical details, see Hargreaves, 1998b; Hargreaves and Earl, in press.
3 Every teacher except one made extensive comments of the same kind – for brevity's sake, just a few are quoted here.
4 For an elaboration of Denzin's (1984) concepts of emotional understanding and emotional misunderstanding applied to teachers within an overall theory of teaching and the emotions, see Hargreaves and Earl (in press).
5 The method of eliciting reported emotions by asking interviewees to describe positive and negative critical incidents is derived from Arlie Hochschild's (1983) classic study of emotional labour in *The Managed Heart*.
6 Other teachers responded to these questions elsewhere in the interview – and their responses are currently under analysis – or provided answers that were too vague for meaningful categorization.
7 In the general school sample, administrators in each school were asked to construct a sample of four teachers including the teachers teaching in the school for the shortest and longest times, a mixture of teachers who favoured change or were sceptical about it, representation of both genders, at least one participant from an ethnic cultural minority; and (in secondary schools) teachers from a range of subject areas.
8 It may also be the case that Lortie undervalued the importance of classroom relationships to teachers because he chose to focus on pride as his only positive emotion – and though warm relationships with pupils may be a source of pleasure and satisfaction for teachers, they will not necessarily be a source of pride as well.

References

Crawford, J., Kippax, S., Onyx, J., Gault, U. and Berton, P. (1992) *Emotion and Gender*, London: Sage.

Denzin, N. (1984) *On Understanding Emotion*, San Francisco: Jossey Bass.

Dinham, S. and Scott, C. (1997) *The Teacher 2000 Project: A Study of Teacher Motivation and Health*, Perth: University of Western Sydney, Nepean.

Elbaz, F. (1991) 'Research on teachers' knowledge', *Journal of Curriculum Studies*, **23**, 1, pp. 1–19.

Goleman, D. (1995) *Emotional Intelligence*, New York: Bantam Books.

Hargreaves, A. (1994) *Changing Teachers, Changing Times*, London: Cassell; New York: Teachers' College Press, pp. 141–59.

Hargreaves, A. (1996) 'Revisiting voice', *Educational Researcher*, **25**, 1, pp. 12–19.

Hargreaves, A. (1998a) 'The emotional politics of teaching and teacher development: implications for leadership', *International Journal of Leadership in Education*, **1**, 4, pp. 315–36.

Hargreaves, A. (1998b) 'The emotions of teaching and educational change', in Hargreaves, A., Lieberman, A., Fullan, M. and Hopkins, D. (eds.), *The International Handbook of Educational Change*, The Netherlands: Kluwer Publications.

Hargreaves, A. and Earl, L., with Moore, S. and Manning, S. (in press) *Beyond Bandwagons: Striving for Success with Curriculum and Assessment Reform*, San Francisco CA: Jossey Bass.

Hochschild, A.R. (1983) *The Managed Heart: The Commercialization of Human Feeling*, Berkeley CA: University of California Press.

Jeffrey, B. and Woods, P. (1996) 'Feeling deprofessionalized: the social construction of emotions during an OFSTED inspection', *Cambridge Journal of Education*, **126**, 3, pp. 235–343.

Kemper, T.K. (1995) 'Sociological models in the explanation of emotions', in Lewis, M. and Haviland, J. (eds), *Handbook of Emotions*, New York and London: Guilford Press.

Lortie, D.C. (1975) *Schoolteacher*, Chicago: University of Chicago Press.

McLaughlin, M. and Talbert, J. (1993) 'What matters most in teachers' workplace context', in Little, J. and McLaughlin, M.W. (eds) *Teachers' Work: Individuals, Colleagues and Contexts*, New York: Teachers' College Press.

Nias, J. (1989) *Primary Teachers Talking*, London: Routledge and Kegan Paul.

Oatley, K. (1991) *Best Laid Schemes: The Psychology of Emotions*, Cambridge: Cambridge University Press.

Sikes, P., Measor, L. and Woods, P. (1985) *Teachers' Lives and Careers*, Lewes: Falmer Press.

Woods, P. (1993) *Critical Events in Teaching and Learning*, Lewes: Falmer Press.

Woods, P. (1995) *Creative Teachers in Primary Schools*, Buckingham: Open University Press.

Woods, P. and Jeffrey, R.J. (1996) *Teachable Moments: The Art of Teaching in Primary Schools*, Buckingham: Open University Press.

Woods, P., Jeffrey, B., Troman, G. and Boyle, M. (1997) *Restructuring Schools, Reconstructing Teachers*, Buckingham: Open University Press.

6 Understanding Teachers' Lives: The Influence of Parenthood

Pat Sikes

In the introductory chapter to his book *Researching the Art of Teaching*, Peter Woods tells of his experiences in the 1940s as a working-class boy at a middle-class grammar school. He notes that 'at the time it was difficult to understand the personal hostility of some of the teachers, especially when we thought we were doing our best' (Woods, 1996, p. 2). Ann Oakley suggests that, frequently, 'academic research projects bear an intimate relationship to the researcher's life . . . personal dramas provoke ideas that generate books and research projects' (Oakley, 1979, p. 4). Although it may be fanciful to make the link, it seems that, throughout his career as an academic and educational researcher, Woods has been seeking to make sense of the attitudes and behaviour of teachers, even after he had himself become one. The outcome of his quest for understanding has been a substantial and significant contribution to the growing body of qualitative research that focuses on teachers and teaching. One strand of this work has been that which takes a biographical and, in particular, a life history approach. Writing in 1985, Woods suggested that 'life histories are due for revival' (Woods, 1985 p. 13). The number of publications describing life history work that have appeared since then suggests that there has been such a revival and, I would argue, Woods has played a significant role in advancing it.

In this chapter the aim is to consider the potential that life history has for studying teachers and teaching, and then to focus on a project that used the approach to explore teachers' perceptions of the ways in which becoming a parent had influenced their professional lives (Sikes, 1997). In doing this I shall also reflect on the way in which life historians' own life histories are intimately connected with their work.

Life History and Teachers

Denzin's (1970) suggestion that 'the life history may be the best method for studying adult socialization, the situational response of self to daily interactional contingencies' echoes Thomas and Znaniecki's (1927) claim that life history is the 'perfect type of sociological material' (p. 1832) and Blumer's (1979) view that the supreme value of life history method is its 'ability to take seriously the subjective factor in social life' (p. 81). With regard to researching and understanding teachers and teaching, a life history approach seems particularly appropriate because of the intensely personal and relationship-based nature of the work. Finding out about the sort of people teachers are, and how they see themselves and the work they do, would seem to be essential. As Hargreaves suggests,

> we are beginning to recognise that, for teachers, what goes on inside the classroom is closely related to what goes on outside it. The quality, range and flexibility of teachers' classroom work are closely tied up with their professional growth – with the way that they develop as people and as professionals. Teachers teach in the way they do not just because of the skills they have or have not learned. The ways they teach are also grounded in their backgrounds, their biographies, in the kinds of teachers they become.
>
> (A. Hargreaves, 1997, p. xi)

This has implications for research into most aspects of schools and schooling, teachers and teaching, which many have recognized. Consequently, since the 1980s, an increasing amount of biographical work dealing with teachers' experience of different aspects of their lives and careers has been undertaken. There are studies that make use of life history to investigate, for example: how secondary art and science teachers at all career stages (from NQT through to retirement) experience and negotiate a way through teaching within particular social, political and economic contexts (Sikes, Measor and Woods, 1985); the ways in which being a parent can influence teachers' pedagogy and professional perceptions (Sikes, 1997); how teachers experience imposed change (Sikes, 1992); the particular problems that PE teachers face as they age (Evans, 1988); women teachers working for social change (Casey, 1993); the experiences of lesbian and gay teachers (Epstein, 1994; Epstein and Johnson, 1998; Sparkes, 1995); primary teaching as work (Nias, 1989); the relationship between teachers' lives, school subjects and curriculum development (Ball and Goodson, 1985; Bell, 1995; Goodson, 1983; Sikes and Everington, 1998; Thomas, 1995); teacher 'socialization' (Bullough, Knowles and Crow, 1991); teachers as researchers (Elliott and Sarland, 1995); teacher professionalization (Goodson and Hargreaves, 1996); the development of personal, professional knowledge (Clandinin, 1989; Elbaz, 1983; A. Hargreaves, 1994; Woods, 1981, 1993); black women teachers (Ostler, 1997); and the use of life history as a strategy for teacher development (Sikes and Troyna, 1991; Woods, 1993; Woods and Sikes, 1987) – to name but a handful of published accounts.

The strengths and weaknesses of life history work have been well rehearsed (see, for example, Bertaux, 1981; Goodson, 1980, 1992; Hatch and Wisniewski, 1995; Plummer, 1983; Smith, 1994; Stronach and MacLure, 1997), as have those of qualitative research more generally. Most writers agree that the key benefits of using life history are that: it is holistic and explicitly recognizes that lives are not hermetically compartmentalized into, for example, a teacher self and a parent self; it is historical and acknowledges the crucial relationship between individuals and social circumstances, present and past; it yields evidence to show how individuals experience, create and make sense of the rules and roles of the social worlds they live in; it yields information that is interesting and meaningful, and may be accessible to a wider audience than is usually the case for research findings; and it may be able to 'give voice' to groups who have tended to be marginalized and who have not had much opportunity to have their cases heard and their experiences recognized.

A frequently cited problem associated with life history work is the tendency towards 'a retreat to personal emotions and interpersonal processes . . . at the cost of addressing important moral, social and political purposes outside the personal domain' (A. Hargreaves, 1994, p. 74). This arises from, first, the individualized nature of the data and, secondly, the intimacy between researcher and informant that is often engendered by the methodology. However, a check can be kept on this if researchers follow Goodson's injunction to:

> locate the teacher's own life story alongside a broader contextual analysis, to tell in Stenhouse's words 'a story of action, within a theory of context'. The distinction between the life story and the life history is therefore absolutely basic. The life story is the 'story we tell about our life'; the life history is a collaborative venture, reviewing a wider range of evidence. The life story teller and another (or others) collaborate in developing this wider account by interviews and discussions and by scrutiny of texts and contexts. The life history is the life story located within its historical context.
>
> (Goodson, 1992, p. 6)

Of course, this 'location' by researchers – and, in a more general sense, the ways in which they tell the story of their research to various audiences – are not exempt from fundamental problems concerning analysis and interpretation. Working from explicitly subjective and personal accounts of lives, and events within them, further complicates the issue. The majority of life historians have confronted the difficulties and have sought strategies to make their work as rigorous and explicit as they can (e.g. Griffiths, 1995; Woods, 1986, 1996). These strategies include triangulation of various kinds, and reflexive accounts that enable readers to gain some insight into the potential biases of the researcher. (That reflexive accounts are

now commonplace and used by researchers taking a variety of methodological approaches is, perhaps, partly due to the influence of life historians.)
The postmodern and post-structuralist position is that the reality of the
text lies in the interaction between the reader and the writer (or the story-
teller and the audience). If this is accepted, then traditional notions of
'validity' can begin to seem less clear cut (see Stronach and MacLure, 1997
for a discussion of these issues), especially as understanding and interpretation can change at both individual and social levels. Plummer (1995)
makes this point forcefully when he states that 'sometimes people hear so
lightly what others say so intensely, and sometimes people hear so intensely
what others say so lightly' (p. 21). This is because our life histories affect
what we see as being salient. That this is indeed the case came home to me
in an obvious way when I became a mother and, as a result, became in
many respects a very different teacher.

Researching Parent Teachers

I have written elsewhere about the way in which my interest in the relationship between personal, parental experience and teachers' professional
practices developed following the birth of my first child and led me to
set up a life history project to see whether it was the same for others
(Packwood and Sikes, 1996; Sikes, 1997; Sikes, 1998). I had been surprised
by the changes I noticed in myself, although perhaps I should not have
been. Some years earlier, together with Lynda Measor and Peter Woods, I
had worked on a research project that used life history to study secondary
school teachers' experiences and perceptions of teaching as a career (Sikes,
Measor and Woods, 1985). This project involved 40 teachers of various
ages and career stages, and around three-quarters of them were parents. All
had mentioned the ways in which they believed they had changed, as
teachers, when they had children. I 'knew' about the phenomenon I was
experiencing, I had talked to teachers about it, I had written about it; but in
some ways it had not registered. The impact of parenthood had only been a
tiny part of the work we were doing and we had not explored it in any
detail. Speaking for myself, I now think that I was involved in what
Michelle Fine (1994) describes as 'othering', that is, seeing the teachers I
was working with as separate, distinct and different from me. Now that
I had become a mother and was aware of what this meant in my professional life, the process of 'othering' was interrupted and I could hear, with
clarity, what those teachers had been saying.

Ten years on, my new parenthood project involved 14 women and 6 men
who had all become parents since starting their teaching careers, and 5
female 'mature' student teachers who had joined the profession after
having children. Informants worked in all sectors of the education system
and occupied a variety of positions, from student to headteacher. They
ranged in age from 22 to 49 and with the exception of one woman on

sabbatical leave from Pakistan, everyone taught in England. All of the men and 17 of the women were white European. One woman was (self-defined) as black British and one was Pakistani. All of the teachers saw themselves as 'middle-class', although the majority said that they had working-class origins, being the first people in their families to go on to higher education. Twenty-three were married, and two were single parents.

Such biographical details are important when it comes to locating the individuals' stories in a broader context. So, as well as considering what people said in the immediate historical context in which we met, it was also possible to situate their experiences within dominant conceptualizations of teachers and teaching, and of motherhood and parenting generally, to which people of different ages and from different social and cultural back-grounds are exposed (see Sikes, 1997 for a discussion).

When I came to examine the data I found, as did Casey, that 'important common verbal patterns [emerged] within the narratives of [this] particular social group of teachers in particular social circumstances' (Casey, 1993, p. 26). It appears that parents who teach, regardless of their position or the type of institution in which they work, share a vocabulary and interests and understandings that are characteristic of, if not distinctive to, them.

Narratives were collected by informal, although focused and in-depth, interviews lasting for between 2 and 10 hours. Some people were seen on a number of occasions, others only once. Informants were simply asked to talk about being parents and teachers, and about the ways in which they felt the two roles interacted. Where appropriate, and when requested, I shared experiences, not least out of a concern to seek respondent validation and to develop a collaborative dialogue in which informants felt able to express their opinions and critique interpretations (cf. Sikes, Troyna and Goodson, 1996, pp. 39–42).

The study yielded a vast amount of detailed and engrossing data. In the context of this chapter, the intention is to present an insight into how informants experienced and perceived the interaction of certain aspects of their roles as parents and as teachers, and also to demonstrate the way in which a life history approach makes this interaction visible.

Parents' Experiences as Teachers

Teaching can be seen as a profession with a gendered and familial nature: with women as mother teachers nurturing and caring; and men as fathers, disciplining and wielding power (cf. Benn, 1989, p. xix). This has, perhaps, been particularly so within the primary sector where, over the past 250 years, a discourse based on a notion of the ideal teacher as the 'mother made conscious' has come to dominate ideology and practice (see, for example, Steedman, 1988; Tyler, 1993; Walkerdine, 1986). Linked as it is to notions of 'normal' and 'natural' femininity, the idea of the teacher as mother is powerful and pervasive, and can be seen to extend its influence beyond the boundaries of the primary school to serve as the organizing metaphor for women's work as teachers in all sectors of the education system. Recognizing the limitations it involves, many women teachers have sought other metaphors to describe their work (cf. Casey, 1990, p. 313).

That teaching, schools and schooling have come to be socially constructed and perceived in this way is ironic, given the way in which teachers' experiences of parenting and the skills and knowledge that can accrue from being a parent are officially, at best, unacknowledged and, at worst, denigrated (e.g. Grumet, 1988; Sikes, 1997). It is, perhaps, especially ironic given the way in which some teachers felt that their professional education and their experiences in school had affected their relationships with their own children. For example:

> The trouble was, having read Piaget and all the rest, and read child development books, you had this sort of feeling you had to do the right thing and I can remember getting to lunch time and thinking, 'God! I haven't said anything to that child for three hours.' You know? 'Coz she'd be happy playing and I'd be doing something else and we hadn't spoken. And I remember thinking it's a wonder this child's oral development isn't arrested. So I think, actually, a little bit of knowledge there was almost, I mean it created an anxiety that needn't have been there. If I hadn't read the books and not known what I should've been doing I'd have gone on doing what naturally felt right for both of us and I don't suppose it made any difference to her, but it certainly would have stopped me getting quite so anxious about, you know, my status as a mother and my inadequacy.
>
> (Rebecca, 46, one child, Further Education lecturer)

> When I was bringing my children up I remember one of the things that stuck in my mind from college, one of the things I encountered there was in the very first week. They were talking about the nature–nurture debate that was very prevalent at the time. And one tutor gave an example of a mother who'd had this child and she wanted the child to grow up and be very intelligent and so, what she did, she spent all her waking hours entertaining the child from it being a baby. And she'd do all her housework when the child slept and the child turned out to be brilliant. This was the story. She read to it, she'd play games, she'd sing to it, she'd just show it things and all this. So I remember thinking at the age of 18, right, when I have a child, I'll do that. And it stuck with me for some reason. And to a large extent I tried to do that with Emma and to a large extent, although I was knackered, I succeeded. I tried it to a lesser extent with Susie and succeeded to a lesser extent because I was even more knackered. So what it meant was the way I sort of interacted with her as a child, as a baby and as a toddler, was sort of, in a teacher role. I mean I'd take her for a walk in the pushchair. She

couldn't speak, she was that young, she couldn't talk, she was four, five months old, and a normal walk, and I saw other mothers taking their babies in pushchairs and they'd cover ten times as much ground as I would in the time available. So I'd walk say, about ten yards, it'd take me about five or ten minutes because I'd be saying, 'Here's a wall. Let's feel the wall', and I'd get her hand, 'Touch the wall. Is it rough? It's rough. This is rough. Look at the trees. Look how tall they are. Tall.' You know? Oh God! I mean it's bloody exhausting and bloody boring. But I did this. I sustained this as far as I was able. I don't know whether it worked or not . . . We'll never know. Who the hell knows? But that's what I was trying to do . . . I would not allow her to sit there, doing nothing, except for the odd minute. I'd be talking to her and the effort would be sheer, bloody boring. I hated it but I would do it. I'd throw a ball up in the air and say 'Up it goes. Down it comes.'

(Lesley, 39, two children, university lecturer)

The eldest is hard work . . . [I think it's due to] the effect of – school, the way that I had to react to the . . . pupils there, because I thought that was the way, was in a very aggressive way. And I didn't realize until it was drummed into me when I got home, that I was doing it when I got home, and I'd got absolutely nothing left for my own kids, well, own kid, then. And I used to shout at him as soon as I walked in the door. Well, he was probably doing something wrong, but the effect of as soon as he saw me, me picking on something that he'd done wrong, was not very good at all. So he ended up not liking me very much for quite a while. But you don't realize that. I was just treating him like a pupil . . . you can't be a teacher with your own . . .

(Christopher, 40, three children, secondary teacher)

Becoming a parent can involve a significant change to one's priorities and values, and to personal identity and sense of self. It can also make a difference to how other people see you, and consequently to the expectations they have of you. In a professional sense this can have positive and negative implications: positive in that it can make it easier to relate to and understand children and, equally significantly, their parents; and negative in that it can cause others to question your commitment to work. This last has been particularly the case for women, many of whose careers have suffered when they became mothers (though it is also true for some men):

I became a different sort of teacher after my children were born and it took me some time to accept that. You can never be the same again because of your relationship to your child, both in your own experience and in how other people see you.

(Janice, 49, three children, independent secondary teacher)

I felt people saw me in a different light, I think, when I had my first child. You have responsibilities which you are expected to fill, but I think there's also the thing, among other men anyway, that you've sort of proved your manhood, you're a 'proper' man.

(Dennis, 42, two children, secondary teacher)

I think the parents see you differently when they know you're pregnant. I felt that people were more friendly. Perhaps because it might be easier for some of them to identify with you. And I felt that they had more respect for me as a teacher too. Even before the baby was born it was as if I had to know more about kids because I was having my own.

(Sylvia, 49, two children, primary head)

I've noticed at parents' evenings, since Sean's been a teenager. I can say, 'Oh yes, we have that. I can say this to you and I know it's not easy. I can't do it myself.' It shows more understanding of their situation and I know that they have a better view than if they think you haven't got any experience of the situation yourself.

(James, 38, two children, secondary teacher)

Jo and Stuart, working in quite different environments, also felt that parenthood had had implications for how their careers developed:

My head of department, when he knew I was pregnant, he said, 'Well, that's your chances of promotion gone because you're bound to have another and then your production will go down.' Since he was the gatekeeper as it were, I took him seriously. Universities aren't equal opps employers at all in my view.

(Jo, 40, two children, university lecturer)

Things changed after the children were born. By then I'd been a deputy head for, what, about 12 years. I had been applying for headships for quite some time and I'd had interviews, but times had changed and I wasn't the sort of person governors were looking for. On one level we could have done with moving because where we lived meant that my wife had an awful amount of travelling to get to her work, but we talked about it and we decided that I'd stop applying. Obviously there were mixed reasons but the main one was that we both wanted me to be there for the kids. If you're a head you have to be out to meetings at night and that means you can't be at home. One of the deputies that used to work with me got a headship and I met him on a course one day and he told me he regretted it. He said his family were suffering. His son had told him that he was going to make an appointment to see him because he never did any more. He'd said, 'you see more of the kids you teach than you do of me', and this had devastated Sam. But he said 'what do you do?'. If you've got the job you have to do it and me being as I am I'd do it up to the hilt and I realized I just didn't want it. I wanted to be at home with the kids . . . It was interesting though, I did apply for a temporary, one-term headship at my school and I did hear that the governors thought that I wouldn't be the right person because it was generally known that I took time off work if necessary to look after the children and because of my views about evening activities.

(Stuart, 46, two children, secondary deputy)

How did the teachers feel that parenthood had changed them in the classroom? Increased patience and tolerance were mentioned by everyone as something that they had been forced to learn as parents and that had spilled over, in a positive sense, to their work:

I'm more patient. I'm more realistic in my expectations of what children can do and what you can ask them to do that they don't think they can do . . . I suppose it's realism sets in, that there are some things that are just unattainable but you can still ask them to have a crack at it as long as you promote it properly . . . I certainly think I'm better at knowing how to see that it isn't like a brick wall in front of them.

(Doreen, 41, two children, student)

I think it's made me a lot more tolerant of children and where they're at and how they feel.

(Sylvia, 49, two children, primary head)

I guess that somewhere along the line it's made me much more tolerant towards individuals because you become more aware of individual circumstances. I'm much more patient, much more tolerant. Whether you would develop anyway with just more experience, more dealings with kids, and as you teach more there's less confrontation, more chance for it, I don't know, but I do think that it's having Sean and Ruby and having to learn to adjust to their pace, in everything, that's just brought it home to me.

(James, 38, two children, secondary teacher)

I'm not a very patient person at all but I think I'm a bit more so since I had the kids. Yes, definitely. Because you have to be. It's no use getting yourself worked up and in a state, perhaps you learn to be more patient as a sort of survival strategy. I do still get impatient but I think I'm not quite so bad and other people tell me I'm not.

(Stuart, 46, two children, secondary deputy)

As was noted earlier, teachers could trace how their professional know-ledge and experience influenced how they related to and educated their own children. They were also able to bring their experience at home to bear on their professional, theoretical knowledge, which they then reflected back on their pupils:

> If you've seen a child develop you know the stages of development, you sort of know where you're at with young children . . . you can look at one and say, well, he should be able to do that. You've got a sort of line to follow, a measure, which sometimes I think you really haven't got because you've only read it in books.
>
> (Jane, 44, one child, nursery teacher)

> What's happened is that as my daughter's grown up and I've seen her go through the classic sort of stages of development, because she's pretty average, fairly bright, but a pretty average sort of young lady, I have been able to see child development as it is perceived for the average. And now, working with youngsters with learning difficulties, I can almost sort of plot their development. My daughter's provided me with the norm if you like, albeit a very rough norm . . . with a sort of personal learning experience that's matched the development of my own career in special needs.
>
> (Rebecca, 46, one child, Further Education lecturer)

It is obviously not necessary to be a parent to love and care for children, but what was interesting was the frequency with which parent teachers said that their loving and caring became more intense when they had their own child, because they saw him or her reflected in their pupils. Grumet (1988) puts it in the following words: 'our relations to other people's children are inextricably linked to our relation to our own progeny, actual and possible, and to the attribution of rights and influences that we attribute to that affiliation' (p. 28). Some of the comments of the informants echo this:

> I think I like children more than I did. I think I was more likely to sort of objectify them and think they were just little objects that could be moulded into what I wanted them to be. I think I probably get on with them better . . . I definitely feel more protective towards them, you can't help it.
>
> (Teresa, 22, one child, student)

> Having your own children must change the way you see children . . . You get an understanding of children but you don't really know where you get it from or how you get it . . . I think having a child of my own helped. And I'm sure I must be more understanding than when I first started to teach.
>
> (Ann, 38, two children, secondary teacher)

I think I have gradually come to see pupils differently . . . at the beginning really there's a tendency to assert some superiority over them, when you first start teaching, when you're young, I suppose, but I tend to feel rather sorry for them now . . . I suppose inevitably, whether I do it consciously or not, I see my own children in them really.

(Margery, 49, two children, secondary teacher)

Conclusion

Hargreaves notes that:

much of the research and writing that has addressed the emotions of teaching has started less from teachers themselves and what they have to say than from pre-constituted theoretical agendas and concepts that have been applied to teachers and teaching . . . There has been less focus on how teachers themselves talk about the emotional dimensions of their work . . . [although] as one scans accounts of teachers and their work, it is clear that teachers do talk extensively about their emotional responses to their work.

(A. Hargreaves, 1994, p. 141)

From what the teachers I spoke with said, it seems that parentally based emotion was an important influence upon their professional practice and philosophy. Of course, being a parent is not a prerequisite for being a 'good' teacher, nor for being able to establish warm and productive relationships with pupils. Nor do perceptions, knowledge, or practices deriving from parental experience always translate positively into the school or college. Carolyn Steedman, for example, writes of,

the mild and genteel methods by which working class children are led to see – out of what kind and painful necessity it is done! – that, really, they aren't very clever, really, can never be like their teacher's own child at home.

(Steedman, 1982, p. 7)

Although I would not have been surprised to hear it, this attitude was not expressed by any of the teachers I interviewed. There are a number of possible reasons for this, including the fact that so many of them had working-class origins themselves.

It is difficult to see how other methodological approaches would have picked up on the intimate, emotional and intricate relationship between parenthood and teaching as effectively as life history appears to have done. Woods (1985) suggests that life histories are 'a natural extension to ethnography, for they offer historical and subjective depth' (p. 13). They certainly do provide insights into the ways in which individuals either attempt to 'bestride the micro–macro interface' (Sikes, Measor and Woods, 1985, p. 14) and 'come to terms with imperatives in the social structure' (Goodson, 1980, p. 74), or 'opt instead for the insubordinate tactic of remaining, impossibly, on both, and neither sides' (Stronach and MacLure, 1997, p. 130).

Over the past 20 years, during which time life history has become accepted as a useful method for investigating aspects of educational life, and as a valuable strategy for teacher development, we have learnt a great deal about what it means to be a teacher and, pertinently, 'a good teacher'. Peter Woods has been a significant contributor to this learning, both from the research he himself has been involved in, and also from his championing of and support for ethnography and life history, which has inspired others to use these approaches.

Unfortunately, though, in Britain we start the new millennium with educational research under attack, and particularly research that uses qualitative approaches (Hillage, Pearson, Anderson and Tamkin, 1998; Tooley, 1998). What we have learnt from life history may lead us to view with concern the government-endorsed exhortation to produce research that:

> (1) demonstrates conclusively that if teachers change their practice from x to y there will be significant and enduring improvement in teaching and learning; and (2) has developed an effective method of convincing teachers of the benefits of, and means to, changing from x to y.
>
> (D. Hargreaves, 1996, p. 5)

Such a view assumes that teachers are a homogeneous group with shared aims, values, abilities and aptitudes. Not so; and life history demonstrates this unequivocally. The research discussed in this chapter reveals the substantial influence that just one, albeit major, change in the personal lives of teachers can have upon their professional work.

As Woods and his colleagues demonstrated in their 1997 book *Restructuring Schools, Reconstructing Teachers*, attempts to change schools and teachers need to take individuals into account if they are not to result in unmanageable stress. Life history offers opportunities to learn more about how to understand and how to get the best out of teachers, to the benefit of everyone, including teachers themselves. It is an opportunity that it would be a shame to neglect.

References

Ball, S. and Goodson, I. (1980) 'Subject disciplines as the opportunity for group action: a measured critique of subject sub-cultures', in Woods, P. (ed.) *Teacher Strategies: Explorations in the Sociology of the School*, London: Croom Helm.

Ball, S. and Goodson, I. (eds) (1985) *Teachers' Lives and Careers*, Lewes: Falmer Press.

Bell, J. (ed.) (1995) *Teachers Talk about Teaching: Coping with Change in Turbulent Times*, Buckingham: Open University Press.

Benn, C. (1989) 'Preface', in DeLyon, H. and Widdowson Migniuolo, F. (eds) *Women Teachers: Issues and Experiences*, Milton Keynes: Open University Press.

Bertaux, D. (ed.) (1981) *Biography and Society: The Life History Approach in the Social Sciences*, California: Sage.

Blumer, H. (1979) *Critiques of Research in the Social Sciences: An Appraisal of Thomas and Znaniecki's 'The Polish Peasant in Europe and America'*, New Jersey: Transaction.

Bullough, R., Knowles, G. and Crow, N. (1991) *Emerging as a Teacher*, London: Routledge.

Casey, K. (1990) 'Teacher as mother: curriculum theorising in the life histories of contemporary women teachers', *Cambridge Journal of Education*, **20**, 3, pp. 301–20.

Casey, K. (1993) *I Answer with My Life: Life Histories of Women Teachers Working for Social Change*, London: Routledge.

Clandinin, D. (1989) 'Developing rhythm in teaching: the narrative study of a beginning teacher's personal, practical knowledge of classrooms', *Curriculum Inquiry*, **19**, pp. 121–41.

Denzin, N. (1970) *The Research Act in Sociology: A Theoretical Introduction to Sociological Methods*, London: Butterworth.

Elbaz, F. (1983) *Teacher Thinking: A Study of Practical Knowledge*, London: Croom Helm.

Elliott, J. and Sarland, C. (1995) 'A study of "teachers as researchers" in the context of award-bearing courses and research degrees', *British Educational Research Journal*, **21**, 3, pp. 371–86.

Epstein, D. (ed.) (1994) *Challenging Lesbian and Gay Inequalities in Education*, Buckingham: Open University Press.

Epstein, D. and Johnson, R. (1998) *Schooling Sexualities*, Buckingham: Open University Press.

Evans, J. (ed.) (1988) *Teachers, Teaching and Control in Physical Education*, Lewes: Falmer Press.

Fine, M. (1994) '"Working the hyphen": reinventing the self and other in qualitative research', in Denzin, N. and Lincoln, Y. (eds) *Handbook of Qualitative Research*, California: Sage, pp. 70–82.

Goodson, I. (1980) 'Life histories and the study of schooling', *Interchange*, **11**, 4, pp. 62–77.

Goodson, I. (1983) *School Subjects and Curriculum Change*, London: Croom Helm.

Goodson, I. (ed.) (1992) *Studying Teachers' Lives*, London: Routledge.

Goodson, I. and Hargreaves, A. (eds) (1996) *Teachers' Professional Lives*, London: Falmer Press.

Griffiths, M. (1995) '(Auto)Biography and epistemology', *Educational Review*, **47**, 1, pp. 75–88.

Grumet, M. (1988) *Bitter Milk: Women and Teaching*, Amherst: University of Massachusetts Press.

Hargreaves, A. (1994) *Changing Teachers, Changing Times: Teachers' Work and Culture in the Post-modern Age*, London: Cassell.

Hargreaves, A. (1997) 'Series editor's introduction', in Sikes, P., *Parents who Teach: Stories from School and from Home*, London: Cassell.

Hargreaves, D. (1996) 'Teaching as a research-based profession: possibilities and prospects', TTA Annual Lecture, London: TTA.

Hatch, J.A. and Wisniewski, R. (eds) (1995) *Life History and Narrative*, London: Falmer Press.

Hillage, J., Pearson, R., Anderson, A. and Tamkin, P. (1998) *Excellence in Research on Schools*, London: Institute for Employment Studies.

Nias, J. (1989) *Primary Teachers Talking: A Study of Teaching as Work*, London: Routledge.

Oakley, A. (1979) *From Here to Maternity: Becoming a Mother*, Harmondsworth: Penguin.

Ostler, A. (1997) *The Education and Careers of Black Teachers*, Buckingham: Open University Press.

Packwood, A. and Sikes, P. (1996) 'Telling our stories: adopting a post-modern approach to research', *International Journal of Qualitative Studies in Education*, **9**, 3, pp. 1–11.

Plummer, K. (1983) *Documents of Life*, London: Allen & Unwin.

Plummer, K. (1995) *Telling Sexual Stories: Power, Change and Social Worlds*, London: Routledge.

Sikes, P. (1985) 'The life-cycle of the teacher', in Ball, S. and Goodson, I. (eds) *Teachers' Lives and Careers*, Lewes: Falmer Press.

Sikes, P. (1992) 'Imposed change and the experienced teacher', in Fullan, M. and Hargreaves, A. (eds) *Teacher Development and Educational Change*, London: Falmer Press, pp. 36–55.

Sikes, P. (1997) *Parents who Teach: Stories from School and from Home*, London: Cassell.

Sikes, P. (1998) 'Parent teachers: reconciling the roles', *Teacher Development: An International Journal of Teachers' Professional Development*, **2**, 1, pp. 87–104.

Sikes, P. and Everington, J. (1998) 'Daring to be an RE teacher?: a life history approach to becoming an RE teacher', Working paper, Coventry: Institute of Education, University of Warwick.

Sikes, P. and Troyna, B. (1991) 'True stories: a case study in the use of life history in initial teacher education', *Educational Review*, **43**, 1, pp. 3–16.

Sikes, P., Measor, L. and Woods, P. (1985) *Teacher Careers: Crises and Continuities*, Lewes: Falmer Press.

Sikes, P., Troyna, B. and Goodson, I. (1996) 'Talking lives: a conversation about life history', *Taboo*, **1**, Spring, pp. 35–54.

Smith, L. (1994) 'Biographical method', in Denzin, N. and Lincoln, Y. (eds) *Handbook of Qualitative Research*, California: Sage, pp. 286–305.

Sparkes, A. (1995) 'Physical education teachers and the search for self: two cases of structured denial', in Armstrong, N. (ed.) *New Directions in Physical Education*, Vol. 3, London: Cassell.

Steedman, C. (1982) *The Tidy House*, London: Virago.

Steedman, C. (1988) 'The mother made conscious: the historical development of a primary school pedagogy', in Woodhead, M. and McGrath, A. (eds) *Family, School and Society*, Milton Keynes: Open University Press.

Stronach, I. and MacLure, M. (1997) *Educational Research Undone*, Buckingham: Open University Press.

Thomas, D. (ed.) (1995) *Teachers' Stories*, Buckingham: Open University Press.

Thomas, W. and Znaniecki, F. (1927) *The Polish Peasant in Europe and America*, New York: Knopf.

Tooley, J. with Darby, D. (1998) *Educational Research: A Critique*, London: Ofsted.

Tyler, D. (1993) 'Setting the child free: teachers, mothers and child-centered pedagogy in the 1930s kindergarten', in Blackmore, J. and Kenway, J. (eds) *Gender Matters in Educational Administration and Policy: A Feminist Introduction*, London: Falmer Pres.

Walkerdine, V. (1986) 'Post-structuralist theory and everyday practices: the family and the school', in Wilkinson, S. (ed.) *Feminist Social Psychology: Development, Theory and Practice*, Milton Keynes: Open University Press.

Woods, P. (1981) 'Strategies, commitment and identity: making and breaking the teacher role', in Barton, L. and Walker, S. (eds) *Schools, Teachers and Teaching*, Lewes: Falmer Press.

Woods, P. (1985) 'Conversations with teachers: some aspects of life history method', *British Educational Research Journal*, **11**, 1, pp. 13–26.

Woods, P. (1986) *Inside Schools: Ethnography in Educational Research*, London: Routledge.

Woods, P. (1993) 'Managing marginality: teacher development through grounded life history', *British Educational Research Journal*, **19**, 5, pp. 447–65.

Woods, P. (1996) *Researching the Art of Teaching: Ethnography for Educational Use*, London: Routledge.

Woods, P. and Sikes, P. (1987) 'The use of teacher biographies in professional self-development', in Todd, F. (ed.) *Planning Continuing Professional Development*, London: Croom Helm.

Woods, P., Jeffrey, B., Troman, G. and Boyle, M. (1997) *Restructuring Schools, Reconstructing Teachers*, Buckingham: Open University Press.

7 Representing Teachers[1]

Ivor F. Goodson

Peter Woods' work on the life histories of teachers has always given considerable attention to their socio-political context, including the effects of education policy. This serves as an important antidote to some of the other approaches that have sought to sponsor teachers' stories in recent years. Indeed, these emerged at a particularly unpropitious time. They set up one of the paradoxes of postmodernism: that at precisely the time teachers are being 'brought back in', their work is being vigorously restructured. Teachers' voices and stories are being pursued as bona fide reflective research data at a time of quite dramatic restructuring. In fact, at precisely the time that the teacher's voice is being pursued and promoted, the teacher's work is being technicized and narrowed. As the movement grows to celebrate teachers' knowledge, it is becoming less and less promising as a focus for research and reflection. Teachers' work intensifies, as more and more centralized edicts and demands impinge on their world, and so the space for reflection and research is progressively squeezed. It is a strange time to leave traditional theory and pursue personal and practical knowledge.

There is the danger of a promising movement 'throwing the baby out with the bathwater'. At a time of rapid restructuring, the timing of these moves seems profoundly unfortunate. To promote stories and narratives, without analysis of structures and systems, shows how the best of intentions can unwittingly complement the moves to uncouple the teacher from the wider picture. Advocacy of stories and narratives can form an unintended coalition with those forces that would divorce the teacher from knowledge of political and micropolitical perspectives, from theory, and from broader cognitive maps of influence and power. It would be an unfortunate fate for a movement that at times embraces the goal of emancipating the teacher, to be implicated in the displacement of theoretical and critical analysis.

The Representational Crisis

Educational study is undergoing one of those recurrent swings of the pendulum for which the field is noted. But as the contemporary world and global economies are transformed by rapid and accelerating change, such pendulum swings in scholarly paradigms seem to be alarmingly exacerbated.

Hence we see a response to a specific structural dilemma in which educational study has become enmeshed; but alongside this, the field is becoming engulfed (though more slowly than many others) by a crisis of scholarly representation. A specific structural dilemma now becomes allied with a wider representational crisis. Jameson (1984) has summarized the latter crisis succinctly as arising from the growing challenge to 'an essentially realistic epistemology, which conceives of representation as the production, for subjectivity, of an objectivity that lies outside it' (p. viii). Jameson wrote this in the foreword to Lyotard's *The Postmodern Condition*. For Lyotard (1984) the old modes of representation no longer work. He calls for an incredulity towards these old canonical meta-narratives and says: 'The grand narrative has lost its credibility, regardless of what mode of unification is used, regardless of whether it is a speculative narrative or a narrative of emancipation' (p. 37).

Returning to the field of educational study, we see that, in response to the distant, divorced and disengaged nature of aspects of educational study in universities, some scholars have responded by embracing the 'practical' by celebrating the teacher as practitioner.

My intention here is to explore in detail one of these movements aiming to focus on teachers' knowledge – particularly the genre that focuses on teachers' stories and narratives. This movement has arisen from the crises of structural displacement and of representation previously outlined – hence the reasons for this new genre are understandable, the motivations creditable. The representational crisis arises from the central dilemma of trying to capture the lived experience of scholars and of teachers within a text. The experience of other lives is, therefore, rendered textual by an author. At root this is a perilously difficult act and Denzin (1993) has cogently inveighed against the very aspiration:

> If the text becomes the agency that records and re-presents the voices of the other, then the other becomes a person who is spoken for. They do not talk, the text talks for them. It is the agency that interprets their words, thoughts, intentions, and meanings. So a doubling of agency occurs, for behind the text as agent-for-the-other, is the author of the text doing the interpreting.
>
> (p. 17)

Denzin, then, is arguing that we have a classic case of academic colonization, or even cannibalization: 'The other becomes an extension of the author's voice. The authority of their "original" voice is now subsumed within the larger text and its double-agency' (p. 17).

Given the scale of this representational crisis one can quickly see how the sympathetic academic might wish to reduce interpretation, even collaboration, and return to the role of 'scribe'. At least in such passivity sits the aspiration to reduce colonization. In this moment of representational crisis the doors open to the educational scholar as facilitator – as conduit for the teacher to tell her or his story or narrative. There is a belief that we can facilitate the genuine voice of the oppressed subject, uncontaminated by the active human collaboration: teachers talking about their practice, providing us with personal and practical insights into their expertise. Here, maybe, is a sanctuary, an inner sanctum, beyond the representational crisis, beyond academic colonization. The nirvana of the narrative, the Valhalla of voice; it is an understandable and appealing project.

The Narrative Turn/The Turn to Narrative

The turn to teachers' narratives and stories is at one level a thoroughly understandable response to the way in which teachers have tended to be represented in so much educational study – where the teacher has been re-presented to serve our scholarly purposes.

Given this history, and the goal displacement of educational study noted, it is therefore laudable that new narrative movements are concentrating on teachers' presentation of themselves. This is a welcome antidote to so much misrepresentation and re-presentation in past scholarship, and it opens up avenues of fruitful investigation and debate. The narrative movement provides, then, a catalyst for pursuing understandings of the teacher's life and work. In many ways, the movement reminds me of the point raised by Andrews (1991) in her elegant study of elderly political activists. She summarizes the posture of those psychologists who have studied such activists:

> When political psychology has taken to analysing the behaviour of political activists it has tended to do so from a thoroughly external perspective. That is to say, that rarely have their thought processes been described, much less analysed, from their own point of view. Yet it is at least possible that a very good way to learn about the psychology of political activists is to listen to what they have to say about their own lives.
>
> (p. 20)

What Andrews says can be seen as analogous to a good deal of our scholarly representation of teachers, where they are seen as interchangeable and essentially depersonalized. In 1981 I argued that many accounts presented teachers as timeless and interchangeable role incumbents, but that:

The pursuit of personal and biographical data might rapidly challenge the assumption of interchangeability. Likewise, by tracing the teacher's life as it evolved over time – throughout the teacher's career and through several generations – the assumption of timelessness might also be remedied. *In understanding something so intensely personal as teaching it is critical we know about the person the teacher is.* Our paucity of knowledge in this area is a manifest indictment of the range of our sociological imagination.

(Goodson, 1981, p. 69)

The argument for listening to teachers is, therefore, a substantial and long overdue one – narratives, stories, journals, action research, phenomenology, have all contributed to a growing movement to provide opportunities for teacher representations.

Story and History

The new emphasis upon teacher stories and narratives, then, encouragingly signifies a new turn in presenting teachers. It is a turn that deserves to be taken very seriously, for we have to be sure that we are turning in the right direction. Like all new genres, stories and narratives are Janus-faced: they may move us forward into new insights or backwards into constrained consciousness, and sometimes simultaneously.

This uncertainty is well stated in Carter's summary of 'The place of story in the study of teaching and teacher education':

Anyone with even a passing familiarity with the literatures on story soon realizes, however, that these are quite turbulent intellectual waters and quickly abandons the expectation of safe passage toward the resolution, once and for all, of the many puzzles and dilemmas we face in advancing our knowledge of teaching. Much needs to be learned about the nature of story and its value to our common enterprise, and about the wide range of purposes, approaches, and claims made by those who have adopted story as a central analytical framework. What does story capture and what does it leave out? How does this notion fit within the emerging sense of the nature of teaching and what it means to educate teachers? These and many other critical questions need to be faced if story is to become more than a loose metaphor for everything from a paradigm or worldview to a technique for bringing home a point in a lecture on a Thursday afternoon.

(Carter, 1993, p.5)

But what is the nature of the turbulence in the intellectual waters surrounding stories, and will it serve to drown the new genre? The turbulence is multifaceted; but here I want to focus on the relationship between stories and the social context in which they are embedded. For stories exist in history – they are in fact deeply located in time and space. Stories work differently in different social contexts and historical times, and can be put to work in different ways. Stories then should not only be *narrated* but *located*. That is, we should move beyond the self-referential individual narration to a wider contextualized collaborative mode. Carter hints at both the enormous appeal, but also the underlying worry, about narrative and story. At the moment the appeal is substantial after long years of silencing, but the dangers are more shadowy. I believe that, unless those dangers are confronted now, narrative and story may end up silencing – or at least marginalizing in new ways – the very people to whom it appears to give voice:

> For many of us, these arguments about the personal, storied nature of teaching and about voice, gender, and power in our professional lives ring very true. We can readily point to instances in which we have felt excluded by researchers' language or powerless in the face of administrative decrees and evaluation instruments presumably bolstered by scientific evidence. And we have experienced the indignities of gender bias and presumptions. We feel these issues deeply, and opening them to public scrutiny, especially through the literature in our field, is a cause for celebration.
>
> At the same time, we must recognize that this line of argument creates a very serious crisis for our community. One can easily imagine that the analysis summarized here, if pushed ever so slightly forward, leads directly to a rejection of all generalizations about teaching as distortions of teachers' real stories and as complicity with the power elite, who would make teachers subservient. From this perspective, only the teacher owns her or his story and its meaning. As researchers and teacher educators, we can only serve by getting this message across to the larger society and, perhaps, by helping teachers to come to know their own stories. Seen in this light, much of the activity in which we engage as scholars in teaching becomes illegitimate if not actually harmful.
>
> (Carter, 1993, p. 8).

Carolyn Steedman (1986) in her marvellous work *Landscape for a Good Woman* speaks of this danger: 'Once a story is told, it ceases to story: it becomes a piece of history, an interpretative device' (p. 143). In this sense, a story 'works' when its rationale is comprehended and its historical significance grasped. As Bristow (1991) has argued, 'The more skilled we become at understanding the history involved in these very broadly defined stories, the more able will we be to identify the ideological function of narratives – how they designate a place for us within their structure of telling' (p. 117). In reviewing Steedman's (1986) work and its power to understand patriarchy and the dignity of womens' lives, Bristow (1991) talks about her unswerving attention to:

> the ways in which life writing can bring its writers to the point of understanding how their lives have already been narrated according to a prefigurative script, Steedman never loses sight of how writers may develop skills to rewrite the life script in which they find themselves.
>
> (p. 114)

This, I think, focuses acutely on the dangers of a belief that merely by allowing people to 'narrate', we in any serious way give them voice *and* agency. The narration of a prefigurative script is a celebration of an existing power relation. Most often, and this is profoundly true for teachers, the question is how to 'rewrite the life script'. Narration, then, can work in many ways; but we must remember that it can work to give voice to a celebration of scripts of domination. It can reinforce or rewrite domination. Stories and narratives are not an unquestioned good: it all depends. And, above all, it depends on how they relate to history, and to social context.

Molly Andrews' (1991) work on the lives of political activists captures the limitation of so much of the developmental psychologists' study of lives; and it is analogous to so much work on teacher narratives:

> In Western capitalist democracies, where most of the work on development originates, many researchers tend to ignore the importance of the society – individual dialectic, choosing to focus instead on more particularized elements, be they personality idiosyncrasies, parental relationships, or cognitive structures, as if such aspects of the individual's make-up could be neatly compartmentalized, existing in a contextual vacuum.
>
> (p. 13)

The version of 'personal' that has been constructed and worked for in some Western countries is a particular, and individualistic, version of being a person. It is unrecognizable to much of the rest of the world. But so many of the stories and narratives we have of teachers' work incorporate, unproblematically and without comment, this version of personal being and personal knowledge. Masking the limits of individualism, such accounts often present 'isolation, estrangement, and loneliness . . . as autonomy, independence and self-reliance' (Andrews, 1991, p. 13). Andrews concludes that if we ignore social context, we deprive ourselves and our collaborators of meaning and understanding. She says:

> It would seem apparent that the context in which human lives are lived is central to the core of meaning in those lives. Researchers should not,

therefore, feel at liberty to discuss or analyse how individuals perceive meaning in their lives and in the world around them, while ignoring the content and context of that meaning.

(p. 13)

This, I believe, has been all too common a response among educational researchers working with teachers' stories and narratives. Content has been embraced and celebrated, context has not been sufficiently developed. Cynthia Chambers (1991) has summarized this posture and its dangers in reviewing work on teacher narratives:

> These authors offer us the naive hope that if teachers learn 'to tell and understand their own story' they will be returned to their rightful place at the centre of curriculum planning and reform. And yet, their method leaves each teacher a 'blackbird singing in the dead of night'; isolated, and sadly ignorant of how his/her song is part of a much larger singing of the world. If everyone is singing their own song, who is listening? How can we hear the larger conversation of humankind in which our own history as teachers is embedded and perhaps concealed?
> (p. 354)

In summary, should stories and narratives be a way of giving voice to a particular way of being, or should the genre serve as an introduction to alternative ways of being? Consciousness is constructed rather than autonomously produced, hence giving voice to consciousness may give voice to the constructor at least as much as to the speaker. If social context is left out this will likely happen.

The truth is that many times a life story-teller will neglect the structural context of his or her life or interpret such contextual forces from a biased point of view. As Denzin (1989) says: 'Many times a person will act as if he or she made his or her own history when, in fact, he or she was forced to make the history he or she lived' (p. 47). He gives an example from his 1986 study of alcoholics: 'You know I made the last four months by myself. I haven't used or drank. I'm really proud of myself. I did it.' A friend, listening to this account commented:

> You know you were under a court order all last year. You didn't do this on your own. You were forced to, whether you want to accept this fact or not. You also went to A.A. and N.A. Listen Buster, you did what you did because you had help and because you were afraid and thought you had no other choice. Don't give me this, 'I did it on my own crap.'

The speaker replies, 'I know. I just don't like to admit it.' Denzin concludes:

This listener invokes two structural forces, the state and A.A., which accounted in part for this speaker's experience. To have secured only the speaker's account, without a knowledge of his biography and personal history, would have produced a biased interpretation of his situation.

(Denzin, 1989, pp. 74–5)

The great virtue of stories is that they particularize and make concrete our experiences. This, however, should be only their *starting point* in our social and educational study. Stories can so richly move us into the terrain of the social, into insights into the socially constructed nature of our experiences. Feminist sociology has often treated stories in this way. As Hilary Graham says: 'stories are pre-eminently ways of relating individuals and events to social contexts, ways of weaving personal experiences into their social fabric' (Armstrong, 1987, p. 14). Carolyn Steedman (1986) speaks of this two-step process. First the story particularizes, details and historicizes – then, at second stage, the 'urgent need' to develop theories of context arises:

The fixed townscapes of Northampton and Leeds that Hoggart and Seabrook have described show endless streets of houses, where mothers who don't go out to work order the domestic day, where men are masters, and children, when they grow older, express gratitude for the harsh discipline meted out to them. The first task is to particularize this profoundly a-historical landscape (and so this book details a mother who was a working woman and a single parent, and a father who wasn't a patriarch). And, once the landscape is detailed and historicized in this way, the urgent need becomes to find a way of theorizing the result of such difference and particularity, not in order to find a description that can be universally applied (the point is not say that all working-class childhoods are the same, nor that experience of them produces unique psychic structures) but so that the people in exile, the inhabitants of the long streets, may start to use the auto-biographical 'I', and tell the stories of their life.

(p. 16)

The story provides a starting point for developing further understandings of the social construction of subjectivity. If the teachers' stories stay at the level of the personal and practical, we forgo that opportunity. Speaking of the narrative method of focusing on personal and practical teachers' knowledge, Willinsky (1989) writes: 'I am concerned that a research process intended to recover the personal and experiential would pave over this construction site in its search for an over-arching unity in the individual's narrative' (p. 259).

Personal and practical, teachers' stories may, therefore, act not to further our understanding, but merely to celebrate the particular constructions of the 'teacher' that have been wrought by political and social contestation. Teachers' stories can be stories of particular political victories and political settlements. Because of their limitation of focus, teachers' stories – as stories of the personal and practical – are likely to be limited in this manner.

A Story of Action within a Story of Context

This sub-heading comes from a phrase often used by Lawrence Stenhouse, who was concerned in much of his work to introduce a historical dimension to our studies of schooling and curriculum (Stenhouse, 1975). Though himself a leading advocate of the teacher as researcher, and a pioneer of that method, he was worried about the proliferation of practical stories of action, individualized and isolated, unique and idiosyncratic, as our stories of action and our lives are. But, as we have seen, lives and stories link with broader social scripts – they are not just individual productions, they are also social constructions. We must make sure that individual and practical stories do not reduce, seduce and reproduce particular teacher mentalities, and lead us away from broader patterns of understanding.

Let us try to situate the narrative moment in this historical moment – for the narrative movement itself could be located in a theory of context. In some ways, the movement has analogies with the existential movement of the 1940s. Existentialists believed that only through our actions can we define ourselves. Our role, existentialists judged, was to invent ourselves as individuals; then, as in Sartre's trilogy *The Roads to Freedom*, we would be 'free', free especially from the claims of society and the 'others'.

Existentialism existed at a particular historical moment, following the massive trauma of the Second World War, and developed most strongly in France, where it followed the protracted German occupation. George Melly (1993) judges that existentialism grew out of this historial context:

> My retrospective explanation is that it provided a way of exorcising the collective guilt of the Occupation, to reduce the betrayals, the colla-boration, the blindeye, the unjustified compromise, to an acceptable level. We know now that the official post-war picture of France under Nazis was a deliberate whitewash and that almost everyone knew it, and suppressed the knowledge. Existentialism, by insisting on the complete isolation of the individual as free to act, but free to do nothing else, as culpable or heroic but *only* within those limits, helped absolve the notion of corporate and national ignominy.

(p. 9)

Above all, then, an individualizing existentialism freed people from the battle of ideologies, freed them from the awfulness of political and military conflict. Individualized existentialism provided a breathing space away from power and politics.

But the end of the Second World War did not provide an end to politics, only a move from hot war to cold war. As we know, ideologies continued their contest in the most potentially deadly manner. During this period narratives of personal life began to blossom. Brightman (see Sage, 1994) has developed a fascinating picture of how Mary McCarthy's personal narratives grew out of the witch-hunting period of Joe McCarthy. Her narratives moved us from the 'contagion of ideas' to the personal 'material world'. Mary McCarthy, Brightman says, could 'strip ideas of their abstract character and return them to the social world from whence they came' (quoted in Sage, 1994, p. 5). In Irving Howe's memorable phrase, as 'ideology crumbled, personality bloomed' (quoted in Sage, 1994, p. 5).

And so with the end of ideology, the end of the cold war, we see the proliferous blooming of personality, not least in the movement towards personal narratives and stories. Once again the personal narrative, the practical story, celebrates the end of the trauma of the cold war, and the need for a human space away from politics, away from power. It is a thoroughly understandable nirvana, but it assumes that power and politics have somehow ended. It assumes, in that wishful phrase, 'the end of history'.

In educational bureaucracies, power continues to be hierarchically administered. I have often asked administrators and educational bureau-crats why they support personal and practical forms of knowledge for teachers in the form of narratives and stories. Their comments often echo those of the 'true believers' in narrative method. But I always go on, after suitable pause and diversion, to ask 'what do you do on your leadership sources?' There it is always 'politics as usual' management skills, quality assurance, micropolitical strategies, personnel training. Personal and practical stories for some, cognitive maps of power for others. So, though the use of stories and narratives can provide a useful breathing space away from power, it does not suspend the continuing administration of power; indeed, it could well make this so much easier. Especially as, over time, teachers' knowledge would become more and more personal and practical – different 'mentalities', wholly different understandings of power would emerge between, say, teachers and school managers, teachers and administrators, teachers and some educational scholars.

Teachers' individual and practical stories certainly provide a breathing space. However, at one and the same time, they reduce the oxygen of broader understandings. The breathing space comes to look awfully like a vacuum, where history and social construction are somehow suspended.

In this way, teachers become divorced from what might be called the 'vernacular of power' – the ways of talking and knowing that then become the prerogative of managers, administrators and academics. In this dis-course, politics and micropolitics are the essence and currency of the interchange. Alongside this, and in a sense facilitating it, a new 'vernacular of the particular, the personal, and the practical' arises, which is specific to teachers.

This form of apartheid could easily emerge if teachers' stories and narratives remain singular and specifically personal and practical, particular and apolitical. Hence it is a matter of some urgency that we develop stories of action within theories of context – contextualizing stories if you like – that act against the kinds of divorce of the discourses, which are all too readily imaginable.

Kathy Carter (1993) had begun to worry about just such a problem in her work on the 'place of story' in the study of teaching:

> And for those of us telling stories in our work, we will not serve the community well if we sanctify story-telling work and build an episte-mology on it to the point that we simply substitute one paradigmatic domination for another *without challenging domination itself.* We must, then, become much more self conscious than we have been in the past about the issues involved in narrative and story, such as interpretation, authenticity, normative value, and what our purposes are for telling stories in the first place.

> (p. 11)

Some of these worries about stories can be explored in scrutinizing the way in which powerful interest groups in society actually promote and employ storied material.

Note

1 This chapter was previously published in *Teaching and Teacher Education* 13, 1, 1991, pp. 111–17.

References

Andrews, M. (1991) *Lifetimes of Commitment: Aging, Politics, Psychology*, Cambridge: Cambridge University Press.

Armstrong, P.F. (1987) *Qualitative Strategies in Social and Educational Research: The Life History Method in Theory and Practice.* Newland Papers No. 14, The University of Hull, School of Adult and Continuing Education.

Bristow, J. (1991) 'Life stories. Carolyn Steedman's history writing', *New Formations,* **13**, Spring, pp. 113–30.

Carter, K. (1993) 'The place of story in the study of teaching and teacher education', *Educational Researcher,* **22**, 1, pp. 5–12, 18.

Chambers, C. (1991) 'Review of teachers as curriculum planners: narratives of experience', *Journal of Education Policy,* **6**, 3, pp. 353–4.

Denzin, N.K. (1989) *Interpretive Biography,* Qualitative Research Methods Series 17, Newbury Park, London: Sage Publications.

Representing Teachers   133

Denzin, N.K. (1993) *On Hearing the Voices of Educational Research*, Review essay, mimeo, University of Illinois at Urbana-Champaign IL.

Goodson, I.F. (1981) 'Life history and the study of schooling', *Interchange*, **2**, 4, p. 69.

Jameson, F. (1984) 'Foreword', in Lyotard, J.F., *The Postmodern Condition: A Report on Knowledge*, Minneapolis: University of Minnesota Press, pp. vii–xxi.

Lyotard, J.F. (1984) *The Postmodern Condition*, Minneapolis: University of Minnesota Press.

Melly, G. (1993) 'Look back in angst', *Sunday Times,* 13 June, p. 9.

Sage, L. (1994) 'How to do the life: Review of C. Brightman's *Writing Dangerously: Mary McCarthy and Her World'*, *London Review of Books*, 10 February, p. 5.

Steedman, C. (1986) *Landscape for a Good Woman*, London: Heinemann.

Stenhouse, L. (1975) *An Introduction to Curriculum Research and Development*, London: Heinemann.

Willinsky, J. (1989) 'Getting personal and practical with personal practical knowledge', *Curriculum Inquiry*, **19**, 3, pp. 247–64.

8 Beyond Reflection: Contingency, Idiosyncrasy and Reflexivity in Initial Teacher Education

Alex Moore

> Fortunately, good teaching does not require us to internalize an endless list of instructional techniques. Much more fundamental is the recognition that human relationships are central to effective instruction.
>
> (Cummins, 1996, p. 73)

> Teaching, in many of its aspects as practised today, is expressive and emergent, intuitive and flexible, spontaneous and emotional.
>
> (Woods, 1996, p. 6)

Dominant Discourses

The last quarter of the twentieth century has seen a plethora of publications about how to teach and how to teach teaching. While many of these publications have concentrated on the organization and broad content of courses of teacher education (Alexander, Craft and Lynch, 1984; Department of Education and Science, 1981; National Union of Teachers, 1976), others have fallen into the category of the teaching *guide*: that is to say, compilations of the wisdom of experienced educators that offer tips and advice to inexperienced teachers on such matters as managing pupils' learning and behaviour, marking and assessing pupils' work, and long- and short-term lesson planning (Cohen and Manion, 1977; Marland, 1975; Stephens and Crawley, 1994). Such publications may be said to both prefigure and support a 'competence-based' model of initial and continuing teacher education: one that prioritizes the notion of the teacher as trained craftsperson (Council for the Accreditation of Teacher Education, 1992; Department for Education and Employment, 1997a and 1997b; Teacher Training Agency, 1998).

Other publications have moved beyond what might be called the skills-based approach to teaching to offer advice about underlying perceptions, procedures and approaches, in what is recognized as a highly complex set of activities. Such publications, eschewing the notion that teaching is reducible to discrete and finite lists of skills and practices, have focused on the importance of informed *reflection* on what one does in the classroom. The notion of 'reflective practice', though already current under different names in the early 1970s (see, for instance, Combs, 1972 and Wragg, 1974), came to the fore in the 1980s and early 1990s through the work of such writers as Schön (1983, 1987), Valli (1992) and Elliott (1993). This notion places as much emphasis on teachers' own *evaluations* of their practice as on the planning and management skills into which such evaluations feed. One of the central techniques recommended in the reflective practitioner discourse is the keeping of diaries or journals by teachers and student-teachers, in which they reflect systematically on their experiences as they perceive them, keeping a record that can be returned to and re-interrogated in the light of subsequent experiences and providing scope for the self-setting of targets and goals. The reflective practitioner discourse continues to show its popular appeal through bookshop shelves (Loughran, 1996; Loughran and Russell, 1997; Mitchell and Weber, 1996), even as it becomes increasingly marginalized by government-sponsored publications favouring the 'competent craftsperson' approach (DfEE, 1997a, 1997b; Office for Standards in Education and Teacher Training Agency, 1996).

It is the suggestion of this chapter that the two discourses of the competent teacher and the reflective practitioner remain the dominant ones in teacher education and, furthermore, that they are equally responsible for marginalizing alternative teacher-education discourses, including discourses that seek to prioritize the idiosyncratic, contingent aspects of teaching and learning (Maguire, 1995; Moore, 1996). I shall argue that both dominant discourses, though often in apparent opposition to one another, are similarly characterized by and rooted in psychological notions of the ideal, unified 'self' (Lacan, 1977, 1979; Walkerdine, 1982, 1990), and in a pseudo-scientific view of teaching and learning that is circumscribed by a notion of closure and of the naming of parts (Hamilton, 1993; Reid, 1993). Both discourses are essentially *symptomatic* in perspective, in that they seek out and identify what is 'wrong' in classroom interactions through explicit reference both to what has 'happened' and to some normalizing notion of what 'ought to have happened'. Both, as a consequence, lend themselves to the danger of pathologizing the individual teacher or pupil in relation to communicative breakdowns or learning difficulties, rather than seeking their causes in the wider, deeper structures and interrelations of society, or indeed in the very complex interrelations between teachers and their pupils. While few people would deny that the competent teacher and the reflective practitioner discourses may offer some help and support to teachers and student-teachers in improving classroom relations and practice, experience suggests that they are just as likely to cause concern, confusion and misguided behaviour through their over-personalization of teaching activity (Mitchell and Weber, 1996).

The 'alternative' discourses that I want to promote in this chapter suggest a revision, though not a wholesale rejection, both of lists of skills and of practice-based journals and diaries. Such alternatives involve re-visiting such discourses as pupil- and student-centred education, and imply the relevance of teachers' re-contextualizing teaching experience within the broader interpersonal experiences of lives lived 'outside' of or prior to the school classroom (Moore, 1997; Quicke, 1988; Schön, 1988; Thomas, 1995): that is to say, teachers perceiving themselves, as well as their class-rooms, as constructed and readable 'texts' (Moore and Atkinson, 1998). Unlike the dominant discourses of the competent teacher and the reflective practitioner, these alternative discourses recognize the fragmented, mate-rial, multifaceted nature of the self, and offer constructive strategies for *de*-pathologizing classroom dysfunction – often, in the process, offering more helpful escape routes for teachers locked into apparent impasses with their pupils.

The Competent Teacher

The recent domination of the competent teacher discourse in initial and continuing teacher development in the UK can be traced to 1992. The discourse was powerful before then, and had already received the full stamp of government approval in the USA (Henry, 1989). However, 1992 marks something of a turning point in the UK, in that the discourse at this point had legitimization bestowed upon it with the full force of the law. The key document in this process was a circular dispatched by the Council for the Accreditation of Teacher Education (CATE) in September of that year to all Higher Education Institutions (HEIs) in the UK providing initial teacher education courses. This circular laid out the basic requirements for all such courses clearly and unambiguously in the terms of the competences discourse:

> The main objective of all courses of initial training is to enable students to become competent teachers who can establish effective working relationships with pupils. To do so, they will need to be knowledgeable in their subjects, to understand how pupils learn, and to acquire teaching skills. . . . It is recognised that . . . the acquisition of competences is not the totality of training [and] each competence is not a discrete unit but one of many whose sum makes for a confident start in teaching.
>
> (CATE, 1992, p. 9)

Emphasis in this circular was placed on key areas of competence that were to become the key 'sub-discourses' of the next six years: 'subject knowledge', 'class management' and 'assessment and recording of pupils' progress'. Since the publication of *Circular 9/92*, the Council for the Accreditation of Teacher Education in the UK has been replaced by the Teacher Training Agency. This change, however, as the new title suggests, has represented not a break from the latter-day discourse of CATE, but rather a natural progression and development of it, in which the identification of 'discrete', universal skills increasingly marginalizes those complex interpersonal relationships and skills that often defy such itemizations in practice (DfEE, 1997a). Such a shift of emphasis, away from the notion of education traditionally favoured by universities and teachers (Alexander et al., 1984; Institute of Education, 1972; National Union of Teachers, 1976; Popkewitz, 1987) towards that of 'training' – always more popular in the official documentation (Allen, 1994; DES, 1981) – also, importantly, marks a shift of emphasis away from debates about the content and structure of pre-service courses, towards issues of assessment and 'quality' *within contents and structures that are 'given'.*

It is not the intention of this chapter to dismiss the competences discourse *in toto.* Much of what is contained within it does, indeed, make relatively uncontentious good sense. Of course teachers do need to have sufficient subject knowledge to teach their pupils effectively; of course they need to be effective planners and classroom managers; of course there was – and still is – some bad teaching in urgent need of having something done about it. The discourse also provides important opposition to another dominant discourse with more immediate popular appeal: that of the 'charismatic subject' (Moore and Atkinson, 1998). The charismatic subject discourse (not to be confused with the reflexive practitioner discourse to which I shall turn later) suggests that good teachers are 'born' rather than 'made', emphasizing mysterious, barely definable 'personal qualities' as the central contributors to success. Within this discourse – arguably responsible for a great deal of poor practice in the past – the effective teacher is often pictured as rejecting what is normally thought of as good practice, succeeding solely through the force of their own unconventional personality. Such a vision of teaching, which remains popular in cinematic representations of schools and classrooms, not uncommonly accompanies student teachers on to their qualifying courses (Moore and Atkinson, 1998; Wragg, 1974), often making life very difficult for them when, in the classroom situation, they discover that they cannot emulate, or be instantly respected in the manner of, the only truly effective teacher they can remember from their own school days.[1]

The power of the competences discourse to 'demystify' teaching processes (Woods, 1996, p. 19), providing for more confident and often more effective teachers, is not to be underestimated. For all its potential, however, the discourse remains problematic. To begin with, there is an obvious difficulty in the way in which it almost inevitably lends itself to misinterpretation. *Circular 9/92* very specifically stated that 'the acquisition of competences is not the totality of training. The criteria do not provide the entire syllabus of initial professional training', and that 'each competence is not a discrete unit but one of many whose sum makes for a confident start in teaching' (CATE, 1992, p. 9). However, the list-like nature of this document has given both teachers and teacher educators a very clear impression that they do, indeed, provide 'the entire syllabus', that the skills listed are indeed 'discrete', and that the lists are intended as finite representations of essential truths (Moore, 1996). This impression, which has been reinforced by subsequent documentation (for example DfEE, 1997a, 1997b), sustains a view – consistently rejected by many teachers and teacher educators – that the ingredients of 'good teaching' can be itemized and that, subject to their being appropriately acquired, anyone can make an effective teacher. The problem with this, of course, is that many student-teachers do appear – to themselves and to others – to acquire, in a satisfactory manner and to a satisfactory degree, the various competences but still have huge difficulties in the classroom and cannot begin to understand why this should be so (Moore, 1996). Similarly, the creators of lists of competences often seem unprepared to accept that language itself defies this kind of inventorizing, so that however many hours go into their construction, such lists will never, finally, be able to answer the question they set themselves: 'What makes an effective teacher?'

A further problem with the competences discourse relates to the very notion of 'competence' itself. Basil Bernstein has addressed this issue through tracing the history of the concept in a variety of fields in the social sciences, including linguistics, sociology and anthropology (Bernstein, 1996, pp. 55–6). Seeking out common ground is the essential difference between various kinds of competence (for example Chomsky's 'linguistic competence' or Saussure's *'langue'*) and various kinds of performance (Chomsky's 'linguistic performance', say, or Saussure's *'parole'*), Bernstein describes competence as 'intrinsically creative and tacitly acquired in informal interactions' (*ibid.*, p. 55). Historically, competence is defined in terms of 'practical accomplishments', constituted by procedures that are essentially 'social'. The universality of competence renders it 'culture free'. Part of its social logic is that 'the subject is active and creative in the construction of a valid world of meanings and practice' and that the development or 'expansion' of this subject is 'not advanced by formal instruction' or 'subject to public regulation' (*ibid.*, p. 56). Competence theories thus have 'an emancipatory flavour', being founded on 'a critical, sceptical view of hierarchical relations'.

This notion of competence – as socially, actively, creatively and yet unconsciously acquired skills, understandings and practices – is critically different from the notion of competences (often conflated with 'competencies') embedded in the competences discourse of CATE and the TTA. Indeed, the term may be said to have been appropriated (Jones and Moore, 1995) to describe something much more closely akin to competence's traditional 'other half': that is to say, 'performance'. The competences (or competencies) discourse as it exists in the areas of teacher education, and – increasingly – in education generally, certainly maintains a somewhat limited notion of the universality and 'culture-freeness' of the old competence discourse, inasmuch as what constitutes effective teaching in one time or place is deemed to constitute it in any other. However, it introduces two important new elements that change its character critically, rendering it anything but 'creative'. These elements are (a) the necessity for competences to be actively, *consciously* taught and learned; and (b) the presentation of *selected lists* of competences whose focus is on the acquisition of 'skills' rather than on understandings or strategies. We might say that through the conflation of competence with performance *combined with* the notion of limited universality, the discourse includes an effective denial of the contingent and idiosyncratic elements that others (Cummins, 1996; Maguire, 1995; Woods, 1996) have placed at the heart of good teaching.

The discourse does more than that, however, as Bernstein has gone on to argue, in that it entails precisely the shift away from 'education' towards 'training' that is implied in the official language of the discourse (in, for example, the shift of terminology from 'the Council for the Accreditation of Teacher *Education*' *to* 'the Teacher *Training* Agency'). Furthermore, this is a highly problematic notion of training, inevitably implying a corresponding notion of 'trainability'. With reference to school pupils – although the same argument holds good for student-teachers – Bernstein argues that:

> The concept of trainability places the emphasis upon 'something' the actor must possess in order for that actor to be appropriately formed and re-formed according to technological, organizational and market contingencies.
>
> (Bernstein, 1996, p. 73)

This reifying quality of trainability and competences leaves 'an emptiness in the concept [of trainability] . . . which makes [it] self-referential and thus excluding'. The nature of that emptiness is that the concept ignores the social world from which it was constructed and in which it resides. In particular, it ignores the concept of identity formation, the context of the 'social *order*', and the particular ways in which identities arise 'through relations which the identity enters into with other identities of reciprocal recognition, support, mutual legitimization and finally through a negotiated collective purpose' (*ibid.*, p. 73). The full significance of the appropriation of the competence concept within the competences discourse immediately becomes clear. On the one hand, the discourse devalues the importance of those interpersonal relationships, perceptual matches and mismatches, notions of self and desire, which are so central a part of effective classroom interaction and which are also at the root of many pupils', teachers' and student-teachers' classroom difficulties. In doing this, it simultaneously encourages individuals to seek reasons for success and failure, and answers to questions and difficulties, within their own 'competence', while discouraging them from seeking such reasons and answers in a 'real world' whose authenticity they come to doubt. On the other hand, the discourse deflects broader debates about ineffectiveness in education away from the 'social context' and therefore, by implication, onto the individual protagonist. The power and importance of this aspect of the discourse from the point of view of the central governments that promote it is plain to see: it is far easier, not to mention more economical, to treat perceived social difficulties symptomatically – for example, to concentrate blame on schools and teachers for educational failures – than it is to take a causal approach that might imply a drastic readjustment in the social distribution of power and wealth. This personalization of the difficulty – implicit in the competences discourse but disguised by its 'abstracted', universalized appearance – has the added impact of effectively disguising broader social problems (Moore, 1996) – what Bernstein refers to as a pointing 'away from the macro blot on the micro context' (*ibid.*, p. 56).

The Reflective Practitioner

Working in parallel with the competences discourse – sometimes in apparent opposition, sometimes in a more complementary way – has been the discourse of the reflective practitioner. This discourse, unlike the competences discourse, emphasizes not discrete skills and areas of knowledge but, rather, the particular skills needed to reflect constructively upon ongoing experience as a way of improving the quality and effectiveness of one's work. Such reflection involves, of course, drawing on the range of strategies and techniques one has at one's disposal, or developing new ones; but it does so selectively, flexibly and strategically – taking full account of the particular circumstances relating to any given problem at any given time. In particular, the discourse encourages teachers and student teachers to take into account the whole picture – analysing the effectiveness of a lesson or series of lessons not simply by measurable outputs such as test scores, but through an attempt to evaluate what was learned, by whom, and how more effective learning might take place in the future. As such, it involves careful evaluation by teachers of their own classroom performance, planning, assessment and so on, in addition to and in conjunction with evaluations of pupils' behaviour and achievement. It also implies a sound understanding on the teacher's part of relevant educational theory and research – including theories of cognitive, linguistic and affective development – in order to address issues not restricted to the 'what' and the 'when' of education but embracing, also, questions of 'how' and even 'why'.

The reflective practitioner discourse is not well favoured within current official discourses of teacher education: the competence category of 'evaluation of one's own teaching', for example, is not included in the Teacher Training Agency's documentation, being relegated in terms of position to the end of another broad area – 'Teaching and Class Management' – and in terms of wordage to '[students must demonstrate that they can] evaluate their own teaching critically and use this to improve effectiveness' (DfEE, 1997a, p. 10; TTA, 1998, p. 8). Such a marginalization only reinforces the notion that the competences discourse is anti-intellectual and anti-theoretical, and that it promotes a view of teachers as, essentially, 'clerks and technicians' (Giroux and McLaren, 1992, p. xiii) rather than thinkers and creators. The reflective practitioner discourse has, however, received much popular support in higher education institutions in Britain offering courses in initial and continuing teacher education, and continues to produce some of the most interesting and insightful practice.

If the competences discourse emphasizes the teacher as technician and 'deliverer', whose 'internalized' skills can be easily monitored through measurable outcomes, the reflective practitioner discourse has always taken a subtler approach to teaching, recognizing the centrality of much-harder-to-identify, codify and quantify skills (concerning communication, presentation, analysis, evaluation and interaction), often promoting, for example, counselling skills on the part of teacher educators and emphasizing the *strategic* aspects of teaching above the acquisition of less flexible methodological approaches (Handal and Lauvas, 1987). Such a difference clearly has implications not only for the way in which teacher education is conducted, but also for research in this domain. The competences discourse, for example, because of its 'self referential' nature (*ibid.*), suggests an evaluative response, sited within a world of skills and capabilities that, as it were, already exists outside of the individual (prompting such questions as 'Which system of competences works best?', 'Which HEIs implement the discourse most effectively?' and so on). The reflective practitioner discourse, on the other hand, suggests a qualitative, research-based response along the lines, say, of ethnography or action research. Such approaches will focus not on measuring success by outcome ('How many students successfully completed this or that course?', 'What gradings were courses given by Ofsted inspectorates?' and so on) but on exploring the *nature* of the teaching and learning processes that are taking place, through an emphasis on 'the processes of meaning-assignation and situation-defining' and on 'how the social world is constructed by people, how they are continually striving to make sense of the world' (Woods, 1979, p. 2).

Competence, Reflection and the Pathologization of the Individual

'Is teaching a science or an art?' asks Woods (1996, p. 14), subsequently concluding: 'it is both a science and an art – and more besides' (*ibid.*, p. 31).

The differing research implications of the two dominant discourses in teacher education represent, of course, no less than a summary of the two contradictory views of human behaviour that underpin those discourses. To use the terms of Peter Woods's question, the competences discourse may be said to represent a quasi-scientific perception of teaching and learning, firmly sited within a paradigm of educational thinking sometimes critiqued under the term 'modernism' (Moore, 1998a). Such a paradigm assumes 'the possibility of completeness' (Standish, 1995, p. 133) through viewing the world as 'an ordered place' and the 'elements of the world of knowledge as topologically invariant' (Hamilton, 1993 p. 55). What is knowable – or what 'needs to be known' – is ultimately definable and susceptible to inventorization and tidy assessment: it is underpinned by a tacit assumption that there is, under passing acknowledgment of the possibility of local variations, only one right way or set of ways of doing things. The discourse of reflection, on the other hand, recognizes what Goodson and Walker have called 'the messy complexity of the classroom' and its only 'partially apprehendable practice' (Goodson and Walker, 1991, p. xii). It is a discourse that gives full recognition to 'the central role that people play in the educational process and educational systems' (*ibid.*, p. 1), that legitimizes a range of approaches and behaviours, and that understands that 'much of the most expert practice in schools is based on intuitive judgment' (McIntyre, Hagger and Burn, 1994, p. 57). Such a discourse is often associated, in the philosophy of education, with the use of the term 'post-modernism' as denoting a 'commitment to notions of process, experience and pleasure' (Green, 1995, p. 402; see also Hargreaves, 1993; Hebdidge, 1986; Levin, 1987; Standish, 1995). As such, it views teaching more as art than as science, lending itself to corresponding modes of research. (The charismatic subject discourse, of course, also views teaching as an art, but as a mysterious art, akin to magic.)

Though clearly separated from one another, the two dominant discourses are not 'oppositional': certainly, they are not mutually exclusive, and most student-teachers these days will find themselves being encouraged and helped to be both 'competent' and 'reflective'. Indeed, in some of its cruder manifestations – in which 'checklists, rankings, peer evaluations, etc.' are prioritized while 'student teachers are seldom given an opportunity to have a concrete understanding of their personalities [and therefore] find it difficult to understand why they react to people, situations, or circumstances as they do' (Johnson, 1989, p. 340) – the reflective practitioner discourse overlaps the competences discourse to such an extent that the two may often appear, to the student, to merge into one. Such convergences suggest that, philosophically, the two discourses may be closer to one another than at first appears. In particular, we might suggest that each of these discourses has its roots in an Enlightenment view of social development, founded on the primacy of private and collective 'reason', and of the notion of the unitary, ideal 'self'. Thus, although the competences discourse may be seen as focusing on universals and the reflective practitioner discourse on the contingent and idiosyncratic, both seem to overemphasize a particular form of agency (that which focuses on 'self-improvement' rather than that which looks 'outward' towards reforming society) through implying the existence of 'detached', 'independent', unified identities. Just as success rests on the student's responsibility, with the aid of tutors, to become 'competent' in the competences discourse, so it is incumbent on individual students to use their own reflective, rational powers in the reflective practitioner discourse. In this way, within either discourse it becomes an easy task to pathologize the individual pupil, teacher or student-teacher for any breakdowns that occur in social interaction (Walkerdine, 1982, 1990). Such pathologizing does two things. First, as has already been suggested, it shifts debate away from issues related to broader socio-economic and cultural relations. Second, through its appeal to ideal, universal 'reason', it promotes the discourse (already very familiar to teachers and pupils) of individual blame. The first diffi-culty, of course, can be addressed initially by ensuring locally that such issues are given adequate coverage as curriculum inputs on courses. The second is rather more difficult to address, since it involves a radical depar-ture for students not only in how they perceive their classrooms but in how they perceive and understand 'themselves'.

Beyond Reflection: Contingency, Idiosyncrasy and Reflexivity

'In the postmodern world', argues Hargreaves, 'multiple rather than singular forms of intelligence are coming to be recognized . . . multiple rather than singular forms of representation of students' work are being advocated and accepted . . . Many ways of knowing, thinking and being moral, not just rational, "logical" ones, are coming to be seen as legitimate' (Hargreaves, 1993, p. 22). Elsewhere, Anthony Giddens has talked of the 'reflexive project of the self, which consists in the sustaining of coherent, yet continuously revised, biographical narratives' (Giddens, 1991, p. 5), while Cole and Knowles (1995, p. 131) have described teaching practice in terms of its 'multiple roles and contexts'.

The notion of multiple identities, the need for flexible responses to meet the demands of changing situations, an emphasis on accommodation (rather than assimilation) and on navigation (rather than control), are concepts that have variously been included under the banners of post-modernism and high modernism.[2] Unlike the notion of self implied in the competences discourse and, to a lesser extent, the reflective practitioner discourse, these notions of self prioritize individual and collective flexibility and collaboration, along with informed understandings of the multiple contexts within which one operates. In doing this, they introduce – in place of the notion of the unified, ideal, 'Cartesian' self – the material, con-structed self: that is, the self as 'text' that is formed (partly *by itself*) at the intersections of various discursive practices and that can be 'read' both by others and 'by the self itself'.

These alternative notions of the self, and of the manner in which it is constructed, have given rise to new modes of practice in initial teacher education as well as to new forms of theoretical enquiry, in which teachers and student-teachers are encouraged to interrogate and critically reflect not only on their pupils' behaviour or upon what happened (in terms of failure and success) in the classroom, but also on their own behaviours – on the ways in which they responded to situations, interacted with other people, experienced emotional responses and so forth. Such practice can be described in terms of a further discourse: that of the *reflexive* practitioner. This discourse, which re-emphasizes the significance of intra- as well as interpersonal relationships in classroom practice, starts from the premise that teachers are, indeed, 'made', though not just in the sense inscribed within the competences discourse. When they come to teaching, for example, teachers already bring with them a history and a culture through which they have negotiated and – however impermanently – 'fixed' meanings, orientations and understandings about such things as how learning works, what schools and education are for and how teachers should conduct themselves, which are immediately subject to revisitations once the practice of teaching begins. (Bourdieu's work on 'habitus' and 'field' provides a useful framework for the exploration of this process: see, for instance, Bourdieu, 1990 and Moore, 1997). Teachers also bring, whether they want to or not, emotional, historical 'baggage' which, in the highly charged atmosphere of the school classroom, can intrude on their practice both positively and negatively (when, for example, the classroom becomes the social space for the playing out or repetition of family-related repressions, irresolutions and role anxieties).

The reflexive discourse encourages teachers, appropriately supported by their tutors (Combs, 1972; Wragg, 1974), not only to reflect critically on ongoing experiences *in themselves*, but to contextualize these experiences within previous experiences as a way of developing more effective teaching strategies (Cole and Knowles, 1995; Quicke, 1988; Schön, 1988; Thomas, 1995). Part of that activity, aimed at helping practitioners to understand more clearly 'the way in which a personal life can be penetrated by the social and the practical' (Thomas, 1995, p. 5) and to make sense of 'prior and current life experiences in the context of the personal as it influences the professional' (Cole and Knowles, 1995, p. 130), involves encouraging individual teachers to critique difficulties they may be experiencing in the here and now within the context of previous roles and experiences they have encountered 'outside' the classroom situation in, for example, their family life or their own schooling. Inevitably, this also introduces issues of *desire* (Hargreaves, 1994; McLaren, 1996) into understandings of practice: 'What do I want from these interactions?' 'What do others want of me?' 'What am I afraid of?' 'What do I want to *do* about the things I don't like here?' With reference to Peter Woods's question we might say that this kind of teaching and research about teaching moves us away from the art/ science dichotomy into his area of the 'more besides' (Woods, 1996, p. 31).

There are, of course, obvious dangers in an approach that invites teachers to interrogate their own behaviours textually. Chief among these are (a) that practitioners and their tutors may engage in ill-informed 'amateur psycho-analysis' that ends up benefiting nobody or even worsening an already difficult situation; (b) that the discourse may slip into the very pathologizations implied by the other discourses we have considered, and provide another way of obscuring the 'macro blot' (Bernstein, 1996, p. 56). Such potential dangers call for care and common sense, however, rather than a dismissal of the discourse. We must never forget that the other discourses are also replete with dangers, not least in their refusal (not always the case with the reflective practitioner discourse) fully to acknowledge, in their obeisance to rationality, either the emotive, autobiographical aspects of classroom interactions or the socio-historical contexts within which classroom practice occurs – omissions which often cut off central avenues of explanation for perplexed teachers when things go wrong. Experience, furthermore, suggests that the incorporation of this third discourse (the 'reflexive' discourse) *along with* those of the competent teacher and the reflective practitioner can, if properly handled,[3] have very beneficial effects – not least for student-teachers experiencing classroom difficulties and for those who, in terms of seeking and responding to advice, seem to have reached an impasse of the kind 'I have tried everything, and everything has failed'. As has already been indicated, this is not a question of *replacing* the competences and reflective practitioner discourses with the reflexive discourse, but rather of adding it *to* those discourses in a way that makes it easier and more profitable for students to 'enter', to understand and to negotiate those discourses; that is to say, it serves as a contextualization function that helps replace morbid, unconstructive 'self' criticism ('Something *in me* is wrong') with constructive, reasoned, 'action' criticism ('Something *that's being done* is wrong').

By way of illustration of how effective such an addition can be in terms of both practice and research, the following brief extracts are drawn from a series of reflexive essays written by students on a one-year course of initial teacher education. (For fuller accounts, see Moore, 1997; Moore, 1998b; Moore and Atkinson, 1998.) These extracts are indicative of the altered 'positioning' of the teacher in the reflexive discourse: that is to say, the way in which teachers simultaneously consider past, present and future actions while looking 'inward' to their own histories and perceived character traits and 'outward' to the behaviours of their pupils and to the social conditions within which they and their pupils operate.

Student A

I was getting angry, and was told that this was exacerbating my problems [with this particular class]. I'd tried to sort this out in my lesson evaluations. I felt I was getting angry because the kids were misbehaving and just refusing to do what I was asking of them. I'd tried being patient, but that hadn't got me anywhere either. With two particular kids, I was rapidly developing a 'relationship' that I would describe as dysfunctional. Not only would they refuse to do anything I told them, but they also continually interfered with other children in the class – but the worst thing was that they started ignoring my presence. In the end, I had them removed from the class, but that just seemed to cause resentment among the rest of the class. I must say that the only thing that really helped, in the end, was when I took the advice to focus on my own anger and ask 'Why am I getting so cross here?' After all, this was only two children not working – and I knew my anger was not out of frustration at them not getting on, or anything like that. It was personal. Thinking about other situations that made me angry like this or had done in the past, and just going through with someone some of the feelings of power and powerlessness I had experienced myself as a child in a working-class home meant that when I went home in the evening I was able to think more clearly, get things in perspective and focus on strategies. It also helped me to stop hating these two and to remember that they were probably behaving the way they did because of the lives they had. I won't say my anger has gone away entirely, but I'm definitely getting better at controlling it and I do have the kids back in the class now and generally enjoy a much better relationship with the class as a whole. In a strange way, it's also helped me to appreciate the politics of the situation. I feel much more clued up now about the way society itself can operate against the interests of some kids, and against teachers who try to do something about it.

Student B

The trouble was, I was taking everything personally, and just taking it home with me. I know we were always told not to do that, but it's easier said than done. Instead of, after a lousy lesson or a rotten day, going away and carefully, rationally thinking what I would do next time to make things work better, I was just wallowing in feelings of inadequacy and dreading the next day – so much so that I went in expecting more trouble, and obviously the kids sensed it and obliged me. The reflexive writing we were asked to do did help, though I was very dubious about it at the start and I don't know how useful it would have been if I'd been forced to show it to anyone rather than volunteering it like this. Just talking through things 'with myself' did help me to appreciate that the kids' behaviour, although I experienced it as being directed against me, was really about something much bigger, and instead of acting confrontationally I had to be sympathetic in my heart and firm and sensible in my manner. Part of what I realised was that I'd had this feeling of kind of being watched all the time – as if there was some expectation of classroom performance that I was constantly not living up to. Another bit, related to that, was that I actually wanted the kids to be 'more personal' to me, if that makes any sense. I think I needed to be liked and respected, and, strange as it seems now, I'd never actually understood that myself – how my need was contributing to the overall problem.

The above examples illustrate the potential helpfulness of the reflexive discourse to student-teachers experiencing classroom impasses when the discourse is appropriately introduced: that is to say, when it is introduced in a way that helps students shift their explanations for and related tactics for dealing with classroom difficulties away from the pathologization of either themselves or their pupils, towards a better understanding of their own and their pupils' behaviours and of the interrelations between these behaviours and the wider social conditions – including social inequalities – in which those behaviours are sited (see also McLaren, 1996, pp. 73–4). When student-teachers are encouraged and allowed to develop reflexivity in this particular way, not only are the dangers of pathologization avoided, but the students are enabled to take a more positive view both of themselves and of the possibilities that are available to them. Indeed, the prioritization of this kind of agency – directed politically outward rather than clinically inward – puts them in a far better position not just to deal sensibly with classroom difficulties but to engage, as 'transformative intellectuals' (Giroux 1988), in wider projects aimed both at 'changing the conditions of their own work . . . and struggling towards a larger vision and realization of human freedom' (Giroux and McLaren, 1992, p. xiii). We should not be surprised if such a struggle, in which teacher education is implicated as a 'progressive force' aimed at 'reaffirming a commitment to justice, equality, and non-exploitive social relations' (Beyer and Zeichner, 1987, p. 298), includes a radical critique of the competences discourse itself as, in essence and in isolation, a tool for social control and cultural reproduction.

Classroom Behaviours: Latent and Manifest Meanings

In addition to indicating the potential helpfulness of the reflexivity discourse to the teacher as practitioner, the examples I have quoted also suggest a *theoretical* paradigm within which to locate research in the field of teaching studies, which is implied in Woods' question 'Is teaching an art or a science?' What Woods' question does, in effect, is to point the way forward very clearly and precisely to where qualitative research in education, no less than education itself, needs to be moving as we enter the twenty-first century: that is to say, towards a post-Enlightenment kind of theorizing, supporting and describing a post-Enlightenment kind of practice, in which questions, perspectives and approaches tied to rationality and reason are no longer allowed to dominate at the expense of questions, perspectives and approaches that prioritize human sensibilities in both the intra-personal and inter-personal contexts. Such a paradigm suggests the adoption of, among other things, a revised notion of the workings of hegemony and of the interrelationships between 'dominant' and 'dominated' cultures in the classroom situation. Rejecting a mechanistic view of the operations of hegemony, for example, this theorizing would focus rather on its dialectical characteristics, exploring ways in which people (pupils, teachers and student-teachers) from marginalized cultures do not simply internalize or reject dominant ideologies, but draw on other voices within their own memories and cultural histories to make sense of what they are shown and told and what they experience (Gramsci, 1985; Martin-Barbero, 1993). With reference to related research practice, this might include explorations of the ways in which the teacher and pupils within a given class may, in different ways, respond to similar hegemonic forces, and the often unnecessary conflicts to which these alternative negotiations can give rise.

Treading just this path between ideological determinism and the emancipatory powers of individual and collective agency, Valerie Walkerdine (1990, pp. 173–204) has adapted concepts from Freud's dream theory to argue for a development of *ethnographic* research that enables researchers, through processes of inter-textualization, to look beyond the 'manifest content' of what they observe and hear, to its 'latent content'; that is to say, both the underlying attitudes, fears and aspirations of the observed actors *and* the power relations in the larger society, for which heard and observed practices and dialogues often act *substitutively*.

Although Walkerdine's work is in the area of audience ethnography, there is clearly much potential value in her work for qualitative research in general and for qualitative educational research in particular. To refer back to the two pieces of student writing quoted above, for example, we might say that the competences and reflective practitioner discourses, in their different ways, revealed to the student-teachers the *manifest* meanings of classroom interaction. The reflexive discourse, which introduced aspects of idiosyncrasy and contingency, suggested *latent* meanings which then enabled a more effective reading of – and, ultimately, response to – the manifest meanings, in both cases facilitating the more effective use of available strategies as a way of helping the students through their impasses. In each case the competences and reflective practitioner discourses were useful – but it was the reflexive discourse that fully 'activated' that usefulness, that made it accessible to the student and that opened the way to a more critical engagement with the interface between personally experienced difficulties and systemic failings.

The notion of an educational theory that recognizes and homes in on the complexity of classroom interrelations, seeking to overcome traditional dichotomies between subjectivity and objectivity, agency and determinism, uniqueness and conformity is, of course, nothing new (e.g. Blumer, 1969; Woods, 1979). In the area of teacher education, however – where, arguably, it has the most to offer and the most to learn (Moore, 1997) – it is in danger of becoming an increasingly overlooked, underdeveloped paradigm with reference both to the education of teachers and to research about the education of teachers. At its centre is the need for teachers to understand their own historical positionings and developments as much as they are able, in addition to trying to understand how their pupils 'tick', and for researchers to explore not only social interactions but also the discourses and contexts within which those interactions take place. From the perspective of manifest and latent content and meaning, classrooms – like cinemas or sitting-rooms – are viewed not just as places of ideological and cultural reproduction and coercion, but also as forums, in which actors with divergent interests, histories, interests and perceptions actively negotiate new meanings and new futures.

Notes

1 The charismatic subject discourse is not to be confused with the notion that teaching is often 'expressive and emergent, intuitive and flexible, spontaneous and emotional' (Woods, 1996, p. 6). The charismatic subject discourse is characterized by an over-reliance on 'personality' and an under-reliance on technique, often involving restrictive efforts to mimic the words and behaviours of teachers remembered from one's own school days. What Woods is suggesting is that teaching is not reducible to learnable competences – although these may be helpful – and that we ignore the specific (and variable) *contexts* of teaching at our peril.
2 I am aware that the terms 'modernism' and 'postmodernism' remain problematic and open to interpretation. 'Modernism' and 'postmodernism' as they are applied to educational settings often have, for example, very different meanings than when they are applied to, say, more directly political situations (Moore, 1998a). As long as we accept and are appropriately wary of this ambiguity, the terms can, however, provide a helpful taxonomy for distinguishing between radically different approaches to education in ways that are potentially more encompassing than those offered in the past by such expressions as 'progressive' and 'traditional' or 'transmissive' and 'pupil-centred'.
3 Related activity must, for instance, have a clear *voluntary* basis and not be subject to formal assessment.

References

Alexander, R.J., Craft, M. and Lynch, J. (eds) (1984) *Change in Teacher Education*, New York: Praeger.

Allen, G. (1994) *Teacher Training: The Education Bill 1993/4: Research Paper 94/58*, London: House of Commons Library.

Bernstein, B. (1996) *Pedagogy, Symbolic Control and Identity*, London: Taylor & Francis.

Beyer, L.E. and Zeichner, K. (1987) 'Teacher education in cultural context: beyond reproduction', in Popkewitz, T.S. (ed.) *Critical Studies in Teacher Education: Its Folklore, Theory and Practice*, London: Falmer Press, pp. 298–334.

Blumer, H. (1969) *Symbolic Interactionism*, Englewood Cliffs: Prentice Hall.

Bourdieu, P. (1990) *In Other Words*, Cambridge: Polity Press.

Cohen, L. and Manion, L. (1977) *A Guide to Teaching Practice*, London: Methuen.

Cole, A.L. and Knowles, J.G. (1995) 'Methods and issues in a life history approach to self-study', in Russell, T. and Korthagen, F. (eds) *Teachers Who Teach Teachers*, London: Falmer Press, pp. 130–54.

Combs, A.W. (1972) 'Some basic concepts for teacher education', *Journal of Teacher Education*, **23** (Fall), pp. 286–90.

Council for the Accreditation of Teacher Education (CATE) (1992) *Circular 9/92*, London: CATE.

Cummins, J. (1996) *Negotiating Identities: Education for Empowerment in a Diverse Society*, California: CABE.

Department for Education and Employment (DfEE) (1997a) *Teaching: High Status, High Standards*, London: DfEE.

Department for Education and Employment (DfEE) (1997b) *Annex A to Teacher Training Circular 1/97: Standards for the Award of Qualified Teacher Status*, London: DfEE.

Department of Education and Science (1981) *Teacher Training and the Secondary School*, London: DES.

Elliott, J. (1993) 'The relationship between "understanding" and "developing" teachers' thinking', in Elliott, J. (ed.) *Reconstructing Teacher Education*, London: Falmer Press.

Giddens, A. (1991) *Modernity and Self-Identity: Self and Society in the Late Modern Age*, Cambridge: Polity Press.

Giroux, H. (1988) 'Critical theory and the politics of culture and voice: rethinking the discourse of educational research', in Sherman, R. and Webb, R. (eds) *Qualitative Research in Education: Focus and Methods*, London: Falmer Press, pp. 190–210.

Giroux, H.A. and McKaren, P.L. (1992) 'Introduction' to Stanley, W.B., *Curriculum For Utopia: Social Reconstruction and Critical Pedagogy in the Postmodern Era*, Albany: State University of New York Press.

Goodson, I.F. and Walker, R. (1991) *Biography, Identity and Schooling*, London: Falmer Press..

Gramsci, A. (1985) *Selections from Cultural Writings*, London: Lawrence and Wishart.

Green, B. (1995) 'English teaching, cultural politics, and the postmodern turn', *Journal of Curriculum Studies*, **27**, 4, pp. 391–409.

Hamilton, D. (1993) 'Texts, literacy and schooling' in Green, B. (ed.) *The Insistence of the Letter*, London: Falmer Press, pp. 46–57.

Handal, G. and Lauvas, P. (1987) *Promoting Reflective Teaching: Supervision in Action*, Milton Keynes and Philadelphia: Society for Research into Higher Education and Open University Press.

Hargreaves, A. (1993) 'Professional development and the politics of desire', in Vasquez, A. and Martinez, I. (eds) *New Paradigms and Practices in Professional Development*, New York: Teachers College Press.

Hargreaves, A. (1994) *Changing Teachers, Changing Times: Teachers' Work and Culture in the Postmodern Age*, London: Cassell.

Hebdidge, D. (1986) 'Postmodernism and "The Other Side"', *Journal of Communication Inquiry*, **10** 2, pp. 78–98.

Henry, M.A. (1989) 'Change in teacher education: focus on field experiences', in

Braun, J.A. Jr (3d.) (1989) *Reforming Teacher Education: Issues and New Directions*, London and New York: Garland Publishing Inc.

Institute of Education (1972) *Education and the Training of Teachers: Statement on the James Report*, London: Institute of Education.

Johnson, B. (1989) 'Developing preservice teachers' self-awareness: an examination of the professional dynametric program', in Braun, J.A. Jr (ed.) (1989) *Reforming Teacher Education: Issues and New Directions*, New York and London: Garland Publishing Inc.

Jones, L. and Moore, R. (1995) 'Appropriating competence: the competency movement, the New Right and the "culture change" project', *British Journal of Education and Work*, **8**, 2, pp. 78–92.

Lacan, J. (1977) *Ecrits*, London: Tavistock.

Lacan, J. (1979) *The Four Fundamental Concepts of Psycho-Analysis*, London: Penguin.

Levin, D.M. (1987) *Pathologies of the Modern Self: Postmodern Studies in Narcissism, Schizophrenia and Depression*, New York: New York University Press.

Loughran, J. (1996) *Developing Reflective Practice: Learning about Teaching and Learning through Modelling*, London: Falmer.

Loughran, J. and Russell, J. (eds) (1997) *Teaching about Teaching: Purpose, Passion and Pedagogy in Teacher Education*, London: Falmer.

Maguire, M. (1995) *Dilemmas in Teaching Teachers: The Tutor's Perspective*, *Teachers and Teaching*, **1**, 1, pp. 119–31.

Marland, M. (1975) *The Craft of the Classroom*, Oxford: Heinemann Educational.

Martin-Barbero, J. (1993) *Communication, Culture and Hegemony: From the Media to Mediations*, London: Sage.

McIntyre, D., Hagger, H. and Burn, K. (1994) *The Management of Student Teachers' Learning*, London and Philadelphia: Kogan Page.

McLaren, P. (1996) *Critical Pedagogy and Predatory Culture*, New York: State University of New York Press.

Mitchell, C. and Weber, S. (1996) *Reinventing Ourselves as Teachers: Private and Social Acts of Memory and Imagination*, London: Falmer Press.

Moore, A. (1996) '"Masking the fissure": some thoughts on competences, reflection and closure in initial teacher education', *British Journal of Educational Studies*, **44**, 2, pp. 200–211.

Moore, A. (1997) 'Unmixing messages: a Bourdieuean approach to tensions and helping-strategies in initial teacher education', unpublished conference paper, International Conference on Bourdieu, Language and Education, University of Southampton.

Moore, A. (1998a) 'English, fetishism and the demand for change: towards a postmodern agenda for the school curriculum', in Edwards, G. and Kelly, A.V. (eds) *Experience and Education*, London: Paul Chapman, pp. 103–25.

Moore, A. (1998b) *Forcing the Issue: An Evaluation of Personal Writing Initiatives with Student Teachers* (updated with new material), University of London, Goldsmiths College.

Moore, A. and Atkinson, D. (1998) 'Charisma, competence and teacher education', *Discourse*, **19**, 2, pp. 171–81.

National Union of Teachers (1976) *Teacher Education: The Way Ahead*, London: National Union of Teachers.

Office for Standards in Education (Ofsted) and Teacher Training Agency (TTA) (1996) *Framework for the Assessment of Quality and Standards in Initial Teacher Training 1996/97*, London: Ofsted.

Popkewitz, T.S. (ed.) (1987) *Critical Studies in Teacher Education: Its Folklore, Theory and Practice*, London: Falmer Press.

Quicke, J. (1988) 'Using structured life histories to teach the sociology and social psychology of education', in Woods, P. and Pollard, A. (eds) *Sociology and Teaching*, London: Croom Helm.

Reid, W. A. (1993) 'Literacy, orality and the functions of curriculum', in Green, B. (ed.) *The Insistence of the Letter*, London: Falmer Press, pp. 13–26.

Schön, D.A. (1983) *The Reflective Practitioner*, New York: Basic Books.

Schön, D.A. (1987) *Educating the Reflective Practitioner*, San Francisco: Jossey-Bass.

Schön, D.A. (1988) 'Coaching reflective teaching', in Grimmett, P.P. and Erickson, G.L. (eds) *Reflection in Teacher Education*, British Columbia: Pacific Educational Press.

Standish, P. (1995) 'Post-modernism and the education of the whole person', *Journal of Philosophy of Education*, **29**, 1, pp. 121–36.

Stephens, P. and Crawley, T. (1994) *Becoming an Effective Teacher*, Cheltenham: Stanley Thornes Ltd.

Teacher Training Agency (TTA) (1998) *National Standards for Qualified Teacher Status*, London: Teacher Training Agency.

Thomas, D. (1995) 'Treasonable or trustworthy text: reflections on teacher narrative studies', in Thomas, D. (ed.) *Teachers' Stories*, Buckingham: Open University Press.

Valli, L. (ed.) (1992) *Reflective Teacher Education*, New York: State University of New York Press.

Walkerdine, V. (1982) 'A psycho-semiotic approach to abstract thought', in Beveridge, M. (ed.) *Children Thinking Through Language*, London: Arnold.

Walkerdine, V. (1990) *Schoolgirl Fictions*, London: Verso.

Woods, P. (1979) *The Divided School*, London: Routledge and Kegan Paul.

Woods, P. (1996) *Researching the Art of Teaching: Ethnography for Educational Use*, London: Routledge.

Wragg, E.C. (1974) *Teaching Teaching*, Newton Abbot: David & Charles.

9 Learning, Policy and Pupil Career: Issues from a Longitudinal Ethnography

Andrew Pollard and Ann Filer

This chapter reviews some of the ways in which symbolic interactionist ethnography, of the type that Peter Woods has done so much to develop throughout his academic career, can illuminate key issues in relation to the major aims of education. Bearing in mind changes in English and Welsh education over the past decade, we argue that the fulfilment of espoused national, system-wide goals requires better understanding of pupils' individual identities, learning strategies, experiences and perceptions in relation to the social contexts that exist in classrooms and schools. In much of his recent work, for instance on creative teaching (Woods, 1995; Woods and Jeffrey, 1996) and school inspection (Jeffrey and Woods, 1998), Peter Woods has shown how the impact of policy can be understood and evaluated in terms of personal, social and educational consequences. Our work echoes this example.

We develop our argument by drawing on what we have called the 'Identity and Learning Programme' (ILP). This is the name coined to describe a series of studies on children's experiences and perspectives on schooling. It had its origins many years ago in Andrew Pollard's 1976 M.Ed. thesis and subsequent Ph.D. – which led eventually to *The Social World of the Primary School* (Pollard, 1985). This book provided a sociological analysis of teacher and pupil perspectives, coping strategies, classroom relationships and processes of social differentiation. However, it did not directly address questions of children's learning, or the development of their identities as learners over time.

Our book *The Social World of Children's Learning* extended that earlier analysis by holistically tracking the early learning experiences of five case-study children from age 4 to 7 at Greenside Primary School (Pollard with Filer, 1996). It explored the ways in which material, physical and intellectual resources, together with gender, socio-political and cultural circumstances, influenced the development and fulfilment of their learning potential. The major focus of the book was on the influence of interpersonal processes in home, classroom and playground. *The Social World of Pupil Careers* (Pollard and Filer, 1999) was a further development of the Greenside study, and focused on the gradual development of the identities and learning dispositions of four children – William, Robert, Sarah and Harriet – as they progressed through their primary schooling. Through accounts of their 'strategic biographies', we documented continuity and change within cases, as well as variations across cases. We described children's emergent sense of self as learners, and their changing conceptions of 'pupil identity'. More analytically, we formalized our understanding of how pupil identity is played out in terms of the *dimensions* and *dynamics* of strategic action.

We are continuing to work on further elements of the Identity and Learning Programme. For instance, our study of children from Greenside Primary School was complemented by a parallel study in a less affluent suburb of Easthampton. Albert Park Primary School provided the context of Ann Filer's Ph.D. study, during which she tracked children's classroom assessment experiences through Key Stage 1 and Key Stage 2. Her thesis showed how teacher-created social and organizational factors could influence pupils' classroom language and responses to tasks, and suggested that teacher assessments should be seen as context-related social accomplishments on the part of pupil, teachers and peers (Filer, 1993). This study was then developed with respect to parental perspectives and as a comparative case-study with Greenside to produce *The Social World of Pupil Assessment* (Filer and Pollard, forthcoming).

The latest phase of the Identity and Learning Programme tracks the secondary school careers of 16 of the children who attended Greenside and Albert Park primary schools. They now attend nine contrasting secondary schools within Easthampton and their experiences will be studied to the end of their compulsory schooling at age 16. Considerable differences in the life experiences and trajectories of the children are already apparent and analysis of this phase of the programme will unite our interest in processes of social differentiation and in social influences on learning.

We see this programme of work as contributing to a tradition of what one might call 'appreciative ethnography', which Peter Woods did so much to establish within the sociology of education. The essence of this is the attempt to both 'hear' and empathize with the perspectives of actors, and take them seriously in analysis. This is an important foundation of the 'new paradigm' in studies of children and childhood (Corsaro, 1997; James and Prout, 1990; James, Jenks and Prout, 1998), a fundamental principle of which is that children should be seen as active in the construction of their own social lives and those of others, rather than as passive subjects of social processes and structures. However, this affirmation has to be balanced by recognition of the wider social, economic, historic, cultural and political factors that frame the structural circumstances in which children act, together with significant forms of discourse, positioning and common-sense conceptions that they experience. The impact of such factors is often embedded in ethnographic publications, but we now approach them more explicitly by relating our analysis of pupil career to three major educational purposes commonly expressed by policy makers: preparation of the workforce for economic production; contributing to social justice and individual rights; and personal development and social integration.

The Purposes of Education

What are the purposes of education? The simplicity of this question is deceptive, for education in modern societies is not just a way of incorporating new members, but a means of building the future. It is a vehicle between 'what is' and 'what ought to be'. This poses important questions of priority and value, with a characteristic distinction being drawn between fulfilling the personal development of individuals and addressing the needs of the society as a whole. Such personal–societal dilemmas tend, quite properly in democratic societies, to be the subject of regular debate, with new settlements to resolve them being attempted by successive ministers and governments.

Through the history of such debates and resolutions, we would suggest that one can detect three major clusters of purpose, the prominence of which changes over time in response to socio-economic circumstance (Green, 1997). These clusters of purposes are all represented in David Blunkett's 'Foreword' to New Labour's 1997 White Paper, *Excellence in Schools*, and we take his expression of them as the organizing device for this chapter.

The Secretary of State expressed the national educational challenge in the following way:

> To compete in the global economy, to live in a civilised society and to develop the talents of each and every one of us, we will have to unlock the potential of every young person.
> (Department for Education and Employment, 1997, p. 3)

First, 'to compete in the global economy' is seen as being dependent on the development in children of basic skills and knowledge, and a positive disposition towards future learning. 'Basic skills' in the elementary school tradition have been seen as a very limited expression of educational goals. However, when seen as a precursor to further learning and explicitly linked to the development of learning dispositions, this concern can be seen as having been updated to reflect the needs of the modern economy.

Second, children's future contribution to 'a civilised society' as responsible citizens raises a range of issues concerning personal, social, moral, spiritual and cultural development. It concerns the broad purposes of education in balancing personal fulfilment and social cohesion. This is particularly important as society becomes increasingly complex, diverse and subject to rapid change. Such concerns have been associated with the 'integrative function' of education, but may also raise the question of the extent to which education is a form of social control.

Third, developing 'the talents of each and every one of us' concerns the rights of children and social justice. In addition to opening opportunities for learning and inclusion, education is also seen as being concerned with issues of confidence, self-esteem, personal judgment, and the development of a spirit of enquiry and challenge. This concern acknowledges the significance of the education system for full participation in the processes of democracy as well as in the formation of the economic life chances of individuals.

In relation to these three educational priorities, we will consider some implications from the Identity and Learning Programme.

'To compete in the global economy': The Preparation of the Workforce

This priority has become the major preoccupation of developed education systems around the world. In the UK, it was a central tenet in the New Right ideology that underpinned the educational reforms of the 1980s and early 1990s. It can be traced back to the post-war 'human capital' theory of the 1960s (Schultz, 1961) in which investment in education was seen as a precondition of economic growth. However, in its 1990s free-market, monetarist manifestation, the concern has been closely related to the emergence of skilled and cheap labour forces in the Pacific Rim and else-where, seen as threatening to the high-cost economies of Western countries such as the UK. As a World Bank review put it, key priorities for education were that:

> It must meet economies' growing demands for adaptable workers who can readily acquire new skills, and it must support the continued expansion of knowledge. Basic education . . . also includes the development of the attitudes necessary for the workplace.
>
> (World Bank, 1995, pp. 1–2)

Similar references to the development of skills, knowledge and positive attitudes to work can be found in the policies of the present 'New Labour' government, for example in statements from the Literacy Task Force (Barber, 1997), the Labour election manifesto (Labour Party, 1997) and the *Excellence in Schools* White Paper (DfEE 1997).

In England and Wales, the dominance of the concern with basic skills is reflected in the ways in which the primary education system has been progressively structured and made accountable in recent years. As we argued in *The Social World of Children's Learning*, this discourse prioritizing the importance of the 'basics' consistently emphasizes teaching and the delivery of the curriculum, and there has been relatively little attention to learners and learning *per se*. The 1997 report of Ofsted's Chief Inspector provides an example, in which 'children' and 'pupils' are mentioned frequently, but only as an adjunct to the dominant discourse about standards. The implicit representation of children is rather like that of industrial raw material awaiting processing and the addition of added value. Various strengths and weaknesses in the functioning of the educational machine are considered, but the assumed passivity of pupils is conveyed by the almost complete absence of any direct account of their perspectives, experiences or quality of life. Education, in this account, is something that is done *to* children, not *with* children, and still less *by* children. Indeed, at a time when the dominant view among many politicians and the media is that the 'old orthodoxies' of teachers cannot be trusted, there seems to be even less reason to listen to the voices of the pupils who are on the receiving end of the pressure for improving standards in basic skills.

There are problems with the consistent emphasis upon teaching, curriculum delivery and assessment for effective learning that continue to inform policy debate. *Children and Their Curriculum* (Pollard, Thiessen and Filer, 1997) is a collection of papers addressing the perceptions of curriculum held by children from the United States, Canada and the UK. The collection focuses most directly on the argument that standards of curriculum learning will rise further and faster if teachers are able to understand the curriculum as experienced by pupils, as distinct from the curriculum as intended by policy makers, at all levels.

Similarly, the Identity and Learning Programme shows the necessity for at least an equal emphasis upon learners and learning as upon teachers and teaching. For instance:

- There are many variations in children's orientations to learning. Individuals develop particular learning agendas in classrooms, and may respond differently to particular motivational and reward systems and to particular patterns of teacher expectation.
- Children's self-esteem and motivation to engage in learning and to seek out challenging tasks are embedded in, and inseparable from, the social structures, relationships, processes and situational opportunities and constraints surrounding learning.

Put very simply, we are arguing that children's strategic orientations towards learning are contextually related. To illustrate this suggestion, we can consider the four case-study children who feature in *The Social World of Pupil Career*. Although the class might be considered to be 'normal' or 'unexceptional', the opportunity to study a few children in detail reveals a range of contextually-related dispositions and strategies. For instance:

Sarah's dominant low-risk, 'conforming' and somewhat passive approach to curricular learning was not replicated in out-of-school learning or in the context of sibling rivalry. Out of school, she set herself new challenges in relation to a range of musical, artistic and physical accomplishments. Most importantly, with her mother's encouragement, she strove to challenge her older, high-achieving brother.

William showed individuality and flair in academic tasks. He positioned himself at the cutting edge of classroom expectations for learning and often negotiated with teachers – which we call 're-defining'. However, he could switch to a low-risk, minimalist conforming approach. This tended to happen when pedagogic expectations denied him opportunities to 'shine' or when the age-composition of his class placed him in a relatively low structural position and undermined his self-confidence.

Robert's usual strategies for learning involved the maintenance of a measure of autonomous self-direction – a form of 'non-conformity'. Some teachers created classroom contexts that were supportive and enabling as he actively created and negotiated opportunities to develop his own slant on the curriculum. Some teachers created contexts that were inhibiting for this, with the result that Robert became demotivated.

Harriet enjoyed being appreciated by teachers for her own distinctive qualities, rather than adapting and pleasing through being 'good', 'first' or 'best' like many of her peers. Each year, she oscillated between enthusiastic participation in classroom life and learning, and private, contemptuous disengagement as teachers variously perceived and related to her independent, non-conforming stance.

The above are simply summarized examples from the child case-studies in the Identity and Learning Programme, each of which forms a narrative of about 20,000 words. They show how children are empowered or de-powered, motivated or demotivated to maximize their learning strategies within particular contexts. Indeed, such longitudinal and holistic analysis traces how children's structural position within peer group, family and classroom statuses changes. Such changes can enable or inhibit individual learning and the development of particular social relationships – and cumulatively form 'pupil career'.

From this discussion, we offer two policy implications. The first is that educational standards are likely to increase more easily if full and appreciative consideration of learners and learning strategies *complements* the present, systemic emphasis on the specification and assessment of curriculum and teaching methods. Second, we note that the early development of positive dispositions to learn as a bedrock for future flexibility and lifelong learning is contingent on social and affective motivation. Such issues need greater consideration than is enabled by present policies.

The attempt at an appreciative ethnography suggests that the policy emphasis on teachers teaching within an increasingly directive framework could eventually become demotivating and counter-productive. Certainly, nation-wide structures and target-setting may have initial sucess in rachet-ing up standards to meet global competition, but this is unlikely to be sustained if it is not possible to fully harness the motivation of children.

This focus on pupils as individuals brings us to the second of our three major educational concerns – personal development and social integration.

'To live in a civilised society': Personal Development and Social Integration

For Durkheim (1961), education was 'the means by which society prepares, within its children, the essential conditions of its own existence'. Within modern Western societies, the socializing role of education has moved beyond responsibility for the inculcation and continuity of some un-problematic notion of 'culture'. Not only has the complex pluralism of the modern world been recognized, but education must now assume a role in transmitting the principles and requirements for a system of participa-tory democracy. In schools in England and Wales, such issues have been most explicitly conceptualized and given expression through the curricu-lum area of 'personal and social education' (PSE).

The Education Reform Act, 1988 made an explicit commitment to breadth and balance in the curriculum. That commitment involved the promotion of the 'spiritual, moral, cultural, mental and physical develop-ment of pupils in school and of society'; and to the preparation of pupils for the 'opportunities, responsibilities and experiences of adult life' (p. 1). However, such concerns were somewhat ill-defined from the start. The underlying purposes of the Education Reform Act were focused rather more prosaically on the creation of curricular and assessment structures that would 'raise standards'. From 1993, however, the introduction of the system for school inspection brought a new official representation of 'pupils' personal development'. This took the form, within the Handbook for Inspection, of 'evaluation criteria' for pupils' spiritual, moral, social and cultural development. Thus, in brief, we had:

Spiritual development: judged by how well the school promotes oppor-tunities for pupils to reflect on aspects of their lives and the human condition . . . and how well the pupils respond.

Moral development: judged on how well the school promotes an under-standing of the moral principles which allow pupils to tell right from wrong, and to respect other people, truth, justice and property; and how well they respond . . .

Social development: judged by how well the school prepares pupils for relating to others in different social settings . . . and how well the pupils respond. It is also to be judged by the extent to which pupils gain an understanding of how societies function and are organised in structures such as the family, the school and local and wider communities.

Cultural development: judged by how well the school prepares pupils to understand aspects of their own and other cultural environments . . . and by the pupils' response to this provision.

(Ofsted, 1994, p. 21)

Subsequent school inspection findings (e.g. Ofsted, 1997) suggested that schools took these matters very seriously. In Ofsted's terms, a majority of schools made 'good' provision in most respects. Provision for cultural development, especially preparing students for a multicultural society, was weaker (Ofsted, 1997).

Superficially, Ofsted's criteria might seem uncontentious. However, they embody some implicit assumptions that are more questionable. First, there is the clear assumption that children and young people are to be socialized into an *adult* frame of reference. Indeed, pupils are predominantly cast as passive, with a social representation that sees them as being deficient and in need of guidance. Thus, for instance, Ofsted requires schools to 'promote' or 'prepare', whereas pupils are to 'respond' or 'gain an understanding'. A second feature is the tacit assumption of consensus and stability about the nature of 'society'. Of course, these two assumptions are connected in exactly the way they were in structural functionalist sociology of the 1950s and 1960s. As then, they fail to represent either the real capacities and activity of children or the capacities young people might need to operate and engage effectively as citizens in such a society. Neither do they fully represent the complexity of our diverse, fractured and rapidly changing societies today.

An alternative conceptualization would be founded on the expectation that children are active, responsible and self-critical. This is the assumption on which Peter Woods based his work and he has offered us plenty of evidence of its potential (e.g. Woods, 1980, 1990). In the more specific area of personal and social education, an influential writer has been Pring (1984, 1988). In contrast to the implicit presumptions of passive socialization offered by Ofsted, Pring's conception is of children as actively engaging with real issues, contradictions and dilemmas, developing responsibility and control in their own lives, and recognizing others as persons. He suggests that four capacities should be developed:

to think, to reflect, to make sense of one's experience, to engage critically with the received values, beliefs, and assumptions that one is confronted with – the development, in other words, of the powers of the mind;

to recognise others as persons – as centres of consciousness and reason like oneself;

to act intentionally, deliberately, and thus to be held responsible for what one does – not simply the unfortunate victim of forces beyond one's control – as the basis of moral attributes;

to maintain consciousness not only of others as persons but of oneself – a sense of one's own capacity to think through a problem, to persevere when things get tough, to establish a platform of values and beliefs whereby one can exercise some control over one's own destiny.

(Pring, 1988, p. 43–4)

A progressive approach has also recently been offered by an Advisory Group on Citizenship (Crick, 1998), whose advice will inform a curriculum review from 2000. Building on some earlier work by SCAA, the Advisory Group suggested that teaching of citizenship and democracy should be a statutory requirement, and in primary schools may be linked to personal, social and health education programmes. They note the importance of the ethos of the school and classroom context, and highlight the first strand of citizenship education as 'social and moral responsibility [in which] children learn from the very beginning self-confidence and socially and morally responsible behaviour both in and beyond the classroom, both towards those in authority and towards each other' (*ibid.*, p. 11).

Turning to the Identity and Learning Programme (ILP), the cumulative arguments suggest that, since children are active in the construction of their own experience, attempts to influence them as if they were passive objects of intervention are likely to fail. In this respect, the thinking of Woods and Pring and the Advisory Group on Citizenship seem to be more constructive and worthwhile than the assumptions embedded in the Ofsted framework. Two particular points are also suggested:

- Active engagement, taking responsibility and self-control will be facilitated by classroom climates within which children are able to manage the personal risk and ambiguity that is inherent in such processes.
- Pupils with the most active strategies for engaging with learning may be positively perceived by teachers – but if teachers are relatively unaware or are routinized in their practices, such activities may also be categorized as 'problems'.

Thus, to manage risk and ambiguity in learning, good classroom relation-ships, self-confidence and trust are needed to complement appropriate intellectual challenge and support. We can illustrate these suggestions with some case studies from *The Social World of Pupil Career*. For instance:

> William's highly interactive and communicative classroom strategies and challenges to teacher definitions were encouraged and viewed as integral to the learning process by some teachers. However, when taught by other classroom teachers, his redefining strategies were experienced as disruptive and perceived as a hindrance to his learning.

> Harriet and Robert adopted independent, autonomous approaches to learning, integrating their own distinct identities into classroom tasks. This independence was sometimes admired by teachers. On the other hand their nonconformity meant that they were also often viewed as exasperating or incomprehensible.

The case studies of such children illustrate transitions between positive or negative cycles of learning, seen as products of classroom interaction processes (Pollard, 1985, p. 239).

The ILP also highlights an important challenge for the personal develop-ment of many pupils concerning the common strategy of 'drifting' through school life in relatively conformist ways – 'keeping one's head down'. Of course, conformity may be a strategic decision and a way of maximizing learning, but for many children it is a low-risk strategy that combines a search for approval and a reluctance to think and operate outside of teacher-given structures and expectations, though it may not be applied in other settings. This is well illustrated by the case study of Sarah, from *The Social World of Pupil Career*:

> Sarah's careful conformity was often regretted by teachers as contri-buting to the risk of underachievement and safe mediocrity. However, her stance was never actively challenged. Indeed, in some years it was encouraged through the often highly rewarded and teacher-approved 'good girl' culture of mainstream girls' groups. On the other hand, within the family context of sibling rivalry, Sarah showed a readiness to employ more active, challenging strategies. Classroom conformity was a contextual strategy.

For Pring's and Crick's characteristics of holistic learners and citizens to be realized, 'conformity', in the form of low-risk minimalism and search for teacher approval, must be challenged in classrooms, even though it is often as 'safe' for the teacher as it is for some pupils. To engage critically with received values, beliefs and assumptions, and to take responsibility and control over one's destiny, implies that pupils begin to venture out of their comfort-zones. 'Conformity' would need to be a less comfortable strategic option – and, conversely, active, autonomous, critical and self-critical learning should be made safer and more viable. Even more challenging is the need to manage this for all children, rather than just for individuals of high status and self-esteem.

In policy terms, we know that civil society requires active citizens who have the self-confidence and social awareness to contribute – as well as the knowledge and skills. The ILP and other ethnographic work suggests that we have to consider the experiences that teachers and schools are able to offer their pupils, given the constraints they face in the modern schooling system. Do these make it possible to fully support children as they prepare to contribute to society's future? Is there a risk that high-stakes assessment, target setting and inspection systems could be counter-productive in this respect? We cannot resolve such issues through this research, but the questions are clearly posed.

In the following section, we move on to consider the third of the Labour Government's educational priorities and the implications of the Identity and Learning Programme for achieving it.

'To develop the talents of each and every one of us': Individual Rights and Social Justice

Several established statements of 'rights', such as the Universal and European Conventions, aspire to set international standards for our citizens. From 1989, the position of children was more specifically enhanced by the Convention on the Rights of the Child. Such agreements have considerable moral force and set important targets, but educational provision in most countries has fallen somewhat short of these ideals.

The case of secondary education in England and Wales provides an example. The 1944 Education Act established a system for selecting children at age 11 for what was thought to be the most appropriate secondary education for their needs. Schools within the 'tripartite' system were to have 'parity of esteem', but this idealistic conception quickly degenerated into a hierarchy placing grammar schools at the top of a pyramid and significantly affecting life-chances. From the 1960s, the comprehensive system was introduced with the explicit goal of providing equality of opportunity within similar institutions across the country. Unfortunately, however, the following decades produced considerable variation in the attainment of different schools and social groups, together with high levels of poor pupil attainment and school failure. The market-led policies of the Conservative governments of the 1980s and early 1990s were supposed to raise standards for all by encouraging excellence, but the problems of less-favoured schools increased. New Labour emphasizes the rights of all children to a high standard of education, and economic and social disadvantage are portrayed as factors that can be overcome in schools by 'target-setting' in relation to educational standards and through 'zero tolerance of failure'. It remains to be seen whether this approach will really work, for an undifferentiated 'pulling up by the bootstraps' approach does not appear to address the specific ways in which our society and our schools continue to fail to provide educational solutions for particular populations of children.

Despite repeated attempts to use the education system as a form of amelioration for social inequalities, schools also perpetuate practices that compound them. Schools strive to change social differences, but they also reproduce them. Gillborn (1995), for example, cites numerous UK studies that depict ways in which even well intentioned teachers, committed to equal opportunities, continue to act to reproduce familiar racial stereotypes. Indeed, Vincent and Tomlinson (1997) suggest that sociological research concerning issues of structural inequalities and power have failed to engage the teaching profession, so that teachers' attitudes concerning social class largely continue to carry a deficit model of working-class parents.

Of course, it could be that the almost continuous focus in recent decades on national policies and school structures may unwittingly have contributed to these problems. Indeed, in an argument with which we certainly agree, Vincent and Tomlinson (1997) suggest that sociologists and others have paid too little attention to the concept of the child and to pupil agency. The problems of inequalities and rights may have been tackled from the structural direction, but with insufficient attention to the perspectives and experiences of individual actors.

The importance of engagement with learners as individuals, recognition of the diversity of identities and of active agency in learning processes has been demonstrated by Peter Woods throughout his career, and we have tried to develop the argument through the Identity and Learning Programme. Through our case studies and analysis, we have drawn the following conclusions:

- Children's sense of self as pupils is shaped by factors such as social class, gender and race within particular politico-cultural contexts. Children progressively develop and maintain their identities as pupils by drawing on their intellectual and physical potential, together with the material, cultural and linguistic resources that are available to them.
- Different classroom and school contexts variously affirm, celebrate, challenge or marginalize children's sense of self derived from family and community.
- Inclusion, affirmation or marginalization of their identity and sense of self has profound implications for children's happiness, their learning and their sense of being valued.

Our case studies are rich with material that, we believe, supports these conclusions. For instance:

> Harriet's sense of self, developed in home and community settings, incorporated a disposition towards autonomy and self-direction in learning and an active involvement in outdoor pursuits, especially horse riding. In some years she was able to draw on this identity in school. She was able to achieve a rapport with her teachers and assert her own distinct identity, which in turn supported her learning. In other years she was unable to draw in that identity, she was often viewed with incomprehension by her teachers and seemed to have no sense of identification or belonging in classrooms. The culture of Greenside School more obviously and readily reflected and supported the expression of a more conventional culture among girls from Greenside families. Harriet's physical and cultural sense of self was at odds with this type of highly gendered style and body consciousness, as well as with the competitive approach to learning and 'goodness' that were characteristic of that culture.

> At home Robert, like Harriet, was a strongly autonomous learner. In shaping his pupil identity, he drew on this autonomy, as well as his computer knowledge and skills. Like Harriet, Robert was dependent on individual teachers for the conditions to assert his distinct identity in the classroom. Without that identity, his marginal position in relation to the dominant boys' culture of physical skills and toughness, meant that he failed to establish satisfying classroom relationships and self-esteem as a pupil and as a boy. In some contexts (though not necessarily in the same contexts) Robert and Harriet were able to give expression to their interests, forge successful pupil identities and, at the same time achieve social integration with peers. In other settings their sense of self as different and marginal to the life and learning of the rest of the class was reinforced.

Social injustice deriving from social or material circumstances was not a threat to the education of children of relatively affluent Greenside families, though this was certainly the case for some of the Albert Park children. However, even within a fairly homogenous socio-cultural group, we found significant differences among pupils, and between girls and boys, in how they related and responded within different teaching contexts and within the dominant cultural expectations of school. We saw through their case-study stories how their sense of themselves as pupils was continuously being shaped and reshaped by relationships and experiences in home, school, playground and community.

The children in the ILP now attend nine different secondary schools, including prestigious independent schools, a grammar school, a City

Technology College and a number of comprehensives. Although they may all have equal rights and benefit from the good intentions of government, it is clear both that their opportunities and structural positions vary considerably and that their dispositions to learn are significantly affected by their feelings and perceptions towards their schools.

This analysis leads us to re-emphasize a need for attention to the individual qualities of learners and their learning. It is important to recognize and 'hear' pupils' individual perspectives as a basis for meeting their educational needs – or negotiating new behaviours if necessary. The respect and dignity that is thereby offered, provides a starting point on which individual children can build as they come to terms with both new learning challenges and the maintenance of their identities within classroom or school settings. This process is particularly important where a child's identity is distinct from, or in tension with, those of the mainstream peer or school culture.

In policy terms, this analysis suggests that we are unlikely to fulfil the potential of children, satisfy individual rights and provide social justice without very careful consideration of the specific needs of individuals, groups and communities. The interaction of socio-cultural contexts and learners is highly complex but extremely powerful. It seems unlikely that system-wide 'solutions' for raising educational standards and providing social justice can work without consideration of such factors. Indeed, initiatives such as the 'New Deal for Communities' (1998) may begin to recognize this.

Conclusion

One way of summarizing the basic message of the Identity and Learning Programme is to say that: Individual capabilities are related to perceptions and self-confidence in particular social contexts.

Teacher actions, expectations, interpretations and responses to pupil strategies affect many aspects of pupil experience – academic progression, approaches to learning, views of selves as learners, self-esteem, relationships with teachers, status with peers, and so on. Our research has been concerned with the extent to which classroom experiences affirm and develop children's sense of self in all these respects, or the way in which that sense of self may become marginalized. In relation to the children that we have studied and come to know so well, such outcomes told us more about whether important academic and social purposes were being met than about National Curriculum levels, league tables and national comparisons. Detailed, qualitative case study can illuminate national policy issues and relate their particular effects to the holistic experience of individual teachers, pupils or parents within their social world.

David Blunkett is certainly correct in his statement that 'to compete in the global economy, to live in a civilized society and to develop the talents of each and every one of us, we will have to unlock the potential of every young person'. But we can only unlock such potential if we attend to school and learning experiences as pupils actually perceive them. The new national requirements for literacy, numeracy, information and communication technology, base-line assessment, target setting, local management of schools, teacher capability, and other initiatives may well begin to increase educational standards, opportunities and social inclusion. However, we would argue that 'unlocking potential' also requires a more personal, appreciative capacity.

What we have here, then, is an application of the type of symbolic interactionist humanism that Peter Woods pioneered in the sociology of education (e.g. Woods, 1983). The basic toolkit is made up of concepts such as self, identity, situation, context, interaction, relationships, meaning, culture and group, and these are deployed to try both to understand the consequences of national policy and to generate suggestions for further development.

References

Barber, M. (1997) *A Reading Revolution: How We Can Teach Every Child to Read Well*, Literacy Task Force, London: Labour Party.

Corsaro, W. (1997) *The Sociology of Childhood*, Thousand Oaks, CA: Pine Forge Press.

Crick, B. (1998) *Final Report of the Advisory Group for Citizenship and Teaching of Democracy in Schools*, London: QCA.

Department for Education and Employment (DfEE) (1997) *Excellence in Schools*, London: DfEE.

Durkheim, E. (1961) *Moral Education*, Glencoe: The Free Press.

Filer, A. (1993) 'Classroom contexts of assessment in a primary school', Ph.D. thesis, University of the West of England.

Filer, A. and Pollard, A. (forthcoming) *The Social World of Pupil Assessment*, London: Cassell.

Gillborn, D. (1995) *Racism and Anti-racism in Real Schools*, Buckingham: Open University Press.

Green, A. (1997) *Education, Globalization and the Nation State*, Basingstoke: Macmillan Press.

James, A. and Prout, A. (eds) (1990) *Constructing and Reconstructing Childhood*, London: Falmer Press.

James, A., Jenks, C. and Prout, A. (1998) *Theorising Childhood*, Cambridge: Polity Press.

Jeffrey, B. and Woods, P. (1997) 'The relevance of creative teaching: pupil views', in Pollard, A., Thiessen, D. and Filer, A. (eds) (1997) *Children and Their Curriculum*, London: Falmer Press.

Jeffrey, B. and Woods, P. (1998) *Testing Teachers: The Effect of School Inspections on Primary Teachers*, London: Falmer Press.

Labour Party (1997) *New Labour: Because Britain Deserves Better*, election manifesto, London: Labour Party.

Ofsted (1994) *Handbook for the Inspection Schools: Part 2*, London: Ofsted.

Ofsted (1997) *The Annual Report of Her Majesty's Chief Inspector of Schools*, London: Ofsted.

Pollard, A. (1985) *The Social World of the Primary School*, London: Cassell.

Pollard, A. with Filer, A. (1996) *The Social World of Children's Learning*, London: Cassell.

Pollard, A. and Filer, A. (1999) *The Social World of Pupil Careers*, London: Cassell.

Pollard, A., Thiessen, D. and Filer, A. (eds) (1997) *Children and Their Curriculum*, London: Falmer Press.

Pring, R. (1984) *Personal and Social Education in the Curriculum*, London: Hodder and Stoughton.

Pring, R. (1988) 'Personal and social education in the primary school', in Lang, P. (ed.) *Thinking about Personal and Social Education in the Primary School*, Oxford: Blackwell.

Schultz, T. (1961) 'Investment in human capital', *American Economic Review*, **51**, pp. 1–17.

Vincent, C. and Tomlinson, S. (1997) 'Home–school relationships: the swarming of disciplinary mechanisms', *British Educational Research Journal*, **23**, 3, pp. 361–77.

Woods, P. (ed.) (1980) *Pupil Strategies*, London: Croom Helm.

Woods, P. (1983) *Sociology and the School: An Interactionist Viewpoint*, London: Routledge and Kegan Paul.

Woods, P. (1990) *The Happiest Days: How Pupils Cope with School*, London: Falmer Press.

Woods, P. (1995) *Creative Teaching in the Primary School*, Buckingham: Open University Press.

Woods, P. and Jeffrey, B. (1996) *Teachable Moments: The Art of Teaching in Primary School*, Buckingham: Open University Press.

World Bank (1995) *The World Bank Review*, Washington, DC: World Bank.

10 Looking Back at the Boys: Reflections on Issues of Gender in Classroom Data

Lynda Measor

In the early 1980s I worked on a piece of research with Peter Woods that resulted in the publication of a book entitled *Changing Schools: Pupil Perspectives on Transfer to a Comprehensive.* The study was framed in the qualitative paradigm and focused, as the title suggests, on pupils' experiences of moving from primary to secondary education (Measor and Woods, 1984). I am currently working on a piece of qualitative research that focuses on sex education programmes in schools, and the responses of adolescents to the programmes they were offered (Measor, Tiffin and Fry, 1996). The approach we adopted in the sex education study, which emphasizes the pupils' perceptions of what was significant in their experiences, owes much to Peter Woods' work. However, theoretical material that we have worked with in this research has encouraged me to look again at some of the data from the *Changing Schools* study.

Adolescent Cultures and Pupil Perspectives

In the introduction to this book, Martyn Hammersley draws our attention to the fact that an interest in pupil perspectives and adolescent cultures was an early and persistent theme in Peter Woods' work. There was a recognition 'that teachers and pupils are not solely, and in some cases not even primarily, concerned with the business of education – narrowly defined'. Almost two decades ago, Peter Woods argued that an understanding of pupils' experience of school was a significant and somewhat unknown area in educational research and he has made a major contribution to exploring it. The *Changing Schools* study reflected this intellectual commitment: the focus was on pupils rather than on teachers, and the central concern of the work was to understand more about pupils' reactions to and feelings about what schools provided for them, at a critical point in their life course. And, in the end, perhaps one of the major effects of this research was to point up the indissoluble connections between the pupils' transfer to the new school and their passage to adolescence. One of the aspects that Peter and I found most fascinating was the interplay between formal and informal cultures in the experiences and adaptations of the pupils as they changed schools.

We argued in 1984 that gender had a formative role in the informal cultures of pupils and was a key element in understanding the formal and informal status passages involved in the process of transition. It is the role of gender in the informal culture of adolescents that I want to concentrate on in this chapter. Since 1984 there has been considerable development in the field of gender studies, in both conceptual and theoretical terms, and those developments have interesting implications for the analysis of data. Qualitative methods imply producing what Woods called a 'rich tapestry of data' (Woods, 1986, p. 63), which is never entirely exhausted by analysis. It is interesting to attempt the re-analysis of that data in the light of new theoretical insights and advances in conceptual thinking. In this chapter, I want to explore some of those issues, and pursue that exercise.

Of course, I do not want to suggest that gender is the only significant factor operating in the schools we studied. Qualitative research has opened our understanding to the wide range of processes that influence inter- actions in classrooms and staffrooms. I do not wish to underplay the interactionist sensitivity to heterogeneity within pupil groups, and to the subtle shifts that variations in context can bring to pupil cultures. Gender and sexuality, which are foregrounded here, are only two of the factors that significantly affect what is going on. They have, however, been neglected aspects of the adolescent world of school, and an analysis of their signifi- cance has real insights to offer.

Gender

The preoccupations of feminist research in the early 1980s involved explor- ing the position of women, and making clear the domination and injustice that operated in their lives. The primary focus in feminist work on educa- tion was on girls, and on documenting the details of the oppression to which they were exposed in school. The girls' powerlessness, in relation to both boys and schools, was of primary interest.

Perhaps the major shift since 1984 concerns the focus on 'gender' as a category, and on relationships between the genders, which has resulted from developments in postmodernist and post-structuralist work. One result of this is that academic research has come to consider masculinities much more carefully than was the case in the earlier work of feminist academics (Griffin and Lees, 1997; Mac an Ghaill, 1994).

It is important to note that significant controversy surrounds these developments. Feminists have argued vociferously about the implications for both understanding and political action that the new intellectual per- spectives hold, and such developments have not gone unquestioned or unchallenged (Jackson, 1992; Ramazanoglu, 1993). Critics have argued that the new focus de-politicizes the issue of gender and draws attention away from the continued injustices faced by women. So the activity of studying masculinities is, it seems, a somewhat fraught task, especially for feminists. But it is nonetheless one that, I want to argue, holds some important insights into the kinds of inequalities that women and girls in schools continue to face.

The new theoretical perspectives emphasize gender as difference, and explore the ways that gender, femininities and masculinities are 'done' in schools and classrooms (Griffin and Lees, 1997, p. 6). By documenting the quotidian details of classroom life, I hope to develop understanding of the 'routine of repeated social actions on a daily basis' that is so powerful in 'reinforcing structures of society and recreating uniform gendered behaviour' (Giddens, 1991, pp. 61–3). The task is to locate the work within both feminist academic preoccupations and the commitments of qualitative research, but to take advantage of some of the new theoretical insights.

Gender Theory

There are theoretical issues in what has just been said about gender that require exploration of what we mean by the concept, and that are central to interpretations of the data presented later in this paper. The starting point is the feminist one, which argues for the difference between sex and gender, and asserts that gender is not simply biologically given or immutable. The argument is controversial, centring on the amount of influence biology has upon gender. Here the position taken is that gender is not solely or simply based on 'natural' differences between the sexes; biological differences are mediated in complicated and powerful ways by influential social processes. Gender is socially constructed as 'two binary categories, hierarchically arranged in relation to each other' (Davies, 1997, p. 11). Furthermore, 'the creation of this binary model is not the result of observation of natural pairs which exist in the world. Rather it is a way of seeing built round an unquestioned assumption of opposition and difference' (*ibid.*, p. 9).

Gender is socially constructed, but it is important to note, though 'The social patterns which construct gender relations do not express natural patterns, neither do they ignore them' (Connell, 1987, p. 80). A structure of symbol and interpretation is woven around natural differences, which can exaggerate or distort them and which count as 'a social transformation of these differences' (*ibid.*, p. 81). The way this symbol and interpretation is selected and employed to weave and construct gender is the main focus of this chapter.

Chodorow's (1971) and Horney's (1932) work, and some of the new material on discourse relating to this topic, are particularly significant in identifying the social patterns involved. Chodorow's work on gender categories is illuminating for our understanding of the way individuals use symbolic resources to signal and express the 'binary divide' in daily life. Horney and Chodorow suggest that a society places items, objects, styles, behaviours and values into categories that are gendered and read in a culture as masculine or feminine. The individual selects from among these 'sets of culturally available, recognised and legitimated themes', which are more or less identified with a specific gender in a particular society. These culturally legitimated ways of living and behaving that signify gender, enable us to 'do' masculinity or femininity. Work that deals with gender, language and discourse has extended our understanding of the processes involved through the concept of 'storylines' relating to gender, and by tracing 'discursive patterns which our culture makes available to us shape us as beings within the two sex model' (Davies, 1997, p. 11). The individual chooses and uses items, styles, storylines and language that signify masculinity or femininity and avoids those that do not signify the appropriate gender.

This approach avoids a determinist view that sees sex roles imposed upon passive individuals. Instead, it emphasizes the notion of individuals as active participants in negotiating a package of gender identity out of the fragments of cultural material they are exposed to. Both symbolic interactionism and some strands within postmodernist thinking suggest that there are in the late twentieth century a series of coexisting versions of gender and sexuality, and that the individual shifts between them. This may not be conscious, or static, and we need to be aware of the flexibility of self, 'negotiated over a whole range of situations' (Morgan, 1992, p. 47). While we want to avoid a view that sees the individual as 'mechanically positioned by the discourses it hears' (Henriques et al., 1984, p. 238), I want to argue that it is important to recognize the power dimensions that configure our choices: 'We confirm ourselves as masculine or feminine in frames of reference which are socially produced and socially regulated' (*ibid.*, p. 241). There are consequences for us from the choice of models we adopt.

This approach also draws attention to the fact that assembling and achieving a gender identity requires that it be communicated to the social world. Morgan writes about the way that gender can be understood as part of a 'Goffmanesque presentation of self' (Morgan, 1992, p. 47). By focusing on the aspects of performance and activity in daily life we can see more about the way that gender, and in this paper masculinity in particular, is 'done'. The way that symbol and interpretation are employed to weave, display and make bids for masculinity and femininity is my main concern.

It is important to make it clear that this process is not a smooth and unproblematic one for succeeding generations of adolescents (Jefferson, 1994, p. 13). Chodorow contends that it is more difficult for boys than it is for girls. The presentation of self that Morgan identifies involves a number of performance aspects that he suggests are troublesome. As Norman Mailer evocatively put it, 'Masculinity is not something given to you, or something you are born with, but something you gain and you gain it by winning small battles with honour' (Mailer, cited in Morgan, 1992). Chodorow suggests that this gives an urgency to social processes for boys, who come to dread association with anything feminine, and act to create distance between it and themselves. Their subjectivity is to be marked as different from and oppositional to that which is associated with the feminine.

However it is important to draw attention to the point that has been basic to the whole feminist project: that 'Masculinity, in all its various forms, is not the same as femininity – it is after all a form of *power* and *privilege*' (Arnot, 1984, p. 53). As Davies comments, 'The binary male–female, coincides with the binary powerful and powerless' (Davies, 1997, p. 11). At a general level this is true, but postmodernist work does force us to give new attention to what this really means. Foucault insists that we look carefully at the ways power threads through our society, and implies that we must recognize that power is only the capacity to do particular sorts of things. Its distribution is a complex matter, and we need to explore not only what powers and privileges are bestowed by masculinity, but also the particular forms of powerlessness that it confers, in relation to other men as well as women. Symbolic interactionism is useful in enabling us to look at the configurations of powerful and powerless in given social situations and to examine the social forces that are at work. It allows us to look at the operation of power in particular circumstances and gain a better purchase on the specifics of how power operates, and fails to operate. Connell (1987) draws our attention to the fact that not all men or adolescent boys have the same relations to power, in connection with either women or other men. Theories of patriarchy make it clear that men have power over women, but they also have power over other men. Connell's work on hegemonic and subordinated masculinities alerts us to the fact that some men have greater entitlement to power and access to resources than others. Though structural factors of class and ethnicity undoubtedly position some men more advantageously than others, nevertheless establishing those hierarchies of masculinities is a lifetime project that repeats the making and remaking of identity on a daily basis.

Masculinities and Pupils in School

Without doubt, some of the concepts and insights that have been developed in this field can be of use here in relation to the micro data I will discuss. What I am suggesting is that pupils actively use aspects of school life as some of the symbolic resources Chodorow identified as being important in constructing their gender identity and their place in the hierarchy. Schools and classrooms are places where pupils and their teachers do a great deal of cultural work on the construction of identity. Connell and Mac an Ghaill have focused on the production of masculinity there (Connell, 1987; Mac an Ghaill, 1994). They argue that in order to be seen and defined by others as properly masculine, boys have to behave in particular ways. And Morgan (1992) has commented on how specific behaviours operate to 'elaborate particular masculine themes'. Others have made the same point: 'At this stage of Western history, hegemonic masculinity mobilises around physical strength, adventurousness, emotional neutrality, certainty, control, assertiveness, self reliance, individuality, competitiveness, instrumental skills, public knowledge, discipline, reason, objectivity and rationality' (Kenway and Fitzclarence, 1997, p. 121).

In this chapter I discuss the actions of boys in classrooms in the *Changing Schools* research in relation to these blueprints for masculinity. I argue that there are a number of arenas and aspects of school life in which these symbolic attributes are worked out, and a number of critical places in which the symbolic messages about gender identification are transmitted. The curriculum clearly has a crucial role to play, and in 1984 we identified and documented the way young adolescents of both sexes used the curriculum to demonstrate gender identity for themselves. The curriculum is not the only issue, however. Other areas of school life are also important. It is clear that the rules by which boys relate to girls in the school setting also have significant social meaning in terms of gender development, and category marking. However, Connell's work in particular has also drawn our attention to the way boys behave to each other as having specific importance for their positioning in a kind of hierarchy of masculinities (Connell, 1987). I will look briefly at the material on the curriculum and teachers that we presented in the *Changing Schools* work; though since this was the area that we devoted most attention to in 1984, it is the other two aspects of school social experience that I will concentrate most on here.

Masculinity and Curriculum

Both boys and girls in the *Changing Schools* research used aspects of the school curriculum to make and signal decisions they had made about their gender identity. This was shown most clearly in their responses to the domestic and physical sciences. Girls made it clear they were uncomfortable in physics and chemistry, although less so in biology, while boys reacted very negatively to the domestic sciences. It is of course important to note that there were differences in reaction to the sciences between individual girls and boys. It is too simple to suggest that all girls and all boys respond in an identical fashion. Some girls were interested in the physical sciences, but here as elsewhere they were in a tiny minority, as we would expect from other research (Kelly, 1981). Boys objected very strongly to one aspect of the design and technology curriculum to which they were exposed. Most of the technology curriculum involved the use of wood, metal or plastic, but one set of lessons involved the use of fabrics and both boys and girls were expected to take the subject. While the girls welcomed the subject and the training in equipment and skills, the boys displayed an absolute hostility to it. In this case it is possible to say that none of the boys expressed positive attitudes towards doing 'needlework', although the amount of active objection they displayed in lessons varied considerably of course (Measor and Woods, 1984).

The point needs to be made that there were, without doubt, factors other than gender that influenced pupil behaviour and activities. We suggested in the *Changing Schools* research that one of the major issues of identity for the pupils concerned their orientation to the school. We were critical of perspectives that categorized pupils as either deviant or conformist in their orientation. Instead, we suggested that in different situations different 'interests at hand' came into play, and pupils used 'knife edging' strategies to display both facets of identity. It was clearly the case that many pupils viewed the technology subjects as being of low status in the school. This meant that they offered an opportunity for a range of pupils to use this school time for the playing out of some of their informal culture concerns.

Masculinity and the Peer Group

One of the issues that gained most academic attention from qualitative researchers at the time of the *Changing Schools* research was friendship patterns among pupils (Davies, 1982; Furlong, 1976; Meyenn, 1980). Classroom observation during our research indicated the clear importance of friendship to pupils of both sexes, but also revealed considerable daily struggles over power, inclusion and friendship. There were some displays of masculine solidarity, but if we focus here on data collected from boys, then the struggles seemed to be an obsessively important part of their school life.

Connell points out that we need to ask about patterns of homophobic sociability and question what patterns of interaction exist between males. The boys seemed to be involved in frequent and significant contests for power and status, and appeared to be rehearsing and discovering their relative places *vis-à-vis* other boys, girls and teachers in what I described at the time as a status hierarchy. I suggest that Connell's work on hegemonic and subordinate masculinity, published in 1987, can throw some fresh insights onto this data and the analysis that was made of it at the time.

Connell's notion of hegemonic and subordinate masculinities draws our attention to the fact that patriarchy is 'about the dominance of men by men as well as the dominance of women by men' (Morgan, 1992, p. 196). The suggestion is that within any given society there is a range of different masculinities, and they are arranged in a hierarchy. In Connell's view heterosexual masculinity is prioritized in the hierarchy. There are, he suggests, ways of establishing and signalling those hierarchies symbolically and actually through various kinds of behaviour. There are real implications for power and privilege attached to the place in the hierarchy that the individual boy achieves in the school setting, and life for those who are allocated to the position of subordinate masculinity is frequently far from easy or pleasant. It is important to note that struggles for masculine status are played out on a daily basis. An individual may aim for hegemonic status but be denied it by his peers, and consistently try to change that status. There is a constant play between the status of masculinity ascribed to a boy, and the definition of masculinity that he accepts.

There were, it seemed, a number of ways of achieving high or hegemonic status within schools. The blueprint that Kenway and Fitzclarence (1997) establish is that to which those who aspire to hegemonic masculinity conform. In the next section of this chapter I look in detail at data from the *Changing Schools* research, with the aim of developing a more informed understanding of the social interactions that went on among boys within and between their friendship groups. It is important to note that status seemed largely to be won through performances that carried weight in the informal culture. The public exhibitions of opposition to teachers and excessive displays of resistance, making loud jokes, showing oneself un-responsive to the control of a woman, could all win status in an informal culture (see Measor and Woods, 1984, for a longer account of how these processes might work). Relationships with peers, however, are of key importance.

It is important again to emphasize that gender and sexuality are not the only important issues of concern to pupils in this situation. Other aspects of identity that we dealt with in greater detail are also important in shaping behaviour. In many of the situations described below the boys are in fact facing situations in which several different types of status hierarchy compete. They have to cope with the complex web of demands and rewards that operate, and as a result the boys are constantly juggling identity in complicated and rapidly shifting ways. Gender is, however, a neglected area of analysis in relation to data of this kind, and in this chapter (in part for reasons of space) I have tried to focus primarily on the role that it plays.

Macho Hierarchies

In the *Changing Schools* research we studied the first year cohort of a comprehensive school. We contacted pupils in one of the feeder primary schools and followed one class, almost 40 pupils, through their first year in secondary school. The primary school class was dispersed into about four classes in secondary school. They were mixed in those four classes, of course, with pupils from other primary schools, making a research group of about 120 pupils. Data is taken from that group.

We witnessed sharp and intense competition for status within groups of boys, and between groups of boys. Status could be won in a number of ways as boys 'did' gender by elaborating the masculine themes that Morgan identified. In the next section I aim to document some of the daily class-room behaviour involved in this activity, and to indicate the range of strategies including humour and sexual success. It is, however, important to take note of the not inconsiderable violence between boys. It seemed to be perhaps the most significant symbolic resource for 'doing masculinity'. Status for boys depended in the last resort on physical toughness and was signalled by the ability to fight, or by having the reputation of such ability. As Willis commented, 'it is the capacity to fight which settles the final pecking order. It is the not often tested ability to fight which valorises status based usually and interestingly on other grounds' (Willis, 1977, p. 30). He draws our attention to the significance of the physical struggles that go on between adolescent boys and indicates the place that violence appears to play there in deciding status. There were a number of different arenas in which such struggles for status went on. The first related to public fights in the school, others to tussles among boys within their friendship groups and between different friendship groups.

The Significance of Violence

On about three occasions during their first year at the comprehensive school, large-scale fights erupted among boys. On each occasion a series of fights occurred one after the other, and there was a kind of 'fights fever'. Some of the fights involved boys from the neighbouring and rival comprehensive school. There were rumours of axes, chains and other weapons being used. First year boys were involved in the early stages of these fights, although later on mostly older boys were involved. The boys whose own identities were largely invested in the informal culture of the school took a great interest in these events. Pete, Roy, Andrew, Keith and Jim had taken part in earlier rounds of this competition and had watched fights in the later stages and knew the results of them all. Status seemed to attach to taking part in the fights and certainly to gaining victory in them; but also it seemed to cling to those who had knowledge of the progress of the rounds of fights that took place.

Status Hierarchies within Friendship Groups

It was possible to discern a kind of status hierarchy within boys' friendship groups, which was based on strength and the willingness or ability to use violence. The first signs of this were displayed in verbal insults to each other, but rapidly developed among the boys into minor aggression, pushing, punching, shoving and taking pieces of equipment from each other, which were then hidden or passed around with a refusal to give it back. By the third week of term Philip had begun to act in this way. He asserted his right to use a piece of equipment out of turn. The other boys in his group fell back and allowed him to bid for this superior status. Roy aimed for the same role in another group. He would push Pete, Andrew and Jim around and specialized in taking chairs away from people as they were about to sit down. It led to Pete confessing in private, 'He do push people around does

Roy.' The demand for toughness and strength therefore applied within the group and a kind of hierarchy was established, status and power being based on physical strength, adroitness and size. Philip and Roy were both noticeably larger-than-average boys.

This kind of activity became increasingly frequent throughout the year in all friendship groups, although in some, leadership status was more contested. The allegation made by a number of researchers is that 'men are made to feel that they must earn their manhood by imposing their will on others, whether by violence or by economic means, perpetuating their superiority' (Tolson, 1977, p. 5). In Chodorow's terms, masculinity is resourced by the individual's ability to impose his will; and, in Connell's argument, hegemonic status is achieved by the individual who can do this. There is evidence of boys developing a process of differentiation between themselves as individuals, and testing out their ability to employ the range of behaviours that signal hegemonic masculinity. It is important to note that control was not the sole aspect of peer relations between boys. We have already said that there were some displays of solidarity among boys and between groups of boys, and friendship groups offered boys opportunities for humour, warmth and strategies for coping with the demands of a new school in a number of emotionally important ways. However, power, control and status within the group was a key aspect of their behaviour and activity at school, and must be emphasized.

Macho Hierarchies between Groups

A kind of status network based on toughness evolved within individual school classes. The pattern of one individual asserting his dominance within a friendship group continued during the first year at comprehensive school. We have described how Philip and Roy had some dominance over others in their friendship group. By February, however, another development had begun, as status hierarchies *between* groups and especially between the leaders of groups began to be tested and established. One day Keith borrowed a pencil from Philip 'without asking'. It clearly represented a challenge, and Philip acted decisively and aggressively. 'You didn't ask!' he bellowed, and 'You'd better do so.' He walked up to Keith and stood looking aggressively at him. Keith backed down, apologized and did not repeat the offence. Mark, a leader in his group, insulted Philip and pushed him. Philip responded decisively to the challenge and swung around and hit him very hard.

Roy had achieved dominance in his own group, and had a school-wide reputation for his success in the public fights we have described. He challenged Philip in a rather different way. He took Giles's eraser and cut it into two pieces with a Stanley knife that he was using in a craft lesson. Giles was part of Philip's friendship group and the latter clearly felt the challenge was directed at him. On other occasions when pupils teased Giles, Philip would intervene to protect him, telling pupils to 'Leave him alone' or 'Give that back.' On this occasion, however, Philip did not challenge Roy. He seemed to accept Roy's claims to greater toughness and ignored a challenge that he was perhaps not sure he would win. Throughout the school year reputations spread to larger and larger circles as identities were tried out. Competition among the boys established status patterns in terms of toughness between as well as within groups.

Some boys won the right to break a number of rules in the informal culture, as a result, perhaps, of their standing in the alternative status network we have called 'macho hierarchy'. One of the strongest rules was that, 'You don't copy.' Roy, however, would lean back and look at answers in Barry's book. Roy felt he was strong enough to insist on these rights for himself. Barry was unlikely to accuse someone as large and tough as Roy of 'copying'. Keith managed to establish a similar prerogative for himself with Erik. The criteria that gave certain boys this status were fairly clear; it is important to note that they involved toughness and not any academic prowess. Roy took answers from Barry, and Keith took answers from Erik, because these boys were known to get good marks in the subjects involved. Roy and Keith were beginning to reap advantages of their position in the class, and Barry and Erik were disadvantaged.

Geoffrey was, however, the best example of a pupil who was unable to use the symbolic resources of masculinity. He was known as a boy who was incapable of being tough. He could not finish the long-distance run, he could not fight, he was persecuted by others, and unable to fight back effectively. His reputation and his title of 'poufter' (gay) were known outside his own class. This had an impact on his alliances: he was isolated and other boys shunned him, he was categorized as the 'outsider' and ignored. The alternative roles of what Connell calls hegemonic and subordinate masculinity were established and recognized within this group of boys, and they had implications for behaviour and action on a daily basis. It is interesting to note that the status and the labels stuck to the boys involved, they were not easy to shake off, nor was it a simple matter to slip between identities in different spheres of life and activity.

The data indicates what failing to achieve hegemonic masculinity means, as well as giving insights into why the struggle is so ferocious among boys. The way this is experienced by boys may be a significant factor in their motivation to behave in this way. Davies points out that 'we should not underestimate the desirability and joyful sense of power that boys can gain from being positioned within dominant forms of discourse which hand them ascendancy over others' (Davies, 1997, p. 15).

I have suggested that violence and the capacity to impose their will on others is an important resource in the 'doing' of masculinity at this stage of early adolescence. And I have tried to show the ways in which violence was part of a range of male activity and experience in the lives of boys in their

first year of a comprehensive school. It is important to look now at some of
the other ways that the 'presentation' of a male self was conducted.

Joking and Teasing

Physical strength and ability was only one of the ways by which masculinity
was displayed: there were other strategies that could win status as a
'proper' male. Morgan has pointed out that being part of a group of males
will also 'provide the opportunity for the elaboration of particular masculine themes through horse play, trading insults, sexual references and mock
homosexual attacks' (Morgan, 1992, p. 92, citing Roy, 1960; Collinson and
Collinson, 1989). There was clear evidence of this kind of gender-based
activity among boys in lessons.

This activity frequently involved aspects of the formal culture of the
school. One way of gaining status within the peer group involved deviant
classroom behaviour, for example behaving outrageously, showing oneself
unresponsive to the control of at least some teachers, and challenging
teachers through rapid-fire joking behaviour. In *Changing Schools* we
devoted considerable attention to the jokes that boys told in classroom
settings. We noted that telling jokes loudly enough so the whole class could
hear and be amused and disturbed by them was primarily a male activity.
We interpreted this activity in a number of ways. It is clearly one of the
situations where several identity issues loom for pupils and several status
hierarchies overlap. We suggested in the book that joke-telling was a way
that pupils avoided boredom in the routine of schools, and also it was a
way of displaying the identity of a deviant: 'Jokes became a popular centre-
stage challenge. Boys learned to inject them into the flow of classroom
discourse. The joke is an astringent weapon for pupil resistance' (Measor
and Woods, 1984, p. 110). However, it is possible to see the jokes also as a
powerful tool in the arsenal of masculinity, indicating a boy's refusal to
passively accept the control of another over him. Also on display was his
ability to demonstrate the centrality of his own adolescent male concerns in
the world through quick responses that allow him to outwit others and
indicate his skills and knowledge of what is expected of him.

It is impossible for reasons of space to give the full flavour of the classroom
jokes. I can only give a few examples. Jokes caused great amusement. On the
occasion described below I suspect the joke-teller aimed to embarrass female
teachers. In the fabrics lesson we referred to earlier a teacher said:

T: Make a knot in the end of that string.
Sean: How do you get knotted miss?

(Measor and Woods, 1984, p. 113)

The use of a term like 'get knotted' is an intrusion of vernacular into a
formal classroom setting and perhaps aimed to confound adult profes-

sionals. Kehily and Nayak talk about the way young boys employ 'acts of transgression', as part of the work of visibly conveying masculine identity. Language is one of the major tactics of 'transgression' and is used as a strategy to invert 'the rules of adult middle class society', and to 'violate social norms' (Kehily and Nayak, 1997, p. 73). These authors suggest that young men celebrate 'vulgarity' in schools and use language for its shock value: this transgression is treasured as a means of displaying masculinity and elaborating one of its themes.

Other joking behaviour we witnessed seemed to be intended to bid for control over a classroom setting:

> A teacher explained a mathematical theory. She explained it very thoroughly and it meant she occupied the centre stage for a long time. She finished brightly:
>
> *T:*   So you could go on doing the square of numbers for ever and ever and ever.
> *David:* Amen.
>
> His timing was perfect and the class collapsed into sustained laughter, after which it was difficult for the teacher to restore the situation.
>
> (Measor and Woods, 1984, p. 112)

The boy shouted the joke loudly in the classroom, and it was sufficiently amusing to the rest of the class so that the teacher's control of the pace of teaching was disturbed and she could not carry on with what she wanted to say. Research like that of Hargreaves (1967) and Willis (1977) has suggested that disorganizing classroom processes is one of the objectives that at least some boys have in the classroom. Their research was more directly concerned with social class than with masculinity, but their data can be reinterpreted to offer insight into gender issues too. Hargreaves and a long list of other researchers have been interested to understand some of the processes of identity construction taking place here, and have seen this kind of activity as crucial in establishing individual pupils' basic orientation to school. However, there are other dimensions that they did not consider. Arnot suggests that proving masculinity 'may require frequent rehearsals of toughness, the exploitation of women and quick aggressive responses' (Arnot, 1984, p. 46). Much of the boys' behaviour fits this blueprint, and can be understood as the public performance of masculine themes. It is also interesting that much of the research celebrated and valorized the boys' behaviour in terms of resistance to social class oppression. A feminist approach throws a more negative light on what is going on, and indicates that we need to ask searching questions about the processes by which masculine identities develop and their implications for the construction of male power and patriarchy. These no doubt inter-weave with social class in complex patterns.

The horseplay and the teasing in the lessons may represent one arena where competition for status within groups of boys, and between groups of boys, is played out. Kehily and Nayak (1997) have developed an analysis of humour and masculinity that is of direct relevance here. They suggest that it represents a discursive practice that plays a significant part in consolidating male peer group cultures in secondary schools. It has a role in organizing, regulating and policing heterosexual masculinities, within pupils' informal culture (Arnot, 1984, p. 48). Humorous exchanges between groups of pupils or between pupils and teachers represent a 'public performance of mas-culinity'. They suggest that boys who are the 'most skilled at employing sophisticated insults had higher status in the group' (Kehily and Nayak, 1997, p. 73). The verbal sparring creates winners and losers in the competi-tion and exposes some boys as vulnerable while others establish reputations as 'hard'.

Masculinity and Girls

It is important to note that status could be won through relationships with girls, as well as with other boys. For some boys at least this was a significant source of status. In *Changing Schools* it was noted that 'within the boys' informal culture status was to be achieved through taking out either a large number of girls or a small number of very attractive girls' (Measor and Woods, 1984, p. 24). Claims for sexual knowledge and expertise, when they were substantiated, had a role in winning a place at the top of the status hierarchy. Some of the boys who were leaders in their group, such as Roy and Keith, were seen to be successful with girls. Roy, in particular, was noted for having taken out 'loads of girls who everybody "fancies"'. By contrast, Geoffrey who had low status in the informal culture, was completely unsuccessful with girls. Indeed the girls taunted him as mer-cilessly as the boys did.

Masculinity can be asserted by expressing power over a woman. While power can be declared in a variety of arenas, nevertheless sexual encounters are one of the most significant. On the basis of empirical research on adolescents, Lees asserts 'It is against women's sexuality that men are motivated to measure their masculinity, and because they must prove this at each such encounter their masculinity never rests assured. It is through their sexuality that men are expected to prove themselves' (Lees, 1986, p. 132).

Sexual Harassment

However, sexual relationships were only one way of behaving that could win status. In the data collection I became aware that harassment and denigration were also important. Other researchers have also found this. Connell (1987) suggests that one of the most significant ways of establishing hierarchies of masculinity is through sexual and other types of harassment. Wood argues that learning to be masculine invariably entails learning to be sexist: being a bit of a lad and being contemptuous of women went naturally together (1984, p. 31). It may also be the case that this way of treating girls is essential to the performance of a 'proper male'. It is difficult, for reasons of space, to include sufficient data to support the analysis that is being made here. But the picture of boys treating girls with disrespect and contempt, seeing them as a source of amusement and entertainment and asserting control over them is familiar from twenty years of feminist research on classrooms, and I will offer only a few examples from the *Changing Schools* data here. There were examples of physical harassment similar to those which researchers like Jones (1985) and Halson (1989) have documented in detail. Boys did touch girls in ways and at times that they did not like, they flicked skirts and straps and pulled ties:

> Amy was walking up the stairs. Alan continually touches her. He touches her on the back of the shoulders and then moves rapidly away before she could hit back. She says to the researcher, 'He is really mithering me'.
>
> (Measor and Woods, 1984, p. 104)

Girls particularly detested Physical Education lessons for the opportunities it gave the boys to tease them:

> Jenny: 'You have to do PE in the hall in shorts, all up on the climbing frame and that. The boys really take the mickey. They all come up and start whistling and that.'
>
> (Measor, 1989, p. 49)

The boys in the *Changing Schools* research attacked girls as 'tarts and slags', a process that Lees (1986) has analysed in detail as involving labelling and policing girls and their sexuality. Some of the jokes we have referred to were directed against girls, and boys were willing to put girls firmly in the place they believed girls should occupy.

Lees returns to Chodorow's analysis to explain this pattern of behaviour from pupils and sees it as part of the category-maintenance work already discussed. 'In adolescence a pattern of male behaviour toward female sexuality evolves. To develop a masculine identity young men need to disassociate themselves from all that is feminine. Boys need to denigrate girls in order to dominate them' (Lees, 1986, p. 301). We can argue that men need women to act as a contrast to themselves and their own activities – they stand defined as masculine in a sharper silhouette against women.

The differences between them underline the meaning of masculinity for men and femininity for women:

> A sense of being a man or less than a man came to the fore in relation to women. What it feels like to be a man can only be fully answered in the context of gender encounters where sexual or gender difference is accented.
>
> (Morgan, 1992, p. 202)

Conclusion

I have argued that the data from the *Changing Schools* project reveals boys and girls acting in accordance with gender codes to which they were attached. We can discern a picture of traditional versions of what it means to be a 'proper' boy or girl through their reactions to the curriculum and to one another. The data needs to be 'understood within a larger social context of reputations, face and relative social status' (Daly and Wilson, 1988, p. 128). I suggest that at this phase in their life cycle, boys and girls are particularly concerned with carving out a valued gender identity. They are, of course, interested in other aspects of identity as well, and *Changing Schools* looked at the range of 'interests at hand' that pupils attempted to juggle. Here I emphasize an area that was neglected in 1984.

The *Changing Schools* fieldwork was completed in 1981 and it is pertinent to ask whether there has been any change in the cultural stereotypes and the behaviour of boys. Giddens (1992) has written hopefully in recent years about the potential for 'the transformation of intimacy'. In other research just completed (Measor and Squires, 1997) there was some evidence of change in middle-class boys' attitudes in the Brighton area. However, signs of change are not widespread, as recent work by Holland and Ramazanoglu (1998) indicates; and there is still clear evidence of 'the toughness and resilience of sexist stereotypes' (Connell, 1987, p. xi).

The data presented here and my analysis of it offers a negative picture of the way adolescent boys behave in schools and classrooms; and when girls are interviewed about the way boys relate to them there is a long catalogue of bitter complaints (Holland and Ramazanoglu, 1998; Jones, 1985; Lees, 1986). However, it is important to acknowledge that we cannot simply condemn male children for their behaviour; as a society we encourage boys to be both aggressive and assertive and by condemning their behaviour and sympathizing with girls we run the risk of simply reinforcing that discourse and failing to view analytically the pressure on all children. Though the assignment of blame is perhaps not part of the analytical task, nevertheless it is important that we look not just at how boys 'do masculinity', but also at the social processes that inform and constrain the choices they make.

Acknowledgments

I would like to thank Martyn Hammersley for his very valuable contribution to an earlier draft of this paper and also the University of Brighton for the funding that made the sex education research possible.

References

Arnot, M. (1984) 'How shall we educate our sons?', in Deem, R. (ed.) *Co-education Reconsidered*, Milton Keynes: Open University Press.

Chodorow, N. (1971) 'Being and doing: a cross cultural examination of the socialisation of males and females', in Gornick, V. and Noran, B.K. (eds) *Women in Sexist Society*, Berkeley, CA: University of California Press.

Collinson, D. L. and Collinson, M. (1989) 'Sexuality in the workplace: the domination of men's sexuality', in Hearn, J., Sheppard, D.L. et al. (eds) *The Sexuality of Organisations*, London: Sage.

Connell, R.W. (1987) *Gender and Power*, Cambridge: Polity Press.

Daly, M. and Wilson, M. (1988) *Homicide*, Aldine de Gruyter.

Davies, B. (1982) *Life in the Classroom and Playground: The Accounts of Primary School Children*, London: Routledge and Kegan Paul.

Davies, B. (1997) 'Constructing and deconstructing masculinities through critical literacy', *Gender and Education*, **9**, 1, pp. 69–87.

Delamont, S. (1990) *Sex Roles and the School*, London: Cassell.

Furlong, J. (1976) 'Interaction sets in the classroom', in Hammersley, M. and Woods, P. (eds) *The Process of Schooling*, London: Routledge and Kegan Paul.

Giddens, A. (1991) *Modernity and Self-identity*, London: Polity Press.

Giddens, A. (1992) *The Transformation of Intimacy*, London: Polity Press.

Griffin, C. and Lees, S. (1997) 'Editorial', *Masculinities in Education*, Special Issue, *Gender and Education*, **9**, 1, March, pp. 5–8.

Halson, J. (1989) 'The sexual harassment of young women', in Holly, L. (ed.) *Girls and Sexuality: Teaching and Learning*, Milton Keynes: Open University Press

Hargreaves, D. (1967) *Social Relations in a Secondary School,* London: Routledge and Kegan Paul.

Henriques, J. et al. (1984) *Changing the Subject*, London: Methuen.

Holland, J. and Ramazanoglu, C. (1998) *The Male in the Head*, London: Tufnell Press.

Horney, K. (1932) 'The dread of women', *International Journal of Psychoanalysis*, **13**, pp. 324–39.

Jackson, S. (1992) 'Amazing deconstructing woman', in *Trouble and Strife*, Winter, **55**, pp. 41–59.

Jefferson, T. (1994) 'Theorising masculine subjectivity', in Stanko, E. et al. (eds) *Just Boys Doing Business*, London: Routledge.

Jones, C. (1985) 'Sexual tyranny in mixed-sex schools: an in-depth study of male violence', in Weiner, G. (ed.) *Just a Bunch of Girls*, Buckingham: Open University Press.

Kehily, M.J. and Nayak, A. (1997) '"Lads and Laughter": humour and the production of heterosexual hierarchies', *Gender and Education*, **9**, 1, pp. 69–87.

Kelly, A. (ed.) (1981) *The Missing Half*, Manchester: Manchester University Press.

Kenway, J. and Fitzclarence, L. (1997) 'Masculinity, violence and schooling: challenging "poisonous pedagogies"', in *Gender and Education*, **9**, 1, pp. 117–33.

Lees, S. (1986) *Losing Out*, London: Heinemann.

Mac an Ghaill, M. (1994) *The Making of Men: Masculinities, Sexualities and Schooling*, Buckingham: Open University Press.

Measor, L. (1989) 'Are you coming to see some dirty films today? Sex education and adolescent sexuality', in Holly, L. (ed.) *Girls and Sexuality: Teaching and Learning*, Milton Keynes: Open University Press.

Measor, L. and Squires, P. (1997) *Juvenile Nuisance*, University of Brighton: HSPRC.

Measor, L. and Woods, P. (1984) *Changing Schools*, Milton Keynes: Open University Press.,

Measor, L., Tiffin, C. and Fry, K. (1996) 'Gender and sex education: a study of adolescent responses', *Gender and Education*, **8**, 3 Oct., pp. 275–89.

Meyenn, G. (1980) 'School girls' peer groups', in Woods, P. (ed.) *Pupil Strategies*, London: Croom Helm.

Morgan, D. (1992) *Discovering Men*, London: Routledge.

Ramazanoglu, C. (1993) *Up Against Foucault: Explorations of Some Tensions Between Foucault and Feminism*, London: Routledge.

Roy, D.F. (1960) 'Banana time: job satisfaction and informal interaction', *Human Organisation*, **18**, pp. 156–68.

Tolson, A. (1977) *The Limits of Masculinity*, London: Tavistock.

Willis, P. (1977) *Learning to Labour*, Farnborough: Saxon House.

Wood, J. (1984) 'Groping towards sexism: boys' sex talk', in McRobbie, A. and Nava, M. (eds) *Gender and Generation*, Basingstoke: Macmillan.

Woods, P. (1986) *Inside Schools*, London: Routledge.

11 Critical Incidents and Learning about Risks: The Case of Young People and Their Health

Martyn Denscombe

Peter Woods has demonstrated that the process of teaching and learning is significantly influenced by both 'critical *events*' and 'critical *incidents*' (Sikes, Measor and Woods, 1985; Woods, 1993). The distinction between the two is that critical events take the shape of planned occasions, such as the production of a drama or a school visit. These events are consciously orchestrated over a period of time; they are intentional and planned. Critical incidents, by contrast, are characteristically 'unplanned, unanticipated and uncontrolled. They are flash-points that illuminate in an electrifying instant' (Woods, 1993, p. 1).

Despite their differences, the two concepts share much in common in regard to the process of learning. First, they both focus on 'highly charged moments and episodes that have enormous consequences for personal change and development' (Sikes et al., 1985, p. 230). They place emphasis on the role of particular occasions in shaping the way people understand their world, rather than treating the learning process as a steady accumulation of knowledge or experience at an even pace. Attitudes and behaviours, from this perspective, are not shaped by a uniform process of socialization but by a sequence of 'high-spots'. Second, the two concepts share a focus on learning through personal experience and through real-world events. Critical incidents and critical events are based on things that actually happen, planned or otherwise. They are neither hypothetical nor abstract. In this sense, they tend to accord with a learning theory that stresses the importance of 'collecting first-hand evidence and material, on doing things oneself, on having a realistic aim. As in research, this heightens the validity of the output. Learning is integrated into the self' (Woods, 1993, p. 4).

Critical incidents, then, might be expected to promote learning in a rather special way, and the purpose of this chapter will be to explore this potential in relation to one specific area: young people's attitudes to taking risks with their health. The study of critical incidents might provide some insight into the way young people develop their attitudes to risk-taking and health. Equally, it might provide a valuable resource in health educators' effort to make young people aware of the dangers associated with health-risk behaviours such as smoking tobacco, drinking alcohol and substance abuse. Either possibility, however, begs the question, 'Do critical incidents actually have an impact on young people's attitudes to taking risks with their health; and, if so, how do they do it?' The purpose of this chapter is to explore this issue.[1]

Health-risking Behaviour and Critical Incidents

Young people seem to be prepared to take risks with their health in a way that defies the logic of health education messages. Though the messages are clear and plentiful, young people seem reluctant to 'learn the lesson'. By the age of 15–16 years, over a quarter of young people in Britain are regular smokers, a similar proportion drink regularly, and a sizeable minority use soft drugs like cannabis (Balding, 1993; Furlong and Cartmel, 1997; Measham, Newcombe and Parker, 1994; Plant and Plant, 1992). Despite health promotion campaigns, despite health education in schools, these young people persist in taking risks with their health.

This has proved to be an intractable problem from the point of view of teachers, health educators and the youth service. Time and again it has been shown that programmes designed to alert young people to the dangers of substance abuse have not been very effective (Lloyd and Lucas, 1998; Lynagh, Schofield and Sanson-Fisher, 1997; May, 1991; Tones, 1993; White and Pitts, 1997). It is not that young people are not exposed to the information. Nor is it that they do not understand the key points that are being put across. The problem is that, despite being aware of the dangers, they go ahead and do it anyway.

The apparent reluctance to learn the lesson of health education owes something to the fact that young people tend to operate with an exaggerated sense of immunity when it comes to risk-taking activity (Elkind, 1967; Jack, 1989). More than at other stages of life, there is a tendency for them to believe that 'it won't happen to me'. However, research on the perception of risk also points to the existence of certain factors that might be expected to weigh against the feeling of 'invulnerability' by *heightening* young people's sensitivity to risks (Denscombe, 1993; Douglas, 1986; Johnson and Covello, 1987). Experience of such events or situations serves to make the risk seem more likely to happen and/or to make people more conscious of the extent to which they personally might be vulnerable to the risk.

The kinds of things that heighten sensitivity to risk broadly comprise two categories – those that contribute to the '*dread factor*' and those that contribute to the '*vividness factor*' (Kahneman, Slovic and Tversky, 1982; Slovic, Fischoff and Lichtenstein, 1980, 1981). The dread factor concerns the depth of fear caused by a risk. It is influenced by a number of variables but, arguably, the primary one is the extent to which people feel *personally vulnerable* to the risk. Where they feel personally vulnerable to a risk it arouses passion, it causes worry, it increases their fear and sense of horror about the risk outcome. The *vividness* of the risk, on the other hand, has a bearing on people's perceptions of how likely it is that a risk outcome will actually happen. Vividness tends to heighten people's awareness of the risk and tends to make them more conscious of its consequences. A risk that is vivid tends to be more easily recalled, easily visualized and clearly imagined. The more people have the risk brought to their attention, for instance through media coverage, and the more dramatically the risk is presented, the easier it becomes to think of the consequences and regard them as a likely possibility (Combs and Slovic, 1979; Thaler 1983).

On the basis of these two factors – dread and vividness – it is reasonable to suppose that where someone has a personal experience of the nasty outcome associated with a given risk, then there is likely to be a heightened sensitivity to that risk. If people know of the dangers at first hand – if they personally have suffered or have close knowledge of someone else who has suffered – the risk is likely to become more real and foreboding for them. The experience might also serve to confront the individual with his or her own mortality and thereby undermine any false sense of invulnerability. To have some loved one – close friend or close family – fall seriously ill or suffer a serious accident or die, whatever the cause, might be expected to bring home to a (young) person the fact that personal health is not something that should be taken for granted. Such an experience would have the constituent features of a *critical incident*,[2] affecting attitudes to personal health through:

- *vivid*, highly-charged moments;
- based on specific *real-world* occurrences (rather than vague and general dispositions); and
- involving things with which those concerned have some *personal experience*.

A Study of Critical Incidents

The proposition that critical incidents in the lives of young people might shape their attitudes to health-risking behaviour has been investigated as part of ongoing research into young people's perceptions of risk. Between January and March 1997 a questionnaire survey of young people aged 15 to 16 years was undertaken in 12 schools in Leicestershire and Rutland – counties in the East Midlands of England. The schools were selected to be representative in terms of their catchment area (social class, ethnic composition, urban/suburban/rural). The questionnaire was distributed to half of the cohort of the Year 11 pupils in the schools via mixed-ability tutor groups. From the 1679 young people who took part in the survey, 1648 usable questionnaires were returned. The questionnaire included items on young people's alcohol and tobacco consumption, attitudes to their own bodies, and perceptions of risks related to health. The survey was followed up with focus groups conducted with a sub-sample of the 15–16-year-olds (n = 123). Two groups, each comprising five or six young people, were used from 11 of the schools (one of the original schools did not take part in this phase of the investigation). Finally, a series of in-depth interviews was conducted with young people from five of the schools in the research (n = 20).

To explore the effect of critical incidents on their willingness to engage in health-risking behaviour, the young people taking part in the survey were asked about any:

- first-hand experience of a serious accident or injury, or
- personal experience of a serious illness or a medical condition affecting their well-being.

They were also asked about any experience they had involving:

- the death of a close friend or someone in the close family, or
- a serious accident or illness affecting someone close to them.

They were asked to recall only situations that had happened since they were aged 10. This restriction on the time period was designed to eliminate from the research those childhood illnesses such as chickenpox and measles which, in the context of contemporary Britain, tend to be rather routine and mundane. Restricting the period to the previous five or six years also placed a reasonable time frame on what it was possible to remember with any clarity, and limited incidents to those that were likely to have had any substantial influence on their developing attitudes to health risks.

Young People Speak about Critical Incidents

The questionnaire survey suggested that most young people had some experience of a serious health-related incident (to themselves, family or a close friend). Responses from the survey revealed that only 12 per cent of the young people had *not* had that experience. Just one in eight, that is, reported that they had suffered no accidents or illness since they were 10 years of age, or had not had someone close to them die or suffer a serious accident or illness. The vast majority, though, had confronted some incident since the age of 10 that had involved some kind of situation which, in principle, might be expected to have had a marked impact on their thinking in relation to health.

There was some evidence from the focus group discussions and interviews that the experience of such incidents could, indeed, have the expected powerful influence on the young people's attitudes to taking risks with their health. For example, one girl described how she had fallen off her pony and suffered considerable bruising as a result:

Sarah: When I got home I thought – what if I had never been able to walk again. And it really freaked me out. Now I don't like jumping. It scares me to think how easily it could happen – I could have been in a wheelchair. (Focus group of four boys and three girls, 15–16 years, white, school 09, 19.3.97)

Falling from ponies, it has to be acknowledged, has not featured prominently in the concerns of health education. But, when it came to the more conventional concerns – such as substance use – other examples illustrated the potential of vivid and horrible realities to act as critical incidents. Frequently, though, the incident revolved around something that had happened to another person. During a focus group an example of this arose in connection with a teacher at the young people's school:

Sajid: We saw this video at school.
Sameena: In tutorial wasn't it?
Sajid: This man lost all his limbs, his legs. He couldn't live without smoking, so they used to get this cigarette and put it through his neck.
Haroon: There's even this teacher in our school. She was a really hard smoker, and unfortunately she lost . . .
Reena: . . . first it was her toe she had to have amputated . . .
Haroon: . . . and now it's part of her leg.
Interviewer: Here? In this school?
Haroon: Yes. She's still working.
Interviewer: Does she ever talk to you about smoking?
Sameena: Yes, she came round once.
Haroon: I think it's good that someone in this school has actually been affected because at least we learn. (Focus group of two girls and four boys, 15–16 years, two Hindus and four Muslims, school 01, 18.11.97)

The young people, here, seemed to have been influenced by the vivid outcome of the risk, coupled with the fact that the risk was brought close to home through the presence of the teacher in the school who had suffered the amputations.

The impact of situations that affect those close to the individual was evident on many occasions when young people referred to things that had happened to members of their family. When someone in the family was affected as a result of smoking, it hit close to home with a message about the risks involved – and this could serve as an effective deterrent:

Emma: My step-granddad died of some illness that he got because he had smoked all his life. So I found that very upsetting, and it put me off smoking.

Laura: Same with me. My granddad died of lung cancer, and we all just had to watch him die and it was really awful. (Shudders) So I'm never going to smoke. (Focus group of three girls and two boys, 15–16 years, white, school 04, 5.2.98)

Or again,

Guy: Well one of my brother's best friends – his mum smoked a lot and she had a leg amputated.

Interviewer: And do you think that really affected you in terms of your decision (not to smoke)?

Guy: Yes, and also my mum. This is why I want her to give up. She sometimes will wake up in the middle of the night, she says, and she can't breathe. And she's had bronchitis, and she said 'I'm never going to smoke again.' And as soon as it went away, as soon as her bronchitis stopped, she went back on to cigarettes again – and every three months or so she'll get it back.

Debbie: My mum's sister died of cancer, actually. But I only ever met her once or twice or something. I think she smoked a lot. But I think it's common sense more than anything. When you see, like, your friends from primary school and, like, they smoke like a chimney, and the way they have changed, it's like . . . I don't want to be like that. My gran always used to say 'If God had wanted you to smoke, he would have given you a chimney in the back of your head.' I've always thought of that – and it's true isn't it? I think that may have influenced me. (Focus group of two girls and two boys, 15–16 years, white, school 05, 16.4.97)

It was not just the tragedy of elderly relatives and cancer that acted as salutary lessons for the young people. Witnessing at first hand the impact of substance use by siblings was also referred to on occasion. In the focus group discussion reported below, the sister's behaviour is treated as a graphic justification for not 'doing [hard] drugs':

Lucy: It's like my sister. She went through the phase when she tried loads of drugs because she was on the dole and she didn't have anything else to do. She went round to somebody else's house and she continually took drugs. She didn't even know what she was taking half the time and she used to come back and she used to go up to my mum and say 'I really hate you. I

	don't want to know you, you're always in my private life.' She turned into a monster.
Jake:	She all right now?
Lucy:	She's all right now, but like she wouldn't do things – she'd hardly have a bath or anything.
Jake:	What was she on?
Lucy:	She don't know – she had cannabis, she had speed once, she had no end of things, she was like someone different. I used to hate it. She'd like come home and she wasn't like my sister anymore. She was someone else.
Interviewer:	So that's had quite an impact on you?
Lucy:	I'd never do that. Cannabis maybe, but nothing else I don't think.
Jake:	I'm going to stick to beer.
Lucy:	Beer and sex I think. (Focus group of three boys and three girls, 15–16 years, four whites and two Hindus, school 10, 27.10.97)

The flash-points that affected the young people's attitudes towards taking risks with their health were not restricted to incidents affecting themselves directly, close friends or close relatives. The focus group discussions and interviews also revealed the impact that certain films or videos could have, specifically in relation to drug use. Powerful imagery coupled with a sense of realism caused films like *Trainspotting* and *Pulp Fiction* to be cited at times as a critical incident influencing a willingness (or otherwise) to take drugs:

| *Meg*: | You might think you're going to get such a wonderful hit from it, but I just wouldn't want the bother. There was a documentary about somebody getting addicted to heroin and they were spitting up black vomit and it was disgusting. |
| *Sandra*: | It's a bit like *Pulp Fiction*. And you see them all injecting themselves and O.D.ing [overdosing]. It puts you off so much. |

[At this point, various horrible bits of the film are recalled by a number of the group.]

Denise:	And, like, if you've seen *Trainspotting*, one of the guys in it can't use his arms any more for injecting because he's used them too much and he's got gangrene in them. So he has to use his leg and there are really vivid descriptions.
Sandra:	I'd never, ever do it.
Caroline:	It's too messy.
Meg:	My brother's got a Sex Pistols video and its got Sid and Nancy sitting in their flat and they're just like . . . in such a state.
Alison:	It's not worth messing up your life is it? You know you're going

to get addicted to it, plus the fact you can get AIDs from needles.

Meg:　　　It's just too risky.

Caroline:　Too much pain. It's not worth it. (Focus group of six girls, 15–16 years, white, school 08, 23.4.97)

Or, in similar vein:

Brian:　　　Films, like *Trainspotting*. Yeah. That really put me off. That bit with the baby crawling along the ceiling. It was really scary.

Interviewer:　Have you ever seen the video about Leah Betts?

All:　　　　They showed it to us last week.

Brian:　　　It was good. *Trainspotting* was better though. That would put more people off doing it. The Leah Betts one was a bit clinical.

[A number of the group murmur agreement with this point.]

Michael:　　No. I thought it [the Leah Betts video] was better because it was based on a real story.

Brian:　　　*Trainspotting* is based on real people. (Focus group of two boys and three girls, 15–16 years, white, school 04, 5.2.98)

The key things that made the videos powerful in terms of their message were, again, the vividness of the images involved and the degree to which the young people could identify with the events as part of the 'real-world' to which they belonged.

To this point, then, there are some indications that young people are encouraged to avoid health-risking behaviour where they come into contact with vivid and horrible incidents that, through their realism or through their proximity, bring home the dangers inherent in the particular activity – whether this be smoking, drinking or using other drugs.

There were, however, plenty of times when the young people drew attention to the way the impact of such critical incidents tended to be short-term. This was particularly the case when it came to the impact of incidents involving alcohol, as the following extracts illustrate:

Jimmy:　　　I was coming down the street and my mate was coming out of a party and like, all you could see was his swaying, and he was steaming – it must have been about 15 [drinks]. All of a sudden, he swerved off a bit . . . knocked his head on the concrete post. I saw the ambulance come and I said 'What's wrong with him' and he said 'Oh, he's in a state of coma.' And he was like that for 32 days nearly. And he had his stomach pumped and everything.

Interviewer: So what impact does that have?

Jimmy: I thought to myself at the time 'Forget it. I'm never going to drink in my life.' . . .

Jake: But that was in Year 10. Everybody's got a bit calmed down – and a bit older. The drinking stopped for about four or five months, and then it started back up. (Focus group of three boys and three girls, 15–16 years, four whites and two Hindus, school 10, 27.10.97)

Jake's comment on Jimmy's story qualifies the extent to which the episode can be considered to have had an influence on any willingness to take risks with health. The comment was not contested by Jimmy. It was tacitly agreed that, though the horror and the closeness of the events really did have an effect, the impact faded after four or five months.

Greg's comments in the extract below indicate a similar recognition that the impact of a critical incident may not be permanent and can fade with time. A bit like driving past the scene of a serious accident on the motorway, a new cautious approach is adopted for a while, but we generally slip back into old habits before too long:

Greg: When we were on holiday in Tenerife we were drinking on the beach. My elder brother got really drunk. He set fire to this palm tree, and then he was so drunk he couldn't move to get out of the way. I had to give him a 'fireman's lift'. We took him to the patio. He said 'Leave me alone for an hour to sleep it off.' When we came back later he still couldn't move.

[Laughter from him and the others.]

Interviewer: Now, everyone's laughing, but what was that like for you?

Greg: It was frightening really. I thought he was really in danger. You can look back and laugh about it, but it wasn't very nice really.

Interviewer: So do you think it's had any impact on you. Would you try to avoid getting that drunk?

Greg: It did for a while, but not now. I probably might get drunk now. (Focus group of five boys, 15–16 years, white, school 04, 6.2.98)

The implications of this for the use of critical incidents might be quite far-reaching. It would suggest that in certain instances the vivid experience of a hazard associated with a health-risking behaviour need *not* lead to any alteration of behaviour beyond the short term. And, certainly, there was evidence from the discussions and interviews with the young people in this research that indicated precisely this:

Joanne: You know Jade – I was there when she had her stomach pumped, and . . . Oh God, it was terrible.

Interviewer: Did you go to hospital with her?

Joanne: No, but I was there when she was drinking. And like the next day she rang everybody up and said like 'Thanks for helping us out.' And then she said to me on the phone 'I'm never going to get drunk again.' And then last night she got steaming with Johnny. (Focus group of three boys and three girls, 15–16 years, four whites and two Hindus, school 10, 27.10.97)

As this extract indicates, direct exposure to the consequences of the health risk does not automatically act as a deterrent. Neither does witnessing such events at close hand, as the comments by Krishna and Meg below illustrate:

Krishna: My grandpa's dying because he's been smoking all his life. He's just had a bypass operation. And my other granddad died of cancer. So I'm, like, 'What the hell am I doing, I'm stupid.' And my dad quit smoking. He used to be on like 40 a day and he quit. I'm stupid smoking – but at the end of the day, I just can't help it. (Focus group of three boys and three girls, 15–16 years, four whites and two Hindus, school 10, 27.10.97)

Meg: I smoke, and my granddad had eight heart attacks off smoking. And that should really teach me a lesson, but it's something that I enjoy – it's sociable, it goes well with a pint and I enjoy it. I like it. (Focus group of six girls, 15–16 years, white, school 08, 23.4.97)

So, the young people did not always 'learn' from the experience of what should be a critical incident in their lives – close contact with the nasty outcome of a health risk. Of this they were quite aware. Indeed, many were able and willing to reflect on the contradiction between their health-risking behaviour and the situations they had witnessed close to hand. They drew on a repertoire of motives and explanations familiar to adults, principal among which was the idea that, even while recognizing that things like smoking increased the likelihood of contracting cancer or heart disease, whether or not any individual was actually smitten by the nasty outcome (e.g. cancer) still depended to some degree on (bad) luck. The young people invoked a spirit of fatalism to justify the dissonance between what their critical incident experience ought to have taught them, and the behaviours they actually engaged in:

Joanne: You can say that like, but my grandma she'd been smoking all her life, from when she was about 15 and she's now 56 and she's been smoking all her life and she's all right. She walks to work and back, she walks everywhere.

Lucy: Another thing. You're going to die of something anyway . . . so if you enjoy it . . . I mean, yeah, it's not advisable.

Jake: You are putting your life at risk . . . you are doing something. But, I mean, you could die any time. You could be run over by a car or something.

Lucy: You could be run over tonight. (Focus group of three boys and three girls, 15–16 years, four whites and two Hindus, school 10, 27.10.97)

Furthermore, even where there was a negative attitude towards taking health risks, it emerged that the critical incidents might not actually play a key role. The incidents, in this respect, could serve to reinforce opinions and behaviour rather than change them:

Sameena: My cousin's brother, he took a lot of drugs and all that. And he had an accident because he got into a fight and he got stabbed. And he went to the hospital but he couldn't be helped because of what the drugs had damaged in his body. Mostly it was his brain that was affected. And he was a really close cousin, and he died. Actually, the whole family got really upset by that. It's the sort of thing that makes you think before doing anything.

Interviewer: Has it made you particularly anti all sorts of drugs then?

Sameena: No, I was anti drugs before, but this has made me even stronger. So if anybody else was doing it, I could actually give them an example – 'Look what happened to him. (Focus group of two girls and four boys, 15–16 years, two Hindus and four Muslims, school 01, 18.11.97)

The reaction to critical incidents, then, is not uniform. As the extracts above indicate, the response to them was not dictated by the nature of the event itself so much as the disposition that the young people brought to it, for instance their existing attitudes. One girl emphasized this point in her account of her reaction to a suicide attempt she had made. For her, the brush with death had not persuaded her of the virtues of safe living, but had caused her to take more risks and 'live life to the full':

Sandra: Well I respect your views but I'm just saying that, what with me being so near to death once in my life, it's made me think that you've got to get out there and have as good a time as you can. I'm enjoying myself now. Before I wasn't and now I'm having a wicked time.

Meg: I mean, tomorrow you could get run over by a school bus.

Sandra: I just think you should go out and do what you want, and get drunk if you want.

Interviewer: Could you tell us a bit more about the incident you just mentioned to us?

Sandra: Sure, yeah. Well, everybody knows about it. I took an overdose of 25 paracetemol just before Christmas. And I got to hospital and the doctor said that he couldn't pump my stomach because I was too far gone and if I'd got in there three quarters of an hour later I would have died. And they still weren't sure if they could save me or not – but they did. Yeah, it was pretty bad.

Interviewer: Has being in such danger altered your perspective on life?

Sandra: It has a lot.

Interviewer: Could you describe that a bit.

Sandra: It made me more easy going. Like, before I was like 'Oh no, I can't go into pubs.' And now I go out and have a laugh with my mates and stuff because I think you should enjoy life more if you have got it.

Meg: Live for the day.

Sandra: Yeah, I agree with you totally. Now I'm really easy going.

Alison: Don't you think that living for the present is a bit dangerous – when you're going to be up half the night after the moment, as it were, throwing up all over the place?

Meg: I've found out if I drink beer, I'm going to be sick.

Sandra: Yeah. If I drink cider, if I drink spirits, I'm going to be sick.

Interviewer: It's interesting the way your experience affected you, Sandra. For some people, you might expect it to make them more cautious – to avoid danger . . .

Sandra: . . . yeah, it's weird, but I just think like that now I just want to go out and have fun whilst I can. (Focus group of six girls, 15–16 years, white, school 08, 23.4.97)

The Social Construction of Critical Incidents

The discussions and interviews serve as a warning against treating health-related critical incidents as having some direct, automatic deterrent effect in relation to risk-taking behaviour. As we have seen, the young people recognized the impact as:

- sometimes being small,
- sometimes being short-term,
- sometimes serving to reinforce attitudes already held,
- even possibly having the effect of encouraging increases in risk-taking behaviour.

From the questionnaire survey part of the research it was evident that the experience of what would appear, on the surface at least, to be a health-related critical incident did not always result in a perceived change of attitude towards taking risks with health. It was found that only 42 per cent of those who had been hospitalized at some point since the age of 10 due to some injury or illness felt that such an experience had affected their attitude to health risks. And, among those with a medical condition affecting their well-being, the proportion was even less (35.8 per cent). Of those reporting a serious accident to a member of the family, just under 50 per cent felt that such an event had influenced their attitudes. And, again, around half of those who reported a serious health-related incident involving a close friend felt that such an event had affected their willingness to take risks with their health.

Ostensibly similar incidents, then, could affect some young people but not others in terms of their attitudes to health and their willingness to take risks with their health. For one half the experience of such an incident was perceived as a flash-point leading to change; for the other half such an incident was not perceived as leading to change.

This carries four important implications for the use of critical incidents as an explanation of learning in relation to personal health, and in terms of its potential value as a vehicle for getting health education messages across to a teenage audience. First, it alerts us to the danger of identifying critical incidents on the basis of objective criteria, to the exclusion of the way the happenings are *interpreted* by those involved. If events that are objectively similar, such as 'the death of a close relative' or 'the personal experience of being hospitalized since the age of 10 because of a serious accident or illness', can have different repercussions for different young people it is because the events carry different meanings for them. So, the focus of attention when dealing with critical incidents needs to include not just the occurrence of specific events but the significance that those happenings have *from the point of view of the young people themselves.*[3]

The second implication, following from this, is that critical incidents in the lives of young people need to be understood in the context of their own health agenda. To focus on critical incidents simply as happenings whose objective features would appear to confront a person with the physical dangers connected with a particular behaviour is to restrict the vision to a medical agenda. A medical agenda would suggest that, having witnessed the horrific consequences of smoking, drinking and drug abuse, young persons should react 'rationally' by doing all they can to protect their health and preserve their lives as long as possible. But this places the protection of health and the pursuit of longevity as top priorities. Now, while this might be true for some of the young people some of the time it is only one part of the whole picture, and needs to be taken in conjunction with other priorities in their lives. Emerging evidence, indeed, points quite strongly to the fact that young people are capable and willing, on occasion, of placing physical appearance above physical health in their sense of priorities. The desire to stay thin can lead young women to smoke even though they acknowledge the likely longer-term risk they are taking with their health. Likewise, the social spin-offs from alcohol, smoking and soft drug use are frequently seen as justifying the longer-term risks to health. It is not the purpose of the current discussion to examine these views in detail; the point is to note the need to include them in any use of critical incidents in relation to health-related behaviour.

The third implication is that the 'critical' nature of the incident for learning is not so much a product of what actually happened as a product of what was *perceived* to have happened and the *meaning* that is attributed in retrospect to such perceived events. As Tripp has noted:

> Critical incidents are not 'things' which exist independently of an observer and are awaiting discovery like gold nuggets or desert islands, but like all data critical incidents are created. Incidents happen, but critical incidents are produced by the way we look at a situation: a critical incident is an interpretation of the significance of an event.
>
> (Tripp, 1993, p. 8)

Finally, if we concede that critical incidents only become critical to the extent that they are perceived as such in retrospect by those involved in the event, we also need to acknowledge that the identification of those features of an incident that mark it out as something special and as 'critical' becomes the province of the respondent in the research rather than of the researcher. The respondent's perspective becomes the crucial factor in deciding what facets of the incident are important and why, not the expert's.[4]

Conclusion

The original conception of critical incidents employed in this research was one deduced from theory and based on previously published research. It seemed reasonable on the basis of the available expert knowledge in the area to regard personal experiences of vivid and severe threats to health as likely flash-points in the learning process concerned with risk-taking behaviour. And there was, indeed, some evidence from the research to support the proposition that health-related critical incidents in the lives of young people could serve to change attitudes towards taking risks with health. As the comments of the young people suggested, the impact of critical incidents reflected the way the incidents were (a) real-world happenings, (b) vivid and memorable and (c) based on personal experience.

However, the evidence coming from the young people equally draws our attention to the limitations inherent in relying exclusively on expert opinion and in treating such incidents as objectively defined moments in the lives of young people. The voices of the young people – those who take the risks or avoid the risks – remind us of the research approach influenced so strongly by Peter Woods during the 1970s, 1980s and 1990s: the need to respect the views of those being studied, to take them seriously and to recognize that their priorities may not accord with official theories.

At a substantial level, the research suggests that the limited success of health education in persuading young people to avoid risk-taking activities might be explained, in part at least, by the degree to which young people do not share the medical agenda that lies behind most health education. Progress in this field, therefore, demands that research focuses on the way young people themselves perceive their lives and the role of their health within it. It is vital that the focus of research turns away from the expert's view, from the medical view, to focus as well on the perspective of the young people themselves. Critical incidents, if their full value is to be realized within health education, need to be placed within the context of the lives of young people, their personal biographies, and the social circumstances influencing their lives.

Notes

1 The research reported here is drawn from the ESRC-funded research project Critical Incidents and Risk-Taking Behaviour Among Schoolchildren (R000 22 1802). Nicky Drucquer was the research officer on this project.
2 The notion of 'critical incidents' and its application to training and learning can be traced back to its use by people like Flanagan (1954) and Herzberg, Mausner and Snyderman (1959). A fuller account of the origins of the critical incident technique and the assumptions underlying its use can be found in Denscombe (1998).
3 This contrasts with some early uses of critical incidents, which preferred to treat critical incidents as objectively verifiable occurrences. Underlying the work of Flanagan and his colleagues, for instance, was a fundamental belief that critical incidents were 'objectively knowable': 'To be critical, an incident must occur in a situation where the purpose or intent of the act seems fairly clear to the observer and where its consequences are sufficiently definite to leave little doubt concerning its effect' (Flanagan, 1954, p. 327). Confusion, disagreement, uncertainty and differing interpretations of occurrences do not sit comfortably with such an approach.
4 Here, again, there is a contrast with some classic uses of critical incidents, which were essentially 'expert orientated'. As Flanagan (1954, p. 355), for example, asserts, 'Reporting should be limited to those behaviors which, according to competent observers, make a significant contribution to the activity.' In this approach, the identification of episodes that could be identified as 'critical' incidents, their significance for the task at hand, and the nature of what was revealed by the incident were all drawn from 'those in the best positions to make the necessary observations and evaluations' – which meant in effect the professionals, the researchers, the experts.

References

Balding, J. (1993) *Young People in 1992*, Schools Health Education Unit, Exeter: University of Exeter.

Combs, B. and Slovic, P. (1979) 'Causes of death: biased newspaper coverage and biased judgments', *Journalism Quarterly*, **56**, pp. 837–43.

Denscombe, M. (1993) 'Personal health and the social psychology of risk taking', *Health Education Research*, **8**, 4, pp. 505–17.

Denscombe, M. (1998) 'Risk-taking and personal health: the role of critical incidents', Paper given to the Association for Public Health: 6th Annual Forum, 'Working Together For Public Health', University of Lancaster, March.

Douglas, M. (1986) *Risk Acceptability According to the Social Sciences*, London: Routledge.

Elkind, D. (1967) 'Egocentrism in adolescence', *Child Development*, **30**, pp. 1025–34.

Flanagan, J. (1954) 'The critical incident technique', *Psychological Bulletin*, **51**, 4, pp. 327–58.

Furlong, A. and Cartmel, F. (1997) *Young People and Social Change: Individualization and Risk in Late Modernity*, Buckingham: Open University Press.

Herzberg, F., Mausner, B. and Snyderman, B. (1959) *The Motivation to Work*, New York: Wiley.

Jack, M.S. (1989) 'Personal fable: a potential explanation for risk-taking behavior in adolescents', *Journal of Paediatric Nursing*, **4**, 5, pp. 334–8.

Johnson, B. and Covello, V. (eds) (1987) *The Social and Cultural Construction of Risk*, Dordrecht: Reidel.

Kahneman, D., Slovic, P. and Tversky, A. (eds) (1982) *Judgment Under Uncertainty: Heuristics and Biases*, New York: Cambridge University Press.

Lloyd, B. and Lucas, K. (1998) *Smoking in Adolescence*, London: Routledge.

Lynagh, M., Schofield, M.J. and Sanson-Fisher, R.W. (1997) 'School health promotion programs over the past decade: a review of the smoking, alcohol and solar protection literature', *Health Promotion International*, **12**, 1, pp. 43–60.

May, C. (1991) 'Research on alcohol education for young people: a critical review of the literature', *Health Education Journal*, **50**, 4, pp. 195–9.

Measham, F., Newcombe, R. and Parker, H. (1994) 'The normalisation of recreational drug use amongst young people in north-west England', *British Journal of Sociology*, **45**, pp. 287–312.

Plant, M.A. and Plant, M. (1992) *Risk Takers. Alcohol, Drugs, Sex and Youth*, London: Routledge.

Sikes, P., Measor, L. and Woods, P. (1985) *Teacher Careers: Crisis and Continuities*, Lewes: Falmer Press.

Slovic, P., Fischoff, B. and Lichtenstein, S. (1980) 'Facts and fears: understanding perceived risk', in Schwing, R. and Albers, W. (eds) *Societal Risk Assessment*, New York: Plenum Press, pp. 187–215.

Slovic, P., Fischoff, B. and Lichtenstein, S. (1981) 'Perceived risk: psychological factors and social implications', *Proceedings of the Royal Society of London*, A376, pp. 17–34.

Thaler, R.H. (1983) 'Illusions and mirages in public policy', *Public Interest*, *73*, pp. 60–74.

Tones, K. (1993) 'Changing theory and practice: trends in methods, strategies and settings in health education', *Health Education Journal*, **52**, 3 (Autumn), pp. 125–39.

Tripp, D. (1993) *Critical Incidents in Teaching*, London: Routledge.

White, D. and Pitts, M. (1997) *Health Promotion with Young People for the Prevention of Substance Misuse*, London: Health Education Authority.

Woods, P. (1993) *Critical Events in Teaching and Learning*, London: Falmer Press.

Appendix

Peter Woods: A Bibliography

Peter Woods is Professor of Education at the Open University. After gaining a degree in history at University College, London, in 1958, and, later, a Certificate in Education at the University of Sheffield, he spent 11 years schoolteaching in Yorkshire. After studying sociology and education at the universities of Leeds and Bradford, he joined the Open University in 1972, where for a number of years he was Director of the Centre for Sociology and Social Research. He has contributed to several courses at the Open University, including chairing 'Contemporary Issues in Education' and 'Exploring Educational Issues'. His main research interest has been school ethnography, and his main subjects of study have been teacher and pupil perspectives, cultures, strategies and careers, and teacher–pupil interaction. Over the past 10 years, he has directed a number of research projects on aspects of creative teaching and learning in the context of recent education policy. He has authored and edited around 30 books and written a large number of articles on the basis of this work.

Authored Books

The Divided School, London: Routledge and Kegan Paul, 1979.

Sociology and the School, London: Routledge and Kegan Paul, 1983.

Changing Schools: Pupil Perspectives on Transfer to a Comprehensive (with L. Measor), Milton Keynes: Open University Press, 1984.

Teacher Careers: Crises and Continuities (with P. Sikes and L. Measor), Lewes: Falmer Press, 1985.

Inside Schools: Ethnography in Educational Research, London: Routledge and Kegan Paul, 1986.

Educating All: Multicultural Perspectives in the Primary School (with E. Grugeon), London: Routledge, 1990.

Teacher Skills and Strategies, Lewes: Falmer Press, 1990.

L'Ethnographie de L'Ecole, Paris: Armand Colin, 1990.

The Happiest Days? How Pupils Cope with School, Lewes: Falmer Press, 1990.

Educational Reform and Educational Sociology in the United Kingdom, Collected Papers Presented in Japan, Nagoya, Japan: Nagoya University, 1990.
Critical Events in Teaching and Learning, London: Falmer Press, 1993.
Creative Teachers in Primary Schools, Buckingham: Open University Press, 1995.
Teachable Moments: The Art of Teaching in Primary Schools (with Bob Jeffrey), Buckingham: Open University Press, 1996.
Researching the Art of Teaching: Ethnography for Educational Use, London: Routledge, 1996. (Translated into Spanish and Portuguese)
Restructuring Schools; Reconstructing Teachers: Responding to Change in the Primary School (with Bob Jeffrey, Geoff Troman and Mari Boyle), Buckingham: Open University Press, 1997.
Testing Teachers: The Impact of School Inspections on Primary Teachers (with Bob Jeffrey), London: Falmer, 1998.
Multicultural Children in the Early Years: Creative Teaching and Meaningful Learning (with Mari Boyle and Nick Hubbard), Clevedon: MultiLingual Matters, 1999.
Successful Writing for Researchers, London: Routledge, 1999.

Edited Books

The Process of Schooling (with M. Hammersley), London: Routledge and Kegan Paul, 1976.
School Experience (with M. Hammersley), London: Croom Helm, 1977.
Teacher Strategies, London: Croom Helm, 1980.
Pupil Strategies, London: Croom Helm, 1980.
Classrooms and Staffrooms: The Sociology of Teachers and Teaching (with A. Hargreaves), Milton Keynes: Open University Press, 1984.
Life in School: The Sociology of Pupil Culture (with M. Hammersley), Milton Keynes: Open University Press, 1985.
Sociology and Teaching: A New Challenge for the Sociology of Education (with A. Pollard), London: Croom Helm, 1988.
Working for Teacher Development, Cambridge: Peter Francis, 1989.
Gender and Ethnicity in Schools (with M. Hammersley), London: Routledge, 1993. (Translated into Spanish)
Educational Research in Action (with R. Gomm), London: Paul Chapman, 1993.
Contemporary Issues in Teaching and Learning, London: Routledge, 1996.

Research Reports

Identity and Culture: The Sociology of Pupil Transfer, Final Report to the SSRC, July 1982.
Crises in Teacher Careers, Final Report to the ESRC, November, 1984.
The Initiation and Management of Change: An Evaluation of an LEA Swann Pilot Project (with C. Bagley, B. Mayor and A. Rattansi), Final Report delivered to the LEA, 1990.
Creative Teaching in the National Curiculum, Final Report to the ESRC, March, 1994.

Child-Meaningful Learning in Bilingual Schools, Final Report to the ESRC, June, 1997.

The Impact of Ofsted Inspections on Primary Teachers and their Work, Final Report to the ESRC, March, 1998.

Articles

'Showing them up in secondary school', in Chanan, G. and Delamont, S. (eds) *Frontiers of Classroom Research*, NFER, 1975, pp. 122–45.

'The myth of subject choice', *British Journal of Sociology*, **27**, 2, June 1976, pp. 130–49. Also in Finch, A. and Scrimshaw, P. (eds), *Standards, Schooling and Education*, Hodder and Stoughton, 1980; in Hammersley, M. and Woods, P. (eds) *Life in School*, Milton Keynes: Open University Press, 1984; and in *The Sociology of the School*, Teaching Unit, Nederlands College of Advanced Education, W. Australia.

'Pupils' views of school', *Educational Review*, **28**, 2, February 1976, pp. 126–37.

'Having a laugh; an antidote to schooling', in Hammersley, M. and Woods, P. (eds), *The Process of Schooling*, London: Routledge and Kegan Paul, 1976, pp. 178–88. (Translated into German and reprinted in the German journal *betrifft: erziehung*)

'How teachers decide pupils' subject choices', *Cambridge Journal of Education*, **7**, 1, March 1977, pp. 21–32. Also in Eggleston, J. (ed.) *Teacher Decision-Making*, London: Routledge and Kegan Paul, 1979. Reproduced in *The Sociology of the School*, Nederlands College.

'Stages in interpretive research', *Research Intelligence*, **3**, 1, February 1977, pp. 17–18.

'Teaching for survival', in Woods, P. and Hammersley, M. (eds) *School Experience*, London: Croom Helm, 1978, pp. 271–93. Also in Hargreaves, A. and Woods, P. (eds) *Classrooms and Staffrooms*, Milton Keynes: Open University Press, 1984; *Teacher Skills and Strategies*, London: Falmer, 1990; and Forquin, J.-C. (ed.) *Les Sociologues de l'Education Americains et Britanniques*, Paris: De Boeck Universite, 1997.

'Relating to schoolwork', *Educational Review*, **30**, 2, June 1978, pp. 167–76.

'Negotiating the demands of schoolwork', *Journal of Curriculum Studies*, **10**, 4, 1978, pp. 309–27. Partially reprinted in Booth, A.J. and Statham, J. (eds), *The Nature of Special Education*, London: Croom Helm, 1982. Also in Hammersley M. and Woods, P. (eds) *Life in School: The Sociology of Pupil Culture*, Milton Keynes: Open University Press, 1984.

'The language of order', in Haig, G. (ed.), *On Our Side*, London: Temple Smith, 1979, pp. 104–20.

'Strategies in teaching and learning', in Woods, P. (ed.), *Teacher Strategies*, 1980, pp. 18–33.

'The development of pupil strategies', in Woods, P. (ed.) *Pupil Strategies*, pp. 11–28.

'Understanding through talk', in Adelman, C. (ed.) *Uttering, Muttering: Collecting, Using and Reporting Talk for Social and Educational Research*, London: Grant McIntyre, 1981, pp. 13–26.

'Strategies, commitment and identity: making and breaking the teacher role', in Barton, L. and Walker, S. (eds) *Schools, Teachers and Teaching*, Ringmer: Falmer Press, 1981, pp. 283–302. Reprinted in Nias, J. (ed.) *Teacher Socialisation: The Individual in the System*, Victoria: Deakin University Press, 1986.

'Coping at school through humour', *British Journal of Sociology of Education*, **4**, 2, 1983, pp. 111–24.

'The interpretation of pupil myths' (with L. Measor), in Hammersley, M. (ed.) *The Ethnography of Schooling*, Driffield: Nafferton, 1983, pp. 55–76.

'A sociology of disruptive incidents', in Frude, N. and Gault, H. (eds) *Children's Aggression at School*, London: Wiley, 1984, pp. 117–35.

'Humour', in Husen, T. and Postlethwaite, T.N. (eds) *International Encyclopaedia of Education*, Oxford: Pergamon Press, 1984, pp. 2358–62. Reprinted in Thomas, R.M. (ed.) *Encyclopaedia of Human Development and Education*, Oxford: Pergamon Press, 1990.

'Teacher self and curriculum', in Ball, S.J. and Goodson, I. (eds) *Defining the Curriculum: Histories and Ethnographies of School Subjects*, Barcombe: Falmer Press, 1984, pp. 239–61.

'Ethnography and theory construction in educational research', in Burgess, R.G. (ed.) *Field Methods in the Study of Education*, Barcombe: Falmer, 1984, pp. 51–78.

'The meaning of staffroom humour' (from *The Divided School*), in Hargreaves, A. and Woods, P. (eds) *Classrooms and Staffrooms*, Milton Keynes: Open University Press, 1984.

'Standards, selection and equality: a test case for educational research', *Journal of Curriculum Studies*, **16**, 2, 1984, pp. 317–25.

'Coping with transfer: pupil perceptions of the passage from middle to upper school' (with L. Measor), in Ball, S. (ed.) *Comprehensive Schools: A Reader*, Falmer Press, 1984, pp. 27–45.

'Educational ethnography in Britain', *Journal of Thought*, **19**, 2, 1984, pp. 75–94. Reprinted in Sherman, R.R. and Webb, R.B., *Qualitative Research in Education: Variety and Unity*, Ringmer: Falmer Press, 1987.

'Cultivating the middle ground: teachers and school ethos' (with L. Measor), in *Research in Education*, **31**, May 1984, pp. 25–40.

'Conversations with teachers: aspects of life history method', *British Educational Research Journal*, **11**, 1, 1985, pp. 13–26.

'Pupil strategies', in Bennett, N. and Desforges, C. (eds) *Recent Advances in Classroom Research, British Journal of Educational Psychology*, Monograph Series No. 2, Scottish Academic Press, 1985, pp. 120–32.

'New songs played skilfully: creativity and technique in writing-up', in Burgess, R. (ed.) *Issues in Educational Research: Qualitative Methods*, Ringner: Falmer Press, 1985, pp. 86–106.

'Sociology, ethnography and teacher practice', *Teaching and Teacher Education: An International Journal of Research and Studies*, **1**, 1, January 1985, pp. 51–62.

'Social interaction in the classroom: the pupil's perspective', in De Corte, E., Lodewijks, J., Parmentier, R. and Span, P., *Learning and Instruction*, A publication of the European Association for Research on Learning and Instruction, Oxford: Pergamon Press, 1986, pp. 217–28.

'The use of teacher biographies in professional self-development' (with P. Sikes), in Todd, F. (ed.) *Planning Continuing Practitioner Education*, London: Croom Helm, 1987, pp. 161–80.

'The management of the primary school teacher's role', in Delamont, S. (ed.) *The Primary School Teacher*, Lewes: Falmer Press, 1987, pp. 120–43; also in Bourne, J. (ed.) *Thinking Through Primary Practice*, London: Routledge, 1994.

'Becoming a junior: pupil development following transfer from infants', in Pollard, A. (ed.) *Children and their Primary Schools*, Lewes: Falmer Press, 1987, pp. 103–20.

'Life-histories and teacher knowledge', in Smyth, W.J. (ed.) *Educating Teachers: Changing the Nature of Professional Knowledge*, Lewes: Falmer Press, 1987, pp. 121–35.

'Ethnography at the crossroads: a reply to Hammersley', *British Educational Research Journal*, **13**, 3, 1987, pp. 297–307.

'Initial fronts' (with L. Measor), in Dale, R., Fergusson R. and Robinson, A. (eds) *Frameworks for Teaching*, London: Hodder and Stoughton, 1988, pp. 53–64.

'Social factors affecting the child's functioning at school', *European Journal of Psychology of Education*, Special Edition on 'The Child's Functioning at School', 1988, pp. 104–6.

'Stress and the teacher role', in Cole, M. and Walker, S. (eds) *Teachers and Stress*, Milton Keynes: Open University Press, 1989, pp. 84–97.

'Towards anti-racist awareness – confessions of some teacher converts' (with C. Burt), in Woods, P. (ed.) *Working for Teacher Development*, Cambridge: Peter Francis, 1989, pp. 205–21.

'Control and choice in the school', in Bergenhenegouwen, G. et al. (eds) *De School: Keuzen en Kansen*, Muiderberg: Continho, 1989, pp. 151–63.

'Opportunities to learn and teach: an interdisciplinary model', *International Journal of Educational Research*, **13**, 6, 1989, pp. 597–606.

'Teaching in crisis? Classroom practice and the Education Reform Act of 1988', Inaugural Lecture, Milton Keynes: Open University, 18 January 1989.

'Social aspects of teacher creativity', in Day, C.W. et al. (eds) *Insights into Teachers' Thinking and Action*, Lewes: Falmer Press, 1990.

'Cold eyes and warm hearts: changing perspectives on teachers' work and careers', *British Journal of Sociology of Education*, **11**, 1, 1990, pp. 101–17.

'Hightown Grammar: a retrospective review', *International Journal of Qualitative Studies in Education*, **4**, 1, 1991, pp. 71–9.

'Breakthroughs and blockages in ethnographic research: contrasting experiences during the "Changing Schools" project' (with L. Measor), in Walford, G. (ed.) *Doing Educational Research*, London: Routledge, 1991.

'Pupils and "Race": integration and disintegration in primary schools' (with E. Grugeon) *British Journal of Sociology of Education*, **11**, 3, 1990, pp. 309–26. Also in Woodhead, M. et al. (eds) *Growing Up in a Changing Society*, London: Hodder and Stoughton, 1991.

'Réflexions sur quelques aspects de l'ethnographie interactionniste de l'école', *Pratiques de Formation*, **20**, 1991, pp. 169–76.

'Symbolic interactionism: theory and method', in Goetz, J., Le Compte, M. and Millroy W. (eds) *The Handbook of Qualitative Research in Education*, New York: Academic Press, 1992. Revised version in Woods, P. *Researching the Art of Teaching*, 1996.

'The conditions for teacher development', Studia de Doctorum Institutione, *International Journal for Teacher Education*, **5**, 1992, pp. 16–29. Also in Grimmett, P.P. and Neufeld, J.P. (eds) *The Struggle for Authenticity; Teacher Development in a Changing Educational* Context, New York: Teachers College Press, 1994.

'Aspectos sociais da criatividade do professor', in Novoa, A. (ed.) *Profissao Professor*, Lisboa: Porto Editora, 1993, pp. 125–53.

'Critical events in education', *British Journal of Sociology of Education*, **14**, 4, 1993, pp. 355–71.

'Managing marginality: teacher development through grounded life history', *British Educational Research Journal*, **19**, 4, 1993, pp. 447–65.

'The magic of Godspell: the educational significance of a dramatic event', in Gomm, R. and Woods, P. (eds) *Educational Research in Action*, London: Paul Chapman, 1993.

'The charisma of the critical other: enhancing the role of the teacher', *Teaching and Teacher Education*, **9**, 5/6, 1993, pp. 545–57.

'Towards a theory of aesthetic learning', *Educational Studies*, **19**, 3, 1993, pp. 323–38.

'Chances of a lifetime: exceptional educational events', in Bourne, J. (ed.) *Thinking through Primary Practice*, London: Routledge, 1993, pp. 168–77. Also in *Topic*, **11**, Spring 1994, pp. 1–6.

'Collaborating in historical ethnography', *International Journal of Qualitative Studies in Education*, **7**, 4, 1994, pp. 309–21.

'Teaching, and researching the teaching of, a history project: an experiment in collaboration' (with P. Wenham), *Curriculum Journal*, **5**, 2, 1994, pp. 133–61.

'Teachers under siege: resistance and appropriation in English primary schools', *Anthropology and Education Quarterly*, **25**, 3, 1994, pp. 250–65.

'Critical students: breakthroughs in learning', *International Studies in Sociology of Education*, **4**, 2, 1994, pp. 123–47. Also in Woods, P. (ed.) *Contemporary Issues in Teaching and Learning*, London: Routledge, 1996.

'Adaptation and self-determination in English primary schools', *Oxford Review of Education*, **20**, 4, 1994, pp. 387–410.

'Adopting ethnography for educational use', in Vasquez, A. and Martinez, I. (eds) *Analyzing Education in the 90s: Ethnographic Perspectives*, Barcelona: Fundacio 'La Caixa', 1994.

'Politics and pedagogy: a case study in appropriation' (with P. Wenham), *Journal of Education Policy*, **10**, 2, 1995, pp. 119–43.

'Seeing into the life of things: ethnography in educational research', *Temps d'Educació*, Divisió de Ciencies de l'Educació, Universitat de Barcelona, **14**, 1995, pp. 107–32. Also in Woods, P. *Researching the Art of Teaching*, 1996.

'Teacher biography and educational process' (with P.J. Woods), *Topic*, **14**, Autumn 1995, pp. 1–6.

'Is teaching a science or an art', in Watson, K., Modgil, S. and Modgil, C. (eds) *Teachers, Teacher Education and Training*, London: Cassell, 1996. Also in Woods, P. *Researching the Art of Teaching*, 1996.

'Creating atmosphere and tone in primary classrooms' (with R. Jeffrey), in Chawla-Duggan, R. and Pole, C. (eds) *Reshaping Education in the 1990s: Perspectives on Primary Schooling*, London: Falmer Press, 1996.

'A new professional discourse? Adjusting to managerialism' (with B. Jeffrey), in Woods, P. (ed.) *Contemporary Issues in Teaching and Learning*, London: Routledge, 1996.

'The composite head: coping with changes in the primary headteacher's role' (with M. Boyle), *British Educational Research Journal*, **22**, 5, 1996, pp. 549–68.

'The relevance of creative teaching: pupils' views' (with B. Jeffrey), in Pollard, A., Thiessen, D. and Filer, A. (eds) *Children and their Curriculum; The Perspectives of Primary and Elementary School Children*, London: Falmer Press, 1997.

'The good times: creative teaching in primary school', *Education 3 to 13*, **24**, 2, 1996, pp. 3–12.

'Feeling de-professionalized: the social construction of teacher emotions during an Ofsted inspection' (with B. Jeffrey), *Cambridge Journal of Education*, **26**, 3, 1996, pp. 325–43.

'Creative teaching in the Primary National Curriculum' (with B. Jeffrey), in Helsby, G. and McCulloch, G. (eds), *Teachers and the National Curriculum*, London: Cassell, 1997.

'Becoming a proper pupil: bilingual children's experiences of starting school' (with M. Boyle), in Walford, G. and Massey, A. (eds) *Children Learning: Ethnographic Explorations*, New York: JAI Press, 1998.

'Critical moments in the "Creative Teaching" research', in Walford, G. (ed.) *Doing Research about Education*, London: Routledge, 1998.

'Team and technology in writing up research' (with M. Boyle, B. Jeffrey and G. Troman), *British Educational Research Journal*, **24**, 5, 1998, pp. 573–92.

'Choosing positions: living the contradictions of Ofsted' (with B. Jeffrey), *British Journal of Sociology of Education*, **19**, 4, 1998, pp. 547–70.

'Talking about Coombes: features of a learning community', in Retallick, J., Cocklin, B. and Coombe, K. (eds) *Learning Communities in Education: Issues and Contexts*, London: Routledge, 1999.

'Intensification and stress in teaching', in Vandenberghe, R. and Huberman, M. *Understanding and Preventing Teacher Burnout: A Sourcebook of International Research and Practice*, Cambridge: Cambridge University Press, 1999.

'A research team in ethnography' (with M. Boyle, B. Jeffrey and G. Troman), *International Journal of Qualitative Studies in Education*, in press.

Shorter Articles

'The generation game', *Youth in Society*, January/February 1975, pp. 15–16.

'School experience', *Education*, September 1975.

'Teachers or survivors?', *Times Educational Supplement*, No. 3221, 25 February 1977, p. 19.

'Mad Mick Tracey and Kamikaze Les', *New Society*, **56**, 968, 4 June, 1981, pp. 385–7; reprinted in Barker, P. (ed.) *The Other Britain*, London: Routledge and Kegan Paul, 1982, pp. 167–73; and in *Leisure Studies*, New Society Publications.

'What's red and screams?', *New Society*, March 1983.

'From child to adolescent: transfer from primary to secondary school, *ESRC Newsletter*, **52**; also in *The Civil Servant Today*, **1**, 4, pp. 59–65; and *Education*, **164**, 23, 1984, p. 468; and *The Educationalist*, Autumn 1984.

'Researching in schools: life in classrooms', in McNeill, P. (ed.) *Society Today*, 2, London: Macmillan, 1991.

'Topical triumphs', *Times Educational Supplement*, 12 February 1993, p. 5.

'Where have all the good times gone?' (with B. Jeffrey), *Times Educational Supplement*, 9 June 1995, p. 6.

'Panic on parade' (with B. Jeffrey), *Times Educational Supplement*, 8 September 1995, Primary Update, p. 13.

Open University Course Material

E352 ('Education, Economy and Politics', 1973)
   Unit 16   Education, Economy and Politics
E202 ('Schooling and Society', 1977)
   Units 7–8   The Ethnography of the School
   Unit 11   The Pupil's Experience
   Units 27–28   Youth, Generations and Social Class
E200 ('Contemporary Issues in Education', 1981)
   Unit 3 Pt I   The Family as Educator (co-author)
   Unit 10 Pt II   Subject and Occupational Choice
   Unit 17   Schools and Deviance
   Unit 22   Marriage and Parenthood
   Unit 24   Careers and Work Cultures
E205 ('Conflict and Change in Education: A Sociological Introduction', 1984)
   Unit 11   Pupil Cultures
E200 ('Contemporary Issues in Education', 1985)
   Units 18–19   Extended Supplementaries on 'Equality, Standards and Educational Research'
EP228 ('Frameworks for Teaching', 1988)
   Unit P3   Pupil Perspectives
ED356 ('"Race", Education and Society', 1992)
   Study Guide 1 Racism and Education: Structure and Strategies (co-author)
E812 ('Classroom Studies', 1993, remade 1996)
   Co-author of MA Module on 'Classroom Studies'
E824 ('Educational Research Methods', 1994)
   Section 5   Qualitative Methods
EU208 ('Exploring Educational Issues', 1996)
   Block 3, Unit 2 Teaching
   Block 3, Unit 3 The Social World of the Pupil
   Block 3, Unit 7 Revision
E835 ('Educational Research Methods', 1996)
   Section 5   Qualitative Methods

Notes on Contributors

Stephen J. Ball is Professor of Sociology of Education at King's College, University of London. He is Director of the newly formed Centre for Public Policy Research and Editor of the *Journal of Education Policy*. His main research interests lie in the areas of education and health policy.

Martyn Denscombe is Professor of Social Research at De Montfort University. He graduated in sociology and then qualified as a teacher at the University of London (Goldsmiths' College). He has a Ph.D. from the University of Leicester for research on the social organization of teaching, and his current research is on perceptions of risk and the health-related behaviour of young people.

Ann Filer is a Research Fellow at the University of Bristol, and a former primary teacher. Her research interests include pupil and peer group perspectives, pedagogy and the sociology of assessment. She is co-director of two ESRC-funded ethnographies, tracking the careers of pupils through their primary and secondary schools. She is co-author (with Andrew Pollard) of *The Social World of Pupil Careers*.

Ivor F. Goodson is Professor of Education at both the University of East Anglia, Norwich, England and the Warner Graduate School at the University of Rochester, USA. He has been director of two research units, most recently at the University of Western Ontario, Canada, where he directed a wide range of research projects on computer education, teachers' lives and careers, case histories of school and curriculum, and racial ethnocultural minority teaching. Among his books are *School Subjects and Curriculum Change*, *The European Dimension and the School*, *The Making of Curriculum*, *Studying School Subjects*, *Studying Teachers' Lives*, *Biography, Identity and Schooling*, and *Studying Curriculum and Subject Knowledge*.

Martyn Hammersley is Professor of Educational and Social Research at the Open University. Much of his recent work has been concerned with methodological issues. With Peter Woods, he edited *The Process of Schooling*, *School Experience*, *Life in School*, and *Gender and Ethnicity in Schools.* He has written several other books, the latest being *Constructing Educational Inequality* (with Peter Foster and Roger Gomm).

Andy Hargreaves is Director of and Professor in the International Centre for Educational Change at the Ontario Institute for Studies in Education. Before moving to North America in 1987, he taught primary school and lectured in several English universities. He is the author and editor of more than 20 books and monographs in education. One of these, *Changing Teachers, Changing Times*, received the 1995 Outstanding Writing Award from the American Association of Colleges for Teacher Education. Among his other recent books are *Schooling for Change* (with Lorna Earl and Jim Ryan), *Teachers' Professional Lives* (edited with Ivor Goodson), *What's Worth Fighting for in Your School?* and *What's Worth Fighting for Out There?* (with Michael Fullan), and *Beyond Educational Reform* (edited with Roy Evans).

Bob Jeffrey, Research Fellow at the Open University, taught in primary schools for more than 20 years. He has published, together with Peter Woods, the findings of research into creative teaching in primary schools and the effects of Ofsted inspections on primary teachers. He was also co-author of *Restructuring Schools; Reconstructing Teachers.* He is currently embarking on a new research project into primary pupils' perspectives on creative learning. He also takes a keen interest in research methodology.

Bethan Marshall taught English in London comprehensives before becoming a lecturer at King's College, University of London, a post she combined until recently with that of an LEA English and Media adviser. Her research interests include the impact of the National Curriculum and its assessment on models of English teaching in the primary and secondary sectors.

Lynda Measor worked as a researcher with Peter Woods on projects that resulted in the publication of two books: *Changing Schools: Pupil Perspectives on Transfer to a Comprehensive*, and *Teachers' Careers: Crisis and Continuities.* She has been a lecturer at the University of Brighton in the School of Applied Social Sciences since 1990, and is currently working on research related to young people's views of the sex education they receive; and a project on the problems that some young people experience and create for their communities as a result of their informal cultures.

Alex Moore is a lecturer in education studies at Goldsmiths College, University of London. Previously, he taught English for 18 years at various inner-London schools. In 1995 he completed his Ph.D. under the supervision of Peter Woods, on the subject of bilingual pupils' experiences of schooling. He has published widely on a variety of educational issues, all linked by an interest in cultural reproduction and hegemony.

Jennifer Nias studied history at university and discovered the value of sociology only when she undertook a Ph.D. as a mature student. Much of her research into the lives, careers and working conditions of primary school teachers has drawn on the skills and perspectives of both disciplines. On the basis of this research she has published extensively. She has also taught children from 3 to 15 and adults from 18 to 56, in several parts of the world; and has worked in schools, colleges of education and universities. She is Visiting Professor at the University of Plymouth, having previously had posts at Liverpool and Cambridge, working in initial and in-service teacher education.

Andrew Pollard is Professor of Education at Bristol University, and a former primary teacher. He is co-director of the Primary Curriculum and Experience project (PACE) and of two longitudinal ethnographies of learning, identity and pupil careers through primary and secondary schools. His interests also include reflective processes in professional development. He is the author (with Ann Filer) of *The Social World of Children's Learning*.

Pat Sikes is a lecturer in the Social Aspects of Education at the Institute of Education, University of Warwick. She has been involved in a number of projects that have used biographical approaches to study aspects of teachers' lives and careers. She is currently using life history methods to investigate what it was like to become a teacher of religious education in English secondary schools at the turn of the century.

Geoff Troman is a Research Fellow and Associate Lecturer in the School of Education at the Open University. Geoff taught science for 20 years in secondary modern, comprehensive and middle schools before moving into higher education in 1989. Throughout his time in schools, he carried out research as a teacher researcher. His recently completed Ph.D., an ethnography of primary school restructuring, was supervised by Peter Woods. He is currently conducting research on the social construction of teacher stress. Among other publications, he co-authored *Restructuring Schools; Reconstructing Teachers*, with Peter Woods, Bob Jeffrey and Mari Boyle.

Index